Thinking About
the Sexually Dangerous

Thinking About the Sexually Dangerous

✦

Answers to Frequently Asked Questions with Case Examples

Edited by
Ellsworth Lapham Fersch

iUniverse, Inc.
New York Lincoln Shanghai

Thinking About the Sexually Dangerous
Answers to Frequently Asked Questions with Case Examples

iUniverse books may be ordered through booksellers or by contacting:

iUniverse
2021 Pine Lake Road, Suite 100
Lincoln, NE 68512
www.iuniverse.com
1-800-Authors (1-800-288-4677)

ISBN-13: 978-0-595-39092-2 (pbk)
ISBN-13: 978-0-595-83481-5 (ebk)
ISBN-10: 0-595-39092-7 (pbk)
ISBN-10: 0-595-83481-7 (ebk)

Printed in the United States of America

Contents

About the Book

This volume grew out of my Harvard seminar on *Confining the Sexually Dangerous* in which the contributors participated by discussing these topics and cases and by writing these materials. Some had previously taken my lecture course on *Psychology and Law,* and others my previous seminar on *The Insanity Defense.* Profiles of all appear in *About the Contributors.*

This volume is modeled on the earlier one that answered ninety-seven frequently asked questions and presented sixteen case studies in nine chapters. This book follows that general organization. Because the answer to each question is self-contained and because readers may choose to explore the book in various ways, some materials are repeated where necessary to answer each question. For simplicity, the masculine pronoun has been used throughout when both males and females may be involved. On some occasions, a plural accompanies a singular to make the same point.

In addition to the questions and answers, this volume also includes a number of case examples. As the contributors to this book began to explore their own potential cases, they realized that the original topic was too confining in itself, and all of us in the seminar discussed expanding the scope of sexual dangerousness. This volume reflects that expansion from more narrow psychological and legal issues to include those of morality, and political and social policy as well. Each contributor then explored a case illuminating an important aspect of the broader topic of sexual dangerousness and wrote an individual study about it. These *Case Studies* are arranged alphabetically. Their subtitles reflect the nature of the primary issue each addresses.

Although this volume includes an extensive *Bibliography,* it does not refer specifically to each listing within the text itself. Intended for the general reader and not for the researcher or the scholar, this volume assists that reader in thinking about sexual dangerousness by presenting varying approaches to the materials. At the same time, it provides a comprehensive list of references for those who may wish to examine further some aspect of the topic of the sexually dangerous. All involved with this volume urge those who read it to explore at length these other works for their interpretations and particular styles. It is the hope of everyone who contributed to *Thinking About the Sexually Dangerous* that this volume will encourage all readers to pursue further the many cases and concepts about which we hear and see so much.

About the Contributors

Randall Adams is a joint concentrator in Social Studies and Psychology at Harvard University. He has worked as a research assistant in Professor Mahzarin Banaji's Harvard Social Cognition Laboratory where he is completing a thesis on racial bias in juries. He has also served as a research assistant to Professor Todd Pittinsky in the Leadership Research Laboratory at the Kennedy School of Government. He is a member of CityStep, which mentors local youth, and the Harvard AIDS Coalition, and he acts as a peer counselor. For this book, he wrote the Mary Kay Letourneau case and contributed to the sections on Conceptions of Dangerousness, and on Media, Political, Social, and Religious Reactions to the Sexually Dangerous, and he compiled the latter section.

Alexander J. Blenkinsopp concentrated in Social Studies at Harvard University. He will pursue further study in Criminology at the University of Oxford. While at Harvard, he worked as a research assistant for Frankfurter Professor of Law Alan Dershowitz and completed a thesis on the civil commitment of sex offenders and the legal rights associated with punishment. He was Executive Editor for *The Harvard Crimson*. He also contributed to and was the Associate Editor of the earlier Harvard seminar book, *Thinking About the Insanity Defense*. For this book, he wrote the Leroy Hendricks case, and contributed to and compiled the section on Attempts to Confine the Sexually Dangerous. He was also the Associate Editor of this entire book.

Irene Choi concentrates in Psychology and is pursuing a foreign language citation in Spanish at Harvard University. An active member of student government and of an all-girl rock band called *Plan B for the Type A's*, she has also played violin in the Harvard-Radcliffe Orchestra and the Mozart Society Orchestra. She has hosted an underground rock radio show for the Harvard University radio station and has boxed with the Harvard Boxing Club. For this book, she wrote the Jesse Timmendequas case and contributed to the section on Statutory, Judicial, and Other Legal Responses to the Sexually Dangerous.

Ellsworth Lapham Fersch has taught at Harvard University in the Medical and Extension Schools and in the College since receiving his J.D. in law and his Ph.D. in clinical psychology there. He has been a visiting faculty member at various colleges and universities, including Boston University, Yale University, and the University of Massachusetts. A licensed clinical psychologist and member of the Massachusetts bar, he served as a long-time director of the Massachusetts Court Clinic. As General Editor of this volume, he guided its preparation in his seminar, contributed material, and wrote the Introduction.

Elizabeth Gamble concentrates in Psychology at Harvard University with a specific interest in psychopathology. She has worked as a research assistant in Professor Matthew Nock's Harvard Laboratory for Clinical Research, and has also volunteered for Echo, a peer counseling group that addresses concerns surrounding eating, body image, and self-esteem. She is a member of the Harvard Women's Varsity Lacrosse Team. For this book, she wrote the Adam Lack case, and contributed to and compiled the section on Psychological Contributions to Treating the Sexually Dangerous.

Jessica Gonzalez in concentrating in Psychology at Harvard University where she is pursuing foreign language citations in both Spanish and Chinese. Her principal area of psychological interest is the development of racial biases in minority children. She also contributed to and helped compile the earlier Harvard seminar book, *Thinking About the Insanity Defense*. For this book, she wrote the Paul Ingram case study, and contributed to and compiled the section on Conceptions of Dangerousness.

Megan Gubbins is concentrating in Psychology at Harvard University with an emphasis on legal applications and psychopathology, where she is also pursuing a foreign language citation in Spanish. She has worked as a research assistant in Professor Wendy Berry Mendes' Harvard Psychophysiology Laboratory, and as a volunteer tutor for Advancement Via Individual Determination, helping prepare underprivileged high school students for college eligibility and success. She is a member of the Harvard Women's Cross Country and Track teams. She also contributed to and helped compile an earlier Harvard seminar book, *Thinking About the Insanity Defense*. For this book, she wrote the Michael Ross case, and contributed to and compiled the section on Statutory, Judicial, and Other Legal Responses to the Sexually Dangerous.

Janet Kwok concentrates in Psychology at Harvard University where she has worked as a research assistant in Professor Matthew Nock's Laboratory for Clinical and Developmental Research, with a focus on self-mutilation and suicide. She is a former editor of the *Harvard Independent*. For this book, she wrote the *Sundance Associates, Inc. v. Reno* case, and contributed to the sections on Media, Political, Social, and Religious Reactions to the Sexually Dangerous, and Psychological Theories of the Causes of Sexual Dangerousness, and compiled the latter section.

Christine Mathieson concentrates in Psychology at Harvard University, where she has worked as a research assistant on ideas surrounding mental control and internal psychological states in Professor Daniel Wegner's Laboratory. She is on the board of Pleiades Society, a Harvard women's group, where she is the head of a non-profit community service branch. She has been a tutor in the Mission Hill After-School Program, and a member of the NCAA Championship Radcliffe crew team. She spent a semester at the University of St. Andrews where she was interested in the theoretical perspectives of psychology and the history of the Scottish castle. For this book, she wrote the Bernard Baran case, and contributed to the sections on Conceptions of Dangerousness, and Attempts to Confine the Sexually Dangerous.

Catherine Matthews concentrates in Psychology at Harvard University, where she has worked in a Cognitive Neuroscience Laboratory and is completing a thesis on the limitations of hippocampal associative learning. Originally from Honolulu, Hawaii, she is active in the Harvard Hawaii Club. She plans to pursue work in the non-profit sector. For this book, she wrote the Larry Don McQuay case and contributed to the section on Attempts to Confine the Sexually Dangerous.

Danila Musante concentrates in psychology at Harvard University where she has conducted research in the Implicit Social Cognition laboratory with a special focus on abnormal psychology. A member of the Harvard Cross-Country and Track teams, she was captain of the Cross Country team, and has taught students in Boston public schools about the Holocaust. For this book, she wrote the Francine Hughes case and contributed to the section on Statutory, Judicial, and Other Legal Responses to the Sexually Dangerous.

Zoe Savitsky is concentrating in Psychology at Harvard University, with an emphasis on the intersection of law and psychiatry, and is also pursuing a foreign language citation in French. She has worked as a research assistant in Professor

Susan Carey's Harvard Laboratory for Developmental Psychology. She is a peer counselor and an aide to a visually-impaired writer. Heavily involved in theatre, she has directed, produced, acted in, and designed close to two dozen productions at Harvard. For this book, she wrote the *Ashcroft v. Free Speech Coalition* case, and contributed to the section on Conceptions of Dangerousness.

Stephanie Sawlit concentrates in psychology at Harvard and has assisted with research on dreams and nightmares in Dr. Richard McNally's laboratory. An active member of the Christian community at Harvard, she has been a leader in the campus fellowship Athletes in Action, as well as a member of the Delta Gamma women's fraternity and a mentor for an inner-city after-school program. For this book, she wrote the John J. Geoghan case and contributed to the section on Media, Political, Social and Religious Responses to the Sexually Dangerous.

Crystal Smith is concentrating in Psychology and pursuing a foreign language citation in Classical Hebrew at Harvard University. She is active in the Harvard-Radcliffe Christian Fellowship and the Harvard chapter of Best Buddies, International, which seeks to foster friendships with intellectually disabled youth. For this book, she wrote the Aileen Wuornos case and contributed to the section on Psychological Theories of the Causes of Sexual Dangerousness.

Jonathan Spiker concentrates in Psychology at Harvard University, where he has been a research assistant in both the Wegner Social Psychology Laboratory and the Snedeker Developmental Psychology Laboratory. From Honolulu, Hawaii, he was a four time undefeated state high school wrestling champion. He plans to pursue business and to start his own company. For this book, he wrote the Salvatore Sicari and Charles Jaynes case and contributed to the section on Psychological Theories of the Causes of Sexual Dangerousness.

HaNhi Tran concentrates in Psychology at Harvard University, with interests in criminal behavior, risk and resilience in immigrant and low-income communities, and legal applications of psychology. She has worked for the Refugee Youth Summer Enrichment program, teaching English as a Second Language to refugee and immigrant high school students from the Boston area, and has volunteered as a big sister for the their Mentoring Program. An active member of the Harvard Vietnamese Association, she has served as one of the Co-Presidents of the organization. For this book, she wrote the Richard Sorrells case, and contributed to the section on Psychological Contributions to Treating the Sexually Dangerous.

Caitlin Watts-FitzGerald concentrates in Psychology at Harvard University, with emphasis on psychopathology and the human conscience. She spent a summer aiding in research at a local trauma center in Florida, and is an active and enthusiastic member of the Harvard Ballroom Dance Team where she has held a number of leadership positions. For this book, she wrote the Benjamin Davis and Stefany Reed case, and contributed to the sections on Conceptions of Dangerousness, and on Media, Political, Social, and Religious Responses to the Sexually Dangerous.

Introduction

This volume addresses a topic constantly in the news and of great concern to people everywhere. It arose from increasing national concern about sexual predators and states' efforts to implement the remedies accepted by the United States Supreme Court in the case of *Kansas v. Hendricks*. This book's initial focus was on legislative, judicial, psychological, and public efforts to continue to detain civilly in a hospital or treatment setting those convicted sex offenders whose criminal sentences of imprisonment were ending.

As work went forward, however, the sixteen case studies and the ninety-eight responses to frequently asked questions led to an expansion of focus from those narrow civil commitment issues to the broader questions addressed now. Those broader questions reflect our interest in three interconnected areas: sexual behavior, issues of consent, and the relation between psychology and law. The responses and the variety of case examples illustrate the complexity of the concept of sexual dangerousness. That complexity derives in part from how broadly or narrowly dangerousness, and even sex, should be defined. After all, many secondary school students, and even a former president, have concluded that sexual relations do not include oral sex. And many people argue that written, pictorial, or auditory representations of sexual activity do not constitute sex itself. It would seem to follow in their narrower view that neither can be sexually dangerous.

But some sexual behaviors are obviously extremely dangerous. They fit any definition of sex, sexual dangerousness, and rape, however narrowly each might be defined. These include the case examples of serial rapists who kill their victims, and of the men who abducted, killed, and then sexually molested a young boy. They also include the woman who killed the men who picked her up while she was hitchhiking as a prostitute. Her claim that she was defending herself against their attempts to rape her did not succeed. Though the behaviors in other cases do not reach the same level of dangerousness, they are often defined as potentially, if not actually, dangerous. These cases involve child pornography, video voyeurism, repressed memory of sexual abuse, and child rape in a daycare center. The last two also raise questions about the validity of the charges.

Beyond clearly dangerous behaviors, debate surrounds other instances of sexual activities considered dangerous by some and not by others. Statutory rape and date or acquaintance rape demonstrate this difference of opinion. Both involve our second area of interest, the idea of consent. Statutory means the law declares that no one below an age determined by the legislature can give consent. That age may be set because of psychological research, political considerations, media-saturated individual cases, or the personal predilections of those who determine the cutoff. In setting an age of consent, society deems sexual activity with a younger person to be physically, psychologically, or morally dangerous. It terms that activity rape even if the participants consider it consensual.

Violation of the age of consent can bring legal consequences as it did in the case example of a female teacher convicted of statutory rape of her young adolescent male former student. Though she was imprisoned, they were married after he reached his majority and she was released. Some commentators argue that, even in instances of a status and power differential, case-by-case considerations of matters beyond age ought to factor in decisions about the nature of consent. And a very few universally condemned individuals have argued for the total abolition of laws governing age of sexual consent.

Sexual activities that many consider so dangerous or at least so immoral as to be impermissible, and others consider matters of individual choice among adults, also test the limits of consent. Yet interpretations of dangerousness and criminality have changed. Some of what were once thought of as criminal behaviors have become matters of individual choice and consent. The United States Supreme Court, for example, had found laws criminalizing consensual homosexual relations between adults constitutional. But more recently, the Court found such laws unconstitutional. Whether laws prohibiting consensual sadomasochistic behavior as sexually dangerous, or classifying the voluntary chemical or surgical castration of offenders as essentially non-consensual, will also change remains to be seen.

Further, the issue of consent divides the public in cases of students accused of sexual assault and acquaintance rape on college campuses. Often involving sexual relations after consumption of considerable amounts of alcohol, these cases have become labeled as he said, she said. Colleges experience conflict about how to handle such matters, even how to define them. Harvard itself conceded the difficulty in discovering the facts in these cases. Because it did not have the investigatory tools at the disposal of law enforcement, it concluded that without corroboration such cases could not occasion disciplinary action. Facing a great outcry, it then set up a commission to determine the proper procedure. Many campuses found that referring all such cases to the police provided a way to proceed.

Our third area of interest involves the relation between psychology and law. This book explores the changing contributions that psychological theories and research have made to understanding the causes of and treatments for sexual dangerousness. Those contributions have followed psychology's path from a psychoanalytic to a behavioral to a cognitive orientation, and now to a neuroscience orientation that employs brain-imaging techniques such as functional Magnetic Resonance Imaging. Through all these changes in focus, the nature versus nurture debate continues.

Yet the law has found psychological science but one source in its efforts to deal with the sexually dangerous. Politics, social policy, religious traditions, and the media play equally important roles in determining what the laws and their interpretations will be. In fact, the controversies surrounding the efforts to confine in mental institutions those individuals whose imprisonment for sexual crimes has ended demonstrate how difficult the balance between protecting the public and protecting offenders' rights can be. While the law has accepted the civil commitment of individuals found dangerous by reason of mental illness, the fact that sexual offenders do not generally fit within the prescribed categories of mental illness has made the effort to confine them civilly more complicated. Either the categories must be reconfigured or the desire to protect the public must be so paramount as to negate the requirement for mental illness at all. In fact, mental aberration, which does not appear in the official Diagnostic and Statistical Manual of Mental Disorders, has conveniently been substituted to permit the institutionalization of sexual offenders after their criminal sentences have ended. Many commentators have contended that it would be better to sentence such individuals to longer terms of criminal confinement than to strain the notion of civil commitment.

From the original focus of this book on this narrow topic of confining the sexually dangerous to the more expansive topics now explored, this volume raises two basic questions. First, when there is controversy, whose view of sexual dangerousness ought to prevail in a pluralistic society with varying social, religious, political, and other norms of sexual behavior? And second, how ought that view to be implemented in the law? In compiling this volume, it is the hope of the contributors that the case examples, the answers to frequently asked questions, and the extensive bibliography will expand the readers' perspectives on the important world where psychology and law, morality, and political and social policy interact and will aid all in thinking more clearly about the sexually dangerous.

Answers to Frequently
Asked Questions

1. CONCEPTIONS OF DANGEROUSNESS

How does the dictionary define dangerousness?

Though dangerousness, the quality of being dangerous, is defined in a variety of ways, some important overarching elements occur in many of the definitions. The first element concerns the power of someone who has jurisdiction or dominion. Another describes danger as the power to dispose of, or to hurt or harm, another at one's mercy. Yet another element describes danger as power to harm an individual, to subdue or subjugate. Thus dangerousness can be thought of as a power dynamic: to be dangerous means to have the power to hurt, dominate, subjugate, or otherwise hold sway over the destiny of another individual.

How does psychology define dangerousness?

Dangerousness entails a combination of factors, including people, the environment, and situational elements. Psychological states which may indicate dangerousness include impulsivity, stress, hostility, and conflict. A psychologist or other mental health professional will typically determine a person to be dangerous if he is at risk of harming himself or others. While psychologists tend to focus more on the well being of the individual with whom they are involved, legal experts and society in general tend to concentrate on the level of potential dangerousness towards others. Because past behavior is the best predictor of future behavior, levels of dangerousness usually are influenced by an evaluation of the likelihood of repeating dangerous or criminal behavior.

How does the law define dangerousness in general?

Dangerousness often refers to the people who are at risk of being physically or psychologically harmful to themselves or others. One common act of harm by dangerous individuals is the sexual offense, often against children or other vulnerable individuals. A definition of dangerousness serves both to help prevent people from committing future harmful acts and to assess responsibility for harmful acts in the past.

How does the law define dangerousness by reason of mental illness?

Generally, statutes consider dangerousness as the likelihood of serious harm resulting from suicidality, homicidality, or the inability to care for oneself in the community. Often the exact form of mental illness is left to the regulations of a Department of Mental Health. In general, if a mental illness is severe enough that the sufferer may potentially harm oneself or others, a person is considered dangerous by reason of mental illness. Once someone receives that label, involuntary hospitalization and treatment can be sought for that person through a court, a therapist, or the police. If a person is determined by the law to be dangerous because of mental illness, they can be civilly committed to an institution.

How does the law define dangerousness by reason of substance abuse?

Studies have shown that substance abuse may be a significant factor propelling people towards violence. As with mental illness, dangerousness refers to a substantial risk of suicidality or homicidality, or a very substantial risk of inability to care for oneself in the community. Misuse of substances may be described as either abuse or dependence and may characterize someone who uses substances excessively enough to interfere with his life or to the point where he loses his ability to control the use. As with mental illness, such persons may be civilly committed to substance abuse facilities or programs.

How does the law define dangerousness by reason of sexuality?

Sexuality refers generally to simply being sexual, or possessing sexual feelings. Throughout history, sexuality has often been considered dangerous in and of itself. In today's world, there are still a number of societies that view sexuality as morally dangerous; in such places, legislation often reflects these fears of sexuality. The United States, for example, has laws against displays of sexuality such as public nudity, or showing uncovered sexual organs or secondary sexual organs in most print or public media. Another, and even stricter, example can be found in certain fundamentalist Islamic regimes. In parts of Iraq and Iran, any hint of feminine sexuality, from makeup to even showing one's hair in public, is viewed as highly dangerous; woman have been injured or even killed for what are viewed as dangerous displays of sexuality.

Sexuality is also a term that is often used as a proxy for sexual preference or sexual orientation. Sexual preference or orientation refers to an individual's sexual identity in regards to the gender or genders of partner to whom the individual is attracted. Being attracted to individuals of the same gender is referred to as homosexuality, or being gay. Until 1973, homosexuality was considered a mental disorder, and persons who identified as such were seen as psychologically disordered. These individuals were also sometimes considered dangerous, unable to control their sexual desires, which were thought to be aberrant. Many individuals who identified as gay were denied legal rights, such as the ability to adopt children, as they were considered unfit legal parents. Since 1973, the psychiatric community has officially ceased to view what are sometimes called alternate sexualities as disorders. However, a great deal of strong feeling still exists in society concerning sexuality and sexual orientation; the United States military, for instance, has a policy against accepting openly gay individuals into their services. Additionally, many states have begun to put forth legislation that would ban gay marriage. Our society seems to believe that legally condoning homosexuality by permitting gay couples to have the same legal rights as heterosexual couples would be inherently dangerous.

Currently, many argue that there should be no legal discrimination against anyone, regardless of sexuality. They conclude that the Fourteenth Amendment should for all intents and purposes preclude such discrimination for citizens of the United States. Many corporations, universities, and other large organizations have put in place anti-discrimination clauses which state that they do not discriminate based on sexuality, among other factors. However, there are laws being suggested or created that would continue to limit the legal rights of those who do not identify as heterosexual. Additionally, laws against public displays of sexuality continue to be written and enforced. The most logical explanation for the continuation of this type of legislation is the sense that sexuality in general and alternative sexual preferences in particular are inherently dangerous.

How do legislatures define dangerousness?

Until the 1980s, most legislatures had a definition of dangerousness that they used to aid in deciding bail, sentencing terms, civil commitments, and other issues. However, an effective, reliable, and valid definition of dangerousness is difficult to find. Rather than focus on actual dangerousness, the legislature and the legal profession turned towards the idea of risk assessment. Risk assessment looks at a variety of factors, from socioeconomic status to medication and hospitalization history, in an attempt to measure dangerousness dynamically on a variety of different dimensions. These efforts may lead to forcibly placing a person in treatment if psychoforensic professionals find that the person is likely, if not given treatment, to lose control over actions and cognition. Dangerousness can be a current or predicted future loss of control due to mental illness or instability.

How do courts define dangerousness?

Courts use legislative and judicial materials as well as relevant facts about the person to determine whether someone is dangerous enough to be denied bail, to be sentenced criminally, or to be committed civilly. Often, courts define dangerousness as the likelihood to cause harm or to commit a crime if released. Courts may rule in favor of protecting community welfare even if at the expense of the offender. If courts deem an offender to be dangerous, they can deny bail and, in the case of sexual offenders, require mental hospitalization even after the convict has served his criminal sentence. Setting a high bail or denying bail altogether for dangerous offenders has fueled criticism from those that feel it violates the Eighth Amendment to the Constitution. However, in 1984 the Bail Reform Act granted judges the power to evaluate potential dangerousness of the defendant as part of bail. Three years later, the Supreme Court ruled in favor of the act. Courts also have the power to commit mentally ill individuals who are deemed dangerous to themselves or others, even if not charged with an offense and even if they have already completed their sentence. However, laws do protect the mentally ill from being involuntarily committed if they are not dangerous.

How does the public define dangerousness?

The public definition of dangerousness is difficult to assess. After all, public opinion is just that: public, on a grand scale, made from general knowledge. The public clearly does have an inherent definition of dangerousness often seen in action when the media pays attention to a particular person or event. The question, however, is whether public opinion on what is dangerous influences what the media covers, or whether media coverage determines what the public pays attention to and finds dangerous. In recent years, coverage of terrorists and sexual perversions has dominated public attention. From the terrorism of September 11, 2001 to the rampant tales of molesting priests, certain stories have captured the public mind. Perhaps the public's definition of dangerousness can be best understood by looking at which people and events cause the public to change their behavior or ask for changes in legislation. The Homeland Security Act, which formalized a number of relatively invasive governmental permissions to intrude on privacy, was passed because people felt that without such legislation, they were in danger. Similarly, the numerous states that have passed increasingly severe laws about sex offender sentencing, registration, and tracking can be thought of as accurately pointing out an arena in which the public sees danger. Current public opinion on the sexually dangerous seems to indicate that people would like to see sexual offenders made undangerous by chemical or medical castration, intensive tracking and registration systems, or, simply, indefinite confinement, as seen in the enactment of the Sexually Violent Predator Laws. Overall, it seems as if the public's definition of dangerousness is impossible to articulate except as an amalgam of the legislation, attention, interest, and fear that the public shows towards given people and events.

What acts are considered dangerous?

An act is considered dangerous if it involves physical violence or aggression by one person against another, and may include verbal threats and destruction of property.

What sexual acts are considered dangerous?

Most simply, sexual acts that are non-consensual are legally considered dangerous; consent, however, is an enormously complicated issue, and some acts, while consensual, are nevertheless considered dangerous because of their very nature or because of attitudes toward them. More specifically, sexual acts that are unwanted, hurtful either physically or psychologically, are considered dangerous. Additionally, sexual acts that might be considered normal or benign may be considered dangerous when performed with an inappropriate partner. And most controversially, the sexual acts that are described as the Diagnostic and Statistical Manual of Mental Disorder's paraphilias are considered aberrant, disordered, and perverse behavior, and dangerous to the self and others.

To what extent is female dangerousness considered different from male dangerousness?

The idea of the dangerous sexual female has taken on multiple forms and idealizations and at different points in history women have been seen as both predators and the victims of sexual aggression. In the Bible and early Western literature, the image of the female vixen is prevalent, a character who can manipulate her sexuality to lead a male hero away from the right path or cloud his judgment. At the same time, women have also been imagined in Western literature and society to be of significantly higher moral sexual character than her male counterparts.

The second idea seems to have become more prevalent in modern America and the stereotype of the sexual predator is certainly a very male figure. When women commit sex crimes, this is considered much more interesting and newsworthy. Incidences of women over thirty having affairs with teenagers become national stories and are treated with intrigue and surprise, rather than disgust or fear. There seems to be something about male sexual dangerousness that makes sense to the American public in a way that female sexual dangerousness does not. The potential for sexual danger appears to be a part of being male, but this does not seem to be the case for women.

A comparison often made after the sentencing of Mary Kay Letourneau, a thirty five year old elementary school teacher who in 1997 was arrested for having a sexual affair with her thirteen year old male student, was between her sentence and that of Steve Billie, a forty two year old teacher who had sex with his fifteen year old female student and was arrested around the same time as Letourneau. Letourneau initially received a suspended sentence and, before her re-arrest, spent only six months in prison. Billie was sentenced to four years in prison.

What is the relation between dangerousness and risk assessment?

Risk assessment attempts to evaluate whether an offender is likely to recommit a crime. Mental health experts have studied various variables from mental health history to family background in an effort to link pertinent variables to predictions of future dangerousness. In the past, these predictions were often incorrect, especially as they overpredicted future dangerousness. Now, however, with the development of standardized procedures, experts can predict future dangerousness significantly better than chance.

Predictions are most successful when clinicians have sufficient information to draw upon. The information can be categorized into static, dynamic and risk management predictors. Static predictors include general information about the offender's background, including past history of violence and presence of mental abnormalities. These variables are often the strongest predictors. Dynamic predictors provide information on the personality of the offender. Personality characteristics that correlate with future dangerousness include impulsivity, lack of insight, and hostility. Finally, risk management predictors involve characteristics of environments that can elevate the probability of violence, such as excessive stress, or lack of social support. The more information an expert is given about the offender, the more accurate they can be in assessing their likelihood to offend in the future.

What is rape?

Rape is legally defined as sexual penetration without a person's consent. While rape is defined in sexual terms, the central intention of rape is to aggressively overpower the victim as opposed to the pursuit of sexual gratification. Rape has increasingly been considered a violent act which involves sex but is directed toward power and control. Rape is punishable as the most serious form of sexual assault in the United States. The punishments and definitions of rape, however, vary from state to state. The one circumstance that is considered and tried as rape in all fifty states occurs when a man forces, against her will, a woman who is not his wife to have sexual intercourse. Some states will define rape in both marital and nonmarital relations, as long as it is not a consensual act of sex. Other states include unwanted sexual acts and sexual assault as forms of rape.

What is statutory rape?

Statutory rape is considered rape based on the relative ages of the two parties who engage in sex. All fifty states have determined an age of sexual consent which typically stands at sixteen or eighteen years of age. Teenagers younger than these ages are legally unable to give consent for sex and thus for an adult to engage in sex with them is legally considered rape. Most states have also now adopted an age window, usually of three to four years, for which these laws do not apply. For instance, in a state where the age of consent is sixteen and the age window is three years, an eighteen year old may engage in sex with a fifteen year old, but a nineteen year old may not. Once the fifteen year old turns sixteen, he or she may engage in sex with persons of any age.

What is pedophilia?

Pedophilia is a psychosexual disorder in which there is a strong preference for sexual activity, desire for or fantasies of sexual activity with prepubescent children. Pedophilia is the paraphilia of being sexually attracted primarily or exclusively to prepubescent children. The Diagnostic and Statistical Manual of Mental Disorders' definition includes the following criteria: that the individual, over a period of at least six months, has had recurrent, intense sexually arousing fantasies, sexual urges, or behaviors involving sexual activity with a prepubescent child or children, normally thirteen years of age or younger; that the person has acted on these urges, or the sexual urges or fantasies cause marked distress or interpersonal difficulty; and that the person is at least sixteen years old and at least five years older than the child or children.

Data have shown that pedophiles are most often males. The children are more often of the opposite sex, though they may be of the same sex. The child or children may be within or outside the pedophile's family. Sexual fantasies, looking, or fondling are more common than genital contact. Pedophilia itself is a psychological term and not a legal term because it does not describe an act but a preference.

The word pedophilia refers strictly to adults' sexual activity with prepubescent children. A separate term, ephebophelia, refers to activity with post-pubescent adolescents. The media and the public at large very frequently use the word pedophilia to refer to both types of behavior, though this conflation is technically inaccurate.

What is sexual assault?

Sexual assault is a statutory offense where a perpetrator knowingly uses force or threat to cause another person to engage in an unwanted sexual act. Most states have replaced the common law definition of rape with statutes defining sexual assault because of the inherent ambiguities of the word rape. Thus substituting for rape the term sexual assault categorizes rape as a sexual crime and an act of violence. A stranger, an acquaintance, and even a spouse can initiate sexual assault. Definitions of sexual assault have drastically changed since the 1980s, when the majority of states required that there be resistance on the part of the victim against the assailant. Presently, resistance plays little role since focus has shifted to the behavior or attitude of the perpetrator and whether coercive means were used to initiate the sexual assault.

What is sexual harassment?

Sexual harassment is the making of unwanted and offensive sexual advances or of sexually offensive remarks or acts, especially by a superior or supervisor. Often, perpetrators sexually coerce the victims with promises or threats relating to their employment or education. The legal foundation of sexual harassment is Title VII of the Civil Rights Act of 1964, which prohibits gender discrimination in the workplace. While the most common sexual harassment occurs with male perpetrators and female victims, male victims may be sexually harassed by a female perpetrator, and perpetrators and victims may also be of the same gender.

What is a sexually hostile climate or environment?

Generally, a sexually hostile climate or environment is a place or space where one feels sexually unwelcome, threatened, harassed, or harmed. There is some legislation that addresses this subject. For example, the U.S. Supreme Court has ruled that the Civil Rights Act of 1964 illegalized behavior such as requests for sexual favors, unwanted sexual advances, and other unwanted sexual conduct in the workplace. Men and women can both create sexually hostile environments and can both report feeling harassed. Some workplaces and schools set more restrictions and include more varieties of behaviors that can be construed as creating a sexually hostile environment, including putting up offensive photographs, holding sexually hostile discussions, and sexual leering.

2. ATTEMPTS TO CONFINE THE SEXUALLY DANGEROUS

What are the forms of confinement?

Confinement restrains a person's ability to live, work, or move in certain ways or in certain places. The legal system can be used to confine individuals in a variety of ways. Perhaps the most widely recognized form is prison, where persons are housed in secure penitentiaries or correctional facilities as punishment for crimes they have committed. Jails are similar to prisons, except they usually detain people for shorter periods of time. For example, jails are often used while an individual awaits trial or serves out a brief sentence for a relatively minor crime. Delinquent minors can similarly be sent to juvenile detention centers. Secure mental institutions are also sometimes used by the legal system to confine individuals, especially those who are considered dangerous to themselves or others. Halfway houses are centers that typically house sex offenders or drug users. They often allow their inhabitants some freedom to work or move outside the center, though they impose other restrictions, such as curfews.

Some forms of confinement do not require an individual to reside in buildings specially designed for imprisonment. Probation and parole, which are often used as components of criminal sentences, require individuals to report to their probation or parole officers at certain times, and often make other limitations on where those individuals may or may not move. For example, individuals on probation or parole may not be able to move across state lines. Courts also issue restraining orders, which prohibit individuals from coming within a certain distance of specific people, or entering certain public places. One controversial type of restraining order disallows those who are considered gang members to congregate in public.

The conviction of celebrity Martha Stewart drew widespread attention to the practice of house arrest. Stewart was required to remain inside her home for a specific period of time, and she wore an electronic ankle bracelet that allowed authorities to track her whereabouts and ensure that she did not violate the terms of her house arrest. Law enforcement officials and correctional officials also can use telephone calls or random visits to ensure that individuals stay in the places where the law has required them to remain. Some laws disallow people who have been convicted of sex offenses and completed their prison sentences to take up residence in proximity to parks and schools.

What are the lengths of confinement?

The length of criminal confinement can range drastically depending on the crime committed, the severity of the crime, record of past offenses, and the state in which the criminal is convicted and sentenced. Often the length of the confinement sentence is left up to the discretion of the judge, though many states have minimum sentencing requirements or rules such as the three strikes rule, which requires long prison sentences for an individual's third criminal offense. In terms of confinement based upon mental illness and civil commitment, the length of the confinement is often indefinite when the individual enters the institution. The length of the individual's confinement is then determined by professionals, whose opinion of the person's mental health is based on their evaluation of the dangerousness risk the professional believes the individual poses to themselves and others.

What is institutional confinement?

Institutional confinement is confinement in a facility which houses individuals who pose a threat to themselves or others, cannot properly take care of themselves, or have committed a crime. These institutions include facilities for individuals who are mentally ill, facilities for the developmentally disabled, nursing homes, juvenile correctional facilities, and adult prisons. Institutional confinement can be in either the realm of the criminal justice system or the mental health system.

What are the forms of non-institutional confinement?

Non-institutional confinement can include restraining orders, home monitoring by bracelet, visits or phone calls, half way houses, and even chemical castration as a condition of release from a prison or other secure facility.

What is global positioning system monitoring?

Global positioning system or GPS is a satellite-based radio navigational system developed by the United States government to give the exact location of an equipped person anywhere in the world. GPS monitoring is the act of equipping a person with a device that connects with the satellite and shows the individual's location at any given moment. GPS monitoring is used with sex offenders to track where they are at all times and to limit their freedom to be in certain areas, such as a schoolyard. If a sexual offender equipped with a GPS device enters into an area that has been determined off limits to him the offender can either be contacted by a supervising agent or be confronted by police who has been alerted of his violation.

What are registration requirements?

Registration requirements are standards of disclosure that a previously convicted sexual offender must conform to. Most states require that at a minimum the sexual offender notify the state of current address and place of employment so that the government can keep track of these individuals. In many states, registries are open to the public. This means that an individual can inquire about an area and learn the name, date of birth, address, physical description, and pertinent criminal record of sex offenders in that given area. In many states a prisoner is required to notify the government of where he expects to live approximately ten days prior to his release. Requiring sex offenders to register before leaving prison is meant to curtail the number of offenders who do not register once they are released.

What is civil commitment?

Civil commitment is the process by which the state confines someone, usually in a mental hospital, because that individual is too unwell to remain in society, as well as a danger to himself or others. The U.S. Supreme Court has ruled that in order to civilly commit someone, the state must show with clear and convincing evidence that the individual meets both the mental illness criterion and the dangerousness requirement. A state may not impose civil commitment upon an individual who can survive safely on his own or with the assistance of family members. Civil commitment requires a hearing before a judge or jury. Civil commitment sometimes requires an individual to undergo treatment outside a hospital setting. This outpatient commitment might include living in supervised or videotaped quarters, taking medication, and attending therapy or counseling sessions. In the 1990s, many states passed laws allowing for the civil commitment of sex offenders. The official purposes of these laws were to treat sex offenders for mental abnormalities and to keep them away from society. In most cases, the civil commitment occurs after a sex offender has completed his prison sentence for his crimes. In 1997, the U.S. Supreme Court upheld the retroactive application of sex offender civil commitment laws.

What are the locations of civil commitment?

Individuals who are civilly committed are usually detained in institutions such as asylums, mental hospitals, or psychiatric wards. While the institutions vary from state to state, many are publicly run. Many serve other types of mentally ill patients as well, including those who are criminally committed, voluntary patients, and people who have been charged with a crime and are under observation to ascertain whether they are competent to stand trial. For example, St. Elizabeths Hospital in Washington D.C., the first mental hospital established by the federal government, accepts both those who have been criminally committed and those who have been civilly committed. For civil commitment on an outpatient basis, individuals are sometimes required to live in supervised group homes, which are usually administered by mental health professionals.

What is criminal commitment?

Criminal commitment is the process by which the state confines someone, usually in a mental hospital, because that person has been acquitted of a crime by reason of insanity, or requires evaluation for competence to stand trial or for criminal responsibility. Some states require that insanity acquittees be automatically committed. The alternative to such commitment, adopted by some states, is to allow for an individual to be released to his community after a brief hospital stay. Those who have been committed would receive treatment, and a judge would later decide whether they are safe enough to be released into the community. One study showed that the average period of confinement in a mental institution for those who have been committed in New York after a finding of not guilty by reason of insanity was three years and increasing. The period of confinement was known to lengthen with the degree of seriousness of the offense.

A common belief of the public is that individuals found not guilty by reason of insanity are quickly released, as in the case of Lorena Bobbitt, who cut off her husband's penis and who was released after only several weeks in a mental institution. At times, however, insanity defendants have been confined more frequently, and for longer periods of time, than non-insanity defendants who have committed similar crimes. For example, Michael Jones was acquitted in Washington, D.C. under a plea of not guilty by reason of insanity for shoplifting but was institutionalized for decades longer than the maximum possible prison sentence for the offense. One explanation for this phenomenon is that under the criminal commitment system, the standard by which the judge decides whether the individual should be released is civil and may be stricter than those for a prison inmate. Though an individual can remain committed to a mental institution only so long as he is considered mentally ill and dangerous, the circumstances which brought an individual to the attention of the police in a misdemeanor case may replay themselves sufficiently to insure longer term commitment to a mental hospital.

What are the locations of criminal commitment?

Criminal commitment usually occurs in the same types of institutions where civil commitment occurs, including asylums, mental hospitals, and psychiatric wards. Sometimes, those who are criminally committed spend a period of time in a jail before being transferred permanently to a mental institution. Other times, criminal committees are housed in the psychiatric wing of a prison. Occasionally, and usually after serving some time in a secure institution, a criminally committed individual might be permitted to live in a supervised group home on an outpatient basis.

What is pre-conviction commitment?

Pre-conviction commitment involves the treatment of an alleged criminal in a psychiatric facility prior to the trial. Individuals who have been arrested for a crime but are not mentally aware enough to go through the trial process are committed to a psychiatric facility and treated until they are able to proceed. The mere presence of a mental disorder or a personality disorder is not sufficient to qualify for pre-conviction commitment. In order to qualify for pre-conviction confinement mental health experts must evaluate the alleged criminal and deem him incompetent to understand the trial procedure or to cooperate in his own defense.

What are the purposes of pre-conviction confinement?

Two major reasons for pre-conviction confinement are to eliminate the risk of flight and to make sure the accused does not harm others, or himself, while he is awaiting trial. Yet another purpose of pre-conviction confinement is to determine whether the person is competent to stand trial or was criminally responsible at the time of an act. Confinement allows psychoforensic professionals to assess the accused's mental state, which could have relevance to the case when it goes to trial.

What are the purposes of post-conviction confinement?

Convicted sex offenders are sometimes held after their jail sentences have been completed for several purposes. One such purpose is to try to treat them and cure them of their pathology or mental disease or abnormality and, in turn, to make them less of a threat to society. Many techniques to cure them or to lessen the likelihood of their reoffending may be employed during this confinement. Another major reason for confinement is to keep the offender off the streets if it is clear that he is dangerous and authorities believe he will most likely reoffend.

What are the similarities between civil and criminal commitment?

Both civil and criminal commitment involve a deprivation of a person's liberty. Both the civilly committed and the criminally committed are usually detained in the same types of settings, such as secure hospitals. Both sets of people are also sometimes granted outpatient status, usually after some time in a secure institution. Treatment depends upon the patient's mental health, rather than on the process by which he was committed.

What are the differences between civil and criminal commitment?

Criminal commitment requires that an individual has some involvement with the criminal justice system, while civil commitment has no such requirement. Criminal commitment can occur if an individual is found incompetent to stand trial, or if an individual needs to be observed before his competency is determined. Civil commitment, in contrast, can occur solely on the basis of an individual's mental health and dangerousness. Also, after an individual launches a successful insanity defense, the prosecution does not bear any burden as statutes may direct that criminal commitment automatically follows. This differs from civil commitment, where the state must provide a certain amount of proof indicating an individual's dangerousness or mental unsoundness. Additionally, after an individual has been criminally committed, some states require that he bear the burden of proving that he is fit to be released. Civil commitment always requires that the state provide proof that confinement should continue.

What changes have taken place in civil commitment?

Civil commitment has a long history in the United States, and the procedure has undergone numerous changes. In the early nineteenth century, the country began to urbanize and the number of mentally ill people grew. There developed a need for a systematized handling of the mentally ill. At first, these people were put in prison. Later, though, religious groups, especially the Quakers, established asylums to take in the insane, the retarded, and other infirm persons. Dorothea Dix, a devout Unitarian, championed the cause of putting the mentally ill in institutions separate from hardened criminals. She and other determined activists petitioned state legislatures, which were ready to establish institutions that responded to the needs of their growing populations. And in the late eighteenth century, Parisian Philippe Pinel and others found that the condition of mentally ill persons could improve through medical and therapeutic treatment rendered in controlled environments. These conclusions also contributed to the asylum movement.

In the first half of the nineteenth century, numerous asylums and, later, state hospitals were established. In many parts of the country, these institutions were quickly filled to capacity. The psychiatrists became the central figures in asylums, and as asylums became more important in U.S. society, so did the psychiatrists. By the middle of the nineteenth century, involuntary commitment became rather common. Patients' families initiated the overwhelming majority of involuntary civil commitments to asylums, and most of those commitments were made only when a family member threatened or committed violent actions. Occasionally, this raised problems, such as in 1860, when Theophilus Packard, Jr. had his wife, Elizabeth Packard, committed to a hospital for the insane in Illinois. The two disagreed about religion, and Theophilus believed that Elizabeth was not appropriately obedient to her husband. The hospital released her after three years of confinement, at which point Theophilus locked Elizabeth in a room. Elizabeth's friends went to the court and filed a petition for a writ of *habeas corpus*, which commands that a detained person be brought to court to examine the grounds of the detention. The judge issued the writ, and at a very heavily publicized and attended trial in a small town's courthouse, Theophilus alleged that his wife was insane. A jury ruled otherwise, however, and Elizabeth Packard's case became a cause célèbre that stirred awareness of the possible misuse of involuntary commitment.

Nonetheless, involuntary commitments continued apace, and laws were made more expansive to allow for the commitment of individuals with or without familial permission, so long as psychiatrists deemed the person mentally ill and in such a condition to merit treatment. This standard was known as the *parens patriae* approach, meaning that the state must interpose or allow another to step in to care for someone unable to care for himself or herself. In a parallel development, many mental hospitals over time became crowded and more focused on efficiency than efficacy. As the environment of asylums changed, though, the commitment laws did not.

Psychiatrists, with their focus on treatment, helped to reconceptualize the handling of sexual psychopaths. Until the 1930s, those who committed crimes involving sex were usually held morally culpable for their crimes and imprisoned. In the 1930s, psychiatrists introduced a therapeutic perspective that viewed sex offenders as suffering from a psychological pathology. As this view gained strength, the legislatures responded. Michigan passed the first sexual psychopath law in 1937, allowing for the civil commitment and treatment of sexual psychopaths. Between 1937 and 1950, twelve states and Washington, D.C. had enacted similar laws. That number had grown to 29 states by 1970. In 1970 few more than half of the states with these laws required conviction before civil commitment could proceed; the other half allowed commitment before conviction.

These laws differ from the sexually violent predator statutes that exist today, and their very names help to make the point. The sexual psychopath laws of the 1930s through the 1970s were meant to address a psychopathy, an illness, through medical treatment. These people were viewed as too unwell to be released into society. Current sexually violent predator laws also allow for the civil commitment of those who have committed sex crimes, but the commitment does not aim at treatment; it is a response to violent predation, to dangerousness. These individuals are viewed as too dangerous to remain at large.

In the latter half of the twentieth century, many called for reforms of civil commitment, with special emphasis on replacing psychiatrists' powers with a more rigid legal process that established procedural safeguards. Some contended that psychiatrists' judgments were often wrong, or based more on personal preferences than on objective medical assessment. In the 1970s, a series of court decisions extended constitutional protections to the mentally ill and eventually shifted the standards for civil commitment to require a finding of dangerousness. In the 1972 case *Jackson v. Indiana*, the U.S. Supreme Court ruled that confining an individual for an indefinite length of time due to his unfitness to stand trial is a violation of due process rights, and that the state must initiate civil commitment proceedings and find the person mentally ill in order to detain such an individual for a long period of time. That same year, a federal district court in Wisconsin ruled that any significant liberty deprivation must be preceded by a hearing in which the necessity of the detention is demonstrated, and that the *parens patriae* standard was unconstitutionally overbroad. Instead, the state must bear the burden of proving that an individual is extremely likely to cause harm to himself or to another before the state may civilly commit him. The Supreme Court finally made a definitive ruling on the dangerousness question in *O'Connor v. Donaldson*, which held that the state cannot confine a person who is not dangerous if he does not require the state's help in order to survive safely. And four years later, in *Addington v. Texas*, the U.S. Supreme Court determined that states must meet a standard of preponderance of the evidence in order to commit an individual. These cases added procedural safeguards modeled upon those employed in the criminal justice system.

State legislatures complemented the judicial decisions by passing laws of their own. In the 1970s, nearly all the states changed their civil commitment codes to include dangerousness requirements. These developments were widely perceived as efforts that successfully wrested control of civil commitment from the psychiatrists and their idiosyncrasies. No longer would the law defer to psychiatrists; henceforth, a judge or jury would have to be satisfied in order for someone's liberty to be abridged. As with deinstitutionalization, it was believed that this reform would reduce the number of people confined to mental hospitals. Many states also repealed their sexual psychopath statutes or stopped exercising them at this time. The American Bar Association and other respected organizations had criticized the laws for being too vague and because they believed treatment to be ineffective.

What changes have taken place in criminal commitment?

In the 1972 case *Jackson v. Indiana*, the U.S. Supreme Court ruled that confining an individual for an indefinite length of time due to his unfitness to stand trial is a violation of due process rights, and that the state must initiate civil commitment proceedings and find the person mentally ill in order to detain such an individual for a long period of time. This decision represented an intersection of criminal commitment and civil commitment. In 1983, the U.S. Supreme Court ruled in *Jones v. United States* that an individual who has been criminally committed after a successful insanity defense may be confined for longer than the maximum prison sentence he could have served if he had instead been found guilty. The decision also stated that the state bears no burden in confining an individual who has successfully launched an insanity defense. This ruling clarified the nature of criminal commitment and is the controlling case on the issue. Since then, some states have noted that the insanity defense is a tool that those accused of misdemeanors should not use, because of the potentially long length of criminal commitment. Some states have attempted to preserve the insanity defense as a viable option for misdemeanants by putting a limit on the length of confinement for those who have been criminally committed.

How are sex offenders dealt with differently from other offenders?

Members of the community are notified when a sex offender moves in. Individuals convicted of other crimes, such as murder or burglary, however, do not have to register, and members of the community therefore do not know about their crimes. Sex offenders also can be civilly committed in many states for an indefinite period of time, something to which other criminals are not subject. Many states have stricter laws for sexual offenders than for other criminals. In 1998, Colorado passed the Lifetime Supervision Act, enacted in part because of the idea that sex offenders can never be cured. People sent to prison under this act cannot be released until the Parole Board deems them no longer a threat. In most cases, offenders will be supervised for life. While in prison, inmates must participate and progress in sex offender therapy if they hope to be paroled. Once offenders are paroled, they are supervised and must continue their therapy. Many other states have passed similar acts for sexual offenders whereas other kinds of criminals are not subject to laws of this type.

What is the role of monitoring the sexually dangerous?

Monitoring the sexually dangerous is an important way of tracking offenders who are in the community on parole or probation. There are many different ways of monitoring sex offenders. One way is to require sex offenders to submit information to sex offender registries. Some states have law enforcement officers sporadically check to make sure that registry information is both current and accurate by visiting the address listed and making sure that the sex offender resides there. Some states are beginning to utilize Global Positioning System or GPS technology to monitor sex offenders. GPS can be used to ensure that the offenders are abiding by the conditions of their release. Many law enforcement officials believe that equipping sex offenders with GPS units will prevent them from violating their parole or probation conditions because they know that they are being watched and will be caught. The other main reason that legislatures feel the need to carefully monitor sex offenders is that many individuals believe that sex offenders cannot be rehabilitated. Equipping sex offenders with GPS units allows law enforcement officers to find the offender if he commits another crime and helps prosecutors build a case by linking the man to the scene of the crime.

How long should monitoring the sexually dangerous continue?

Though some people believe that monitoring sex offenders after release from confinement is wrong it seems that public opinion and therefore legislation supports the long term monitoring of sex offenders at the very least through registries. In Massachusetts, sex offenders who are required to register may only be removed from the registry after the board of registration approves a written request to remove the offender. Sex offenders must submit their petition for removal at least ten days before their annual registration date, and must submit documented evidence supporting their reasons for removal. The board will only grant removal from the registry to people who they believe will not reoffend. Sex offenders who have been deemed sexually violent predators, have committed a sexually violent offense, or been convicted of multiple sex offenses may never be removed by the registry.

Besides registration, many states have looked into using Global Positioning Satellites to monitor sex offenders. Questions remain about who should be monitored and for how long. Many GPS supporters feel that GPS units should be used to monitor sexually violent offenders at least throughout the duration of their parole. Others believe that certain sex offenders should be monitored for a much longer period of time, if not indefinitely. At least four states passed laws in 2005 requiring lifetime electronic monitoring of certain sex offenders.

What are boards of registration of sexual offenders?

A board of registration consists of the people responsible for maintaining accurate registries of sexual offenders and for updating and verifying the information provided to the registry. Each state has its own board that oversees the registration process and ensures that it proceeds as dictated by the law.

Should names, photos, and data on sexual offenders be placed on the internet?

Many states have made their sex offender registry open to the public via the internet. Online registries often include personal information about the sex offender, including a physical description, photograph, current home address, current work address, and the offense committed. In most cases anyone with internet access can type in a zip code and see a list of all the sex offenders living in that zip code. Most states have notification requirements stating that neighbors of sex offenders must be notified that a sex offender has moved into the area. Before online registries were implemented, law enforcement officers visited houses in the neighborhood to inform residents of the presence of the sex offender. The online registry streamlines this process and allows law enforcement officers to better use their time. Proponents of online registries believe that they provide essential information to residents and allow them to better protect themselves and their children.

Others feel, for various reasons, that online registries should not be used as notification devices. The two main issues of contention are insufficient notification and over-notification. Those who believe that online registries provide insufficient notification point out that residents must seek out the information themselves. They say that many may not know that the online registries exist, and although it is a very technologically advanced world, they argue that it seems inappropriate to assume that every household has access to the internet. Those who believe that online registries over-notify point out that anyone with an internet connection can access registries from multiple states. Notification laws usually assert that people living near sex offenders have a right to know, but do not imply that people from any state, or even country should be able to access this information.

Should neighbors and others be warned of the presence of sexual offenders?

The clear argument for notifying neighbors that they are living near a sexual offender is demonstrated by the legal case that inspired notification laws. Megan Kanka was seven years old when a sex offender neighbor raped and murdered her. Her murder sparked a national outcry demanding change. Since her death in 1994, all fifty states have adopted laws on registration and notification of sex offenders, dubbed Megan's laws. Public opinion concurs that it is the right of the public to know that a sex offender is living among them and that this outweighs the privacy rights of the individual offender. There have been challenges to registration and notification laws but they have been largely unsuccessful. The major arguments against such laws are that they violate the rights of an individual, and that they could also lead to vigilantism. Opponents of the laws contend that, according to the legal system, once a lawbreaker's punishment has ended that individual should be given another chance. Registries, many argue, keep sex offenders from getting a fair chance to start over by leading to social persecution. Critics of registration and notification laws point out that the public is not notified when persons convicted of other crimes, such as spousal abuse and drug dealing or assault and battery, move into a neighborhood and thus it is unfair to notify the public about the presence of a convicted sex offender.

Should data banks of DNA be kept of those suspected of or convicted of sexual offenses?

The primary argument in favor of maintaining DNA data banks for suspected or convicted sex offenders is that these data banks are likely to prevent or solve future crimes. The assumption is that sex offenses frequently result in DNA evidence, especially in the form of semen or blood, being left behind by the perpetrator. If these pieces of evidence can be compared to a data bank, then a match can be found and the identity of the perpetrator can be determined. Some have noted that DNA databases could work in much the same way as fingerprint databases; samples collected at the scene of a crime can be quickly compared to samples collected previously. Also, people whose DNA has already been included in the data bank are less likely to commit sex offenses in the future because they run a greater risk of getting caught. This incentive is especially important given the widespread perception that recidivism rates for sex offenders are very high. In 1989, Virginia became the first state to pass laws requiring the collection of DNA from certain categories of criminals. Within nine years, every state had passed a similar provision.

The primary argument against these data banks is that they violate individuals' right to privacy. DNA, unlike fingerprints, contains an enormous amount of information about the individual from whom it is collected. As scientific researchers learn more about DNA, these samples could conceivably be used to find out even more information about suspects and their predispositions. Because individuals who are related share certain genetic characteristics, DNA could be used to find out about one's relatives. Thus, it is conceivable that law enforcement agents could extract information from DNA samples of the relatives of the suspects in a case, rather than of the suspects themselves. This would abridge the privacy of individuals who had never even been arrested for a crime. Additionally, the practice of collecting DNA samples upon arrest, rather than upon conviction, has been subject to especially sharp criticism. More than half the states also collect samples from juvenile offenders, and, unlike other components of the juvenile's record, these samples are not destroyed when the offender becomes an adult. This has prompted objections from those who believe that one is permitted to start over with a clean slate when one becomes an adult. An additional argument against these databases is that when a match is found, law enforcement agents and jurors will jump to the conclusion that the individual did in fact commit the crime, even though problems with the quality and maintenance of the samples might have erroneously resulted in the match. Moreover, some have wondered whether the line between acceptable law enforcement uses of the DNA data banks, and unacceptable or unrelated purposes for accessing the information, might become blurred in the future.

Should data banks of DNA be kept of everyone?

Those who favor maintaining DNA records for everyone argue that such information could easily be used to identify individuals who were killed or seriously injured, especially in catastrophes or disasters. They also argue that crimes could be more readily solved, and that innocent people in jail would be set free or would not have been accused or convicted in the first place if a wider sample of DNA were obtained. Supporters also argue that it would be easy to carry out such a collection if, at birth, a DNA sample were taken from everyone. Arguments against keeping data banks of all people's DNA center around the idea that making all people submit their DNA is an infringement of their civil liberties and an invasion of their privacy. They also contend that keeping data banks of hundreds of millions of people's DNA would be logistically too difficult to carry out and would also be prohibitively expensive. Those who disagree also contend that it would be hard to enforce a law requiring everyone to submit DNA samples, and the chance for fraud or simple carelessness in sampling procedure would make the whole enterprise ultimately invalid.

3. PSYCHOLOGICAL THEORIES OF THE CAUSES OF SEXUAL DANGEROUSNESS

How does the Diagnostic and Statistical Manual of Mental Disorders define sexual disorders?

In the American Psychiatric Association's official listing of mental disorders, the Diagnostic and Statistical Manual of Mental Disorders, sexual disorders refer to a larger category of psychopathology associated with sexual desire or behaviors. Within this group are sexual dysfunctions and paraphilias. Sexual dysfunctions manifest themselves as disturbances in sexual desire and in the psychophysiological changes that affect sexual response and cause significant distress and interpersonal difficulty, such as male erectile dysfunction. Paraphilias are intense, recurring sexual urges or behaviors directed towards unusual objects, scenarios or activities that cause marked distress or disruption in social, occupational, or other important functioning, such as voyeurism. Sexual disorders not described within these categories can also be considered, but concepts of acceptable sexual behavior may vary among cultures.

To what extent does the Diagnostic and Statistical Manual of Mental Disorders refer to dangerousness arising from sexual disorders?

Dangerousness associated with sexual disorders is mentioned in the diagnosis of paraphilias. Certain paraphilias, especially pedophilia, include a possible condition for diagnosis when these urges are performed with a nonconsenting individual. The majority of all sex offenders are afflicted by exhibitionism, voyeurism, and pedophilia. Individuals with paraphilic behavior are seldom self-referred and are recommended for treatment only after their behavior has resulted in conflict with sexual partners or society. Sexual behaviors are considered disorders only when the patient is disturbed by them, if he or she has compelled another to participate without consent, if the behavior has resulted in criminal activity, and if the patient suffers from disruption in work or social life as a result of the behavior. Not all sex crimes, however, involve a paraphilia, as substance abuse or opportunistic behavior may have a more significant role.

How have changes in the Diagnostic and Statistical Manual of Mental Disorders' classification of homosexuality illustrated shifts in psychiatric and psychological approaches to sexual behavior?

What is fascinating, helpful, and arguably disconcerting about the Diagnostic and Statistical Manual of Mental Disorders is that its definitions of mental disorders and criteria for them change, often drastically, over time. Until 1973, the Diagnostic and Statistical Manual of Mental Disorders included homosexuality as a full mental disorder. Yet a shift in the psychological community towards accepting homosexuality had been gaining momentum for some time, as the American Psychiatric Association had started meeting with groups sympathetic to homosexuality to discuss petitioning the Nomenclature Committee of the APA to modify the Diagnostic and Statistical Manual of Mental Disorders. Although some psychologists were still advocating psychotherapy as a treatment for homosexuality, the revised nomenclature met little opposition.

In 1973, as a result of a public demonstration against the American Psychiatric Association and a subsequent vote taken by it, the Association declared that homosexuality was not per se a mental disorder, yet the Manual retained a partial category. It included among its disorders the category egodystonic homosexuality to account for the discomfort some felt in their sexual preference for those of the same gender, suggesting some sort of mental and psychological imbalance as the causative factor. Though it was not explicitly stated, if an individual's homosexuality were personally acceptable, or egosyntonic, then it was not deemed a mental disorder, and thus was not listed in the Manual. Then, in 1987, as a result of the combined weight of social, political, and scientific pressures concerning the elements and diagnosis of sexuality and sexual preferences, the Manual did not even list egodystonic homosexuality. While similar pressures have arisen over recent years to change the interpretation and listing of fetishism and transvestitism, no ensuing changes have gained favor.

What has Freudian psychology contributed to theories of causation?

According to Freudian psychology, causation for sexual dangerousness comes from that fact that each person goes through several stages of psychosexual development throughout their early life. In order of occurrence these phases are the oral, anal, phallic, and genital phase. These stages indicate where a person's desires are focused at different points in his life. If a person moves onto the next successive stage without completely overcoming and resolving any problems from the previous stage, then sexual problems will occur later on in life and this person may have difficulties in certain situations such as controlling their sexual urges and sexual attitudes. A weak or absent father and a strong or domineering mother were considered, for example, to cause homosexuality, considered a mental disorder and potentially sexually dangerous behavior.

What have biology and related sciences contributed to theories of causation?

According to biology and related sciences, causation for sexual dangerousness comes from a biological disturbance. Specifically hormones can cause sexual dangerousness and aggressive sexual feelings and attitudes. For instance too much testosterone in men may cause them to have an overaggressive or uncontrollable sex drive and lead to deviant and dangerous sexual behavior. There are also many biological factors such as a history of prior violence, a major mental disorder, and being an abuse victim that may cause one to become sexually dangerous.

What has brain science contributed to theories of causation?

According to brain science, causation for sexual dangerousness comes from a chemical imbalance of hormones within the brain. In the pituitary, the Gonadotropin releasing hormone stimulates synthesis and release of follicle stimulating hormones and luteinizing hormone, a process that is controlled by the frequency and amplitude of Gonadotropin releasing hormone pulses, as well as androgens and estrogens. If any of these hormones fail to work properly one may become sexually dangerous, have problems functioning sexually, and/or be unable to control their sexual urges.

What has cognitive neuroscience contributed to theories of causation?

According to cognitive neuroscience, causation for sexual dangerousness comes from one's negative and harmful beliefs and attitudes towards females, children, males, or objects. Negative, inappropriate thoughts may lead to inappropriate beliefs which may lead to one acting on these beliefs and becoming sexually dangerous. Problems with one's cognition often result in an unrealistic view of sexuality. This contributes to poor decision making in sexual situations, which can in turn make a person sexually dangerous.

What has learning theory contributed to theories of causation?

According to the learning theory, causation for sexual dangerousness comes from constructing and organizing one's knowledge from previous experiences. This is a personalized process, and the person applies their concepts, rules, and general principles in daily life. In essence the learning theory involves learning from one's own mistakes. However, the sexual dangerous fail to learn from their mistakes either by choice or because they are mentally ill. Subscribing to ideologies and attitudes that are negative towards women may also cause sexual dangerousness.

What has behaviorism contributed to theories of causation?

In the context of criminality and, in particular, the sexually dangerous criminal, behaviorism concerns itself with how the offender's behavior is a product of his response to stimuli, or conditions in his outer environment and inner environment, which are his biological processes.

What has sociology contributed to theories of causation?

Sociology is the source of theories that explain criminal behavior as an adaptive mechanism of the social environment of the offender. Differential association suggests that all criminal behavior is a learned behavior. The process of learned behavior depends on the degree to which the individual is exposed to individuals whose behavior adheres or does not adhere in varying degrees to morals and laws. The theory of anomie suggests that an individual who is unable to attain the goals that society expects from him by socially acceptable ways will resort to criminal behavior. The example for this theory commonly used is gangs in the United States. Control theory suggests that a person's ability to resist the propensity to commit crime is reliant upon the strength of his attachment to parents, his participation with common and acceptable activities and progressive endeavors, and his resolve to align with established and strict moral values that forbid criminal behavior. Labeling theory, however, purports that criminality results from society's reaction to the individual, not the individual's own unlawful actions or criminally-minded personality. So the individual becomes more and more socialized into criminal behavior as he is rejected by law-abiding people and accepted by other delinquents.

What common elements are there in the various theories?

All of these theories deal with how the individual reacts to an outer or inner condition or how those conditions influence the individual with results in criminal behavior.

What differences are there in the various theories?

The theories of causation relating to brain science, biology, cognitive neuroscience, and other similar sciences deal with physical processes within the individual which contributes to criminal behavior. Theories of causation related to learning theory, behaviorism, and sociology emphasize the external aspects that influence individuals to engage in and continue in criminal behavior.

What explains the apparent Dr. Jekyll and Mr. Hyde nature of many serially sexually dangerous persons?

Psychopaths are frequently able to lead a double-life, whether they are sexually dangerous persons or even murderers. According to the Diagnostic and Statistical Manual of Mental Disorders, the condition that may afflict such individuals would be antisocial personality disorder, where the individual has little concern for others, no remorse, and frequently breaks the law. Psychopaths excel at cultivating a superficial charm and become experts at manipulating human interactions to their advantage. Their impulsivity and lack of empathy makes it possible for them to commit crimes without a conscience, yet continue to blend in with society because they appear to be perfectly rational.

Why are serially sexually dangerous persons overwhelmingly male?

A recent Canadian study found that less than one percent of sex offenders serving prison sentences of two or more years were female. The reason may be rooted in the reproductive conflict between men and women. Males have a larger potential reproductive rate than females, as it is in their survival interests to mate with as many females as possible to ensure that their genetic material is passed on. Females have a higher parental investment in raising offspring as they can only reproduce with one partner at a time, and thus are more selective. For males, there is competition to reproduce with as many females as possible to prevent other males from reproducing, but for females, there is a scarcity of suitable mates. In the animal world, males do try to force copulation with females, but the latter have usually evolved to possess the most effective defense features.

In humans, high mating effort is an important feature of male psychopathy. The phenomenon of Young Male Syndrome has been proposed, where mating effort and intrasex competition spike during late adolescence and early adulthood for men in general, which accounts for adolescence-limited offending. Two smaller groups of men emerge with more unusual behavior in that one exhibits high-mating effort likely because of competitive disadvantage, and the other high-risk and antisocial behavior as part of an alternative social strategy their whole lifetimes.

What characterizes female sexually dangerous persons?

There are three basic types of female offenders that have emerged in research literature, and they differ slightly from those of the male offenders. The largest group of female offenders molests children under the age of six, often their own, as a result of seeing themselves merged with their children and also unable to function in a maternal role. Another group is a teacher-lover group that pursues teenage victims. Women in this category are older, usually in their thirties, and romanticize their involvement with the victim. The third group consists of women who were initially coerced into sexual relations with a child by a male partner. The women usually comply out of a fear of abandonment and desire to please. Eventually, many of these women develop an enjoyment of these encounters and begin molesting children independently.

What is the role of fantasy in sexual dangerousness?

Fantasy has a central role in the creation of compulsive sex offenders, although not every person who has these fantasies will act upon them. Offenders' fantasies differ from those of nonoffenders by their prevalence, obsessiveness, and importance to the individual. In fact, for many offenders, the fantasy itself may be more important than the act itself, which is primarily a source of new material. The individual constantly bombarded by sexual fantasies becomes fixated with the resulting sexual excitement, and compulsively seeks the fulfillment of that thrill by enacting the fantasy.

What is the role of power and control in sexual dangerousness?

Power and control are often keystones of sexual struggle and dangerousness as it applies to cases which attract the attention of law enforcement and the courts. Power and the desire for control are frequently aphrodisiacs to the criminal; they may either be something that the criminal lacks under normal circumstances and seeks to enforce under conditions of his own making, or contrarily may be a state of his normal personality which simply loses inhibition and treads over the line that separates safe and consensual expression of relationship dominance, and that of sexual dangerousness. The expression of power over another human being, in most cases of sexual dangerousness (specifically instances of molestation, rape and abuse), involves both a power imbalance which usually places the sexual predator as the dominant of the two, as well as an attempt to wrest an acknowledgement of that place of power from the victim. In situations of parent-child molestation, it is not uncommon for the parent to remind the child of their helplessness, that no one would believe their claims, and that it is the parent's good graces which prevent worse from taking place. This perceived helplessness is a byproduct of the power dynamic which often renders the victim incapable of action which would otherwise deter the sexual predator. It is often the case with many sexual preda-tors that any concerted act of rebellion or resistance on the part of the object of their attentions will discourage their attempts, yet the manner in which they exert power and attempt to establish the predator-victim control dynamic is geared toward lulling the victim into an awareness of their own defenselessness. Power often, therefore, plays a central role both in the initial drive and intentions of the sexually dangerous predator, as well in the actions and arousals, both physical and mental, which may follow.

What is the role of narcissism in sexual dangerousness?

Narcissistic traits and a conception of self-grandiosity tend to foster Malignant Narcissism, elaborated upon by a noted personality disorder scholar, who distin-guishes those whose misanthropy leads them to devalue the rights and signifi-cance of others to the point of manipulation, even violence. However, no confirmed links have been made between this form of narcissism and sexual dan-gerousness.

To what extent are sexually dangerous persons mentally disordered?

In the United States, a sexually dangerous person is one who has a history of committing sexual violence; a current mental, personality, or sexual disorder or dysfunction; and the likelihood of future sexual dangerousness. The inclusion of mental disorder in the legal definition of a sexually dangerous person was initi-ated in the 1990s, when legislators were under pressure to keep sex offenders incarcerated for longer periods of time. In response to this unease, numerous states passed legislation permitting the civil commitment of sex offenders to men-tal institutions. In order for this legislation to be effective, however, the definition of sexual dangerousness had to be redefined because civil commitment to a men-tal institution required that an individual was both mentally ill and dangerous. The most significant impact of defining the sexually dangerous as mentally ill is that medicalizing their behavior permits the offender's involuntary and indefinite commitment to a mental institution.

What is the relation among the sexual psychopath, the sexual predator, and the sexually dangerous person?

The sexual psychopath may not be a criminal, but enjoys manipulating others into either being taken advantage of sexually or being the victim of a sexual offense. The sexual predator may or may not be a psychopath, but participates in criminal sexual behavior. Both may be described as sexually dangerous, as may be those who threaten others' well-being through unwanted sexual behavior, such as pedophiles.

How broad is the definition of mental disorder in the sexually dangerous?

If a sex offender is considered afflicted with a mental disease or defect, the individual may not be asked to stand trial, may be involuntarily hospitalized or confined, and all contracts involved may be nullified. There is no listing of the particular diseases or defects that qualify as mental disorders in the legal sense, but the effects of these disorders are considered when issues of insanity arise. A test such as M'Naghten test or the American Law Institute test is applied to determine whether the offense occurred while the individual was incapacitated by a mental disorder. There is disagreement over whether the definition of mental disorder should be defined only along standard clinical terms, such as those provided in the Diagnostic and Statistical Manual of Mental Disorders. In *McDonald v. United States*, for example, the court argued that the definition of what constituted a mental disease or defect could not be left entirely up to science because clinical definitions were designed with regard to treatment, whereas the jury was weighing the disorder's role in affecting criminal responsibility and judgment.

Following the John Hinckley trial, the American Psychiatric Association recommended that only serious mental disorders be grounds for acquittal by reason of insanity. Relevant disorders would be those that impaired cognition but not control; that meant that personality disorders and antisocial personalities would not be recognized in a legal defense. Around the same time, the American Bar Association also proposed that mental impairment must be the result of an organic or functional defect, rather than an issue of character or uncontrollable passion. The Diagnostic and Statistical Manual of Mental Disorders admits that although it cannot provide a consistent practical definition for all situations, a disorder is a clinically important behavioral or psychological syndrome or pattern that is associated with distress or disability, or with a markedly increased risk of death, pain, disability, or interference with normal occupational or social functioning, including criminal behavior.

Many argue that the definition of mental disorder with regard to the sexually dangerous should only be applied if the mental illness in question genuinely contributed to causing the sexual offense in question. It is not productive, they contend, to allow leniency or give treatment to a convicted sex offender whose behavior was not the product of a mental disorder. An indirect but major concern of theirs is ensuring that a mentally disordered sex offender will receive treatment while incarcerated. This is to avoid the practice where mental disorder labeling is used as a means of extending incarceration after time served in prison through civil confinement.

4. PSYCHOLOGICAL CONTRIBUTIONS TO TREATING THE SEXUALLY DANGEROUS

What are the elements of cognitive behavioral therapy?

Cognitive behavioral therapy can be broken into several domains of therapy. Cognitive restructuring aims to address the offender's sexual interests and distorted attitudes. Behavioral therapy's goal is to improve interpersonal functioning and behavior management. There are several goals in cognitive-behavioral therapy. They include enabling the offender to accept responsibility for his offenses; to deal with his emotions, including separation of his anger from sexual thoughts; to develop a supportive social network; to recognize and change cognitive distortions; and to develop and use interventions to avoid future deviant acts. The first domain of treatment addresses the deviant sexual interests of the offender. Treatment aims to decrease deviant sexual arousal by increasing arousal to non-deviant sexual stimuli. The assumption here is that deviant sexual arousal is learned behavior and can therefore be unlearned. Different types of therapy can be used in this domain such as aversion therapy to decrease arousal to deviant thoughts and acts. The second domain of cognitive-behavioral treatment tries to address the distorted attitudes of sex offenders. The focus is mainly directed at victimization awareness and empathy training. The third domain of treatment addresses the improvement of interpersonal functioning through role playing. This domain also includes assertiveness training since many offenders suffer from low self-esteem. The fourth and final domain of treatment is behavior management through covert sensitization and relapse prevention training. Covert sensitization requires the offender to work through the thoughts prior to his offense, allowing the offender to recognize the negative consequences which many offenders often ignore. Relapse prevention training aims to help offenders understand that prevention is a life-long process, and that certain situations threaten to trigger a new offense. However, when these trigger situations occur, he can prevent himself from committing the act through positive coping strategies which he has been taught in therapy.

Either a combination or all four of these domains are employed in order to restructure the offender's cognition and behavior. This treatment may be used in conjunction with other forms of therapy such as family therapy and group therapy.

What are the elements of group therapy?

Group therapy is the most commonly used treatment for sex offenders in the United States. Group therapy is based on the notion that offenders need to confront their manipulative tendencies in a group setting. However, this is based on the assumption that all offenders demonstrate manipulative tendencies. Group therapy is intended to set up an environment in which people can speak honestly and openly about their socially unacceptable sexual tendencies. Hostile confrontation and punitive measures are often employed, and too often there is no effort at providing a theoretical base for the program. Group therapy is often used in conjunction with other forms of therapy such as cognitive-behavioral therapy.

What are the elements of electroconvulsive therapy (ECT)?

Electroconvulsive therapy (ECT) is used sparingly in the treatment of sex offenders. There is insufficient evidence of its efficacy. Electrodes are affixed to a patient's head, and an electric current passes through the electrodes and through the patient's brain, which induces a grand mal seizure. Experts are still unsure as to how ECT actually works, but it has been shown to be effective in cases of severe depression and anecdotal evidence shows that it is effective in treating sex offenders.

What are the elements of chemical castration?

Chemical castration involves administration of drugs that reduce the testosterone levels in sex offenders. Lower testosterone levels reduce sex drive, ease of achieving erection, sexual fantasies, and aggression levels in males. Drugs such as cyproterone and medroxyprogesterone, more commonly known as Depo-Provera, are normally used to lower testosterone to pre-puberty levels. Offenders need to continue taking these drugs in order to maintain low testosterone levels. Chemical castration can be reversed by ending drug treatment.

Chemical castration is available only for repeat sex offenders or pedophiles. Patients typically go to treatment centers once a month for an injection of Depo-Provera.

California promulgated the first chemical castration law in January 1997, requiring that repeat sex offenders receive Depo-Provera in order to be eligible for parole. Florida followed suit in October 1997, allowing chemical castration as part of the punishments for those convicted of sexual battery, and requiring the administration of Depo-Provera to repeat offenders. This would occur subsequent to the approval of a court-appointed medical expert. Georgia, Louisiana, Montana, Oregon, Texas, and Wisconsin have since enacted laws similar to California's and Florida's.

What are the elements of surgical castration?

Another type of castration is surgical castration, which involves removing the testicles. The process, called orchiectomy, is done through small incisions in the scrotum, similar to those required during a vasectomy, to remove the testicles. Chemical and surgical castration therapies are available widely in Europe. In the United States, they may be performed only on repeat sex offenders.

What are the elements of relapse prevention programs?

Relapse-prevention programs teach offenders to anticipate and avoid situations, cues, and behaviors that would lead them to reoffend. Offenders also learn how to cope with their feelings or behaviors that precede sexual offense in order to prevent the offense from occurring. These programs are usually an element of sex offender treatment programs and are available widely.

What are the elements of sexual abuse cycle education?

Offenders participate in programs that teach them about the sexual abuse cycle in order to become aware of the causal factors behind their sexually deviant behavior. The theory behind the sexual abuse cycle is that individuals who are victims of childhood sexual abuse are more likely to sexually abuse others, either because the individual believes such behavior is acceptable, or because the individual is venting his feelings of anger towards his offender by abusing others.

How evidence-based are the results of research on the various programs or treatments?

There is little credible evidence available to support the efficacy of any particular sex offender treatment program. However, there is also no evidence that these programs do not work. One of the issues with the evidence that has been collected is that there is not a legitimate control group for comparison. Many studies do not use a control group at all, and those that do usually use offenders who either drop out of treatment or decline to participate in treatment.

Despite lack of evidence in relation to the effectiveness of group therapy in curing sexual abuse and preventing recidivism, it is often the type of intervention mandated by the criminal system. There is no empirical support for the claim that group therapy is effective in confronting manipulative or deceptive tendencies of sex offenders.

How successful are programs or treatments?

The main goal of treatment for sex offenders is to protect society by preventing future acts of sexual violence. This goal overshadows consideration for the patient's emotional health or adjustment. Someone who is accused of sexual abuse may be required to enter a treatment program even before he is proven guilty. Therefore, there is the chance that innocent people are being forced into treatment programs that often rely on the person's admittance to their own guilt as part of their recovery. Therapy may become punitive in nature when it is used in place of more aversive consequences such as imprisonment, removal from children, loss of job, or loss of money through trial expenses. When treatment is mandated through sentencing or as part of a plea bargain, it undermines the value of the actual treatment. In this situation, the therapist is aligned with the law, causing issues in therapist-patient relationships. The therapist is required to report any additional offenses that are mentioned by the patient. The therapist also is responsible for making regular reports to parole officers, judges, and child protection workers which puts them in a place of great authority. Some evidence has shown that this power can cause therapy to be destructive and damaging to the patient when the therapist takes on a hostile style. Also, research suggests that offenders will often adopt the terminology and explanations of their behavior from their therapist in order to meet their therapist's expectations or to secure an early release. Individually tailored cognitive-behavioral treatment is shown to be highly effective in some research with success rates between eighty-five and ninety-five percent. A cost-benefit analysis performed in one study shows that sex-offender treatment programs are likely to be more than compensated by the benefits they produce, measured by recidivism rates. A national study of programs, however, found that few provided continued follow-up, monitoring, and aftercare services. The minimal amount of credible evidence that has been collected supports the efficacy of cognitive-behavioral treatments. Most research also shows that pure relapse prevention programs are not effective.

What causes the failure of programs or treatments?

Sex offender treatment programs are evaluated based on several criteria, the most essential is whether they have prevented sex offenders from recidivating in the future. Treatment programs also seek to rehabilitate sex offenders to normal functioning, which is measured by how their behaviors and desires comply with social norms. Treatment is normally coerced and ordered by the court; therefore therapists have to deal with patients who might be in denial or who are not very cooperative. Therapy may become punishment itself, and patients cannot choose which programs or therapists to treat them. Agencies normally approve the therapist or treatment program, and the danger with this is that sex offenders may be channeled to only a handful of therapists. The therapist serves as a double agent, a therapist and a jailer, because he has responsibility to the court and society. The patient does not have full confidentiality because anything he discloses under treatment that reveals further offenses he committed must be reported by the therapist to the court. From the patient's perspective, it is difficult to fully trust the therapist, to disclose information about himself and his true feelings. On the therapist's part, there is the possibility that he will develop hostile feelings and counter transference that could interfere with therapy. Oftentimes there is no time limit on the sex offender treatment, or the patient has to stay in treatment only during his incarceration. Therefore, sometimes patients need to withdraw from treatment before they complete the program.

A treatment might also fail if it is not the one best suited to the sex offender. For example, a pedophile with strong physiological sexual urges to molest children that are beyond his control may not be helped simply with psychotherapy, group therapy, talk therapy, cognitive restructuring, or victim empathy. The desire may be so strong that only chemical or pharmacological treatment that changes his physiological composition may be the only treatment that is helpful. The danger is having the pedophile placed in an unsuitable treatment program. Another cause of failure of treatment is that the court may order the sex offender to undergo only castration and no other treatment, thinking that castration will be sufficient. However, though castration lowers the sex offender's sex drive, the sex offender may still continue to molest children to fulfill his mental desires. There is also usually no follow-up treatment after programs end, perhaps leading the sex offender to relapse without additional help from treatment programs. Even with patients who undergo a suitable, comprehensive treatment, the effectiveness rate of these treatment programs is variable. Other problems that could lead to the failure of treatment programs is the lack of theoretical basis behind treatment programs, and a disconnect between the treatment facility and the real world, which would make it difficult for the sex offender to readjust to the real world after treatment ends.

How scientific is the evaluation of programs or treatments?

Sex offender treatment programs are evaluated on their efficacy, whether they have prevented their patients from recidivating, and whether they have succeeded in rehabilitating their patients for society. Studies are done to measure the rate of recidivism once patients leave the treatment program. Studies attempt to have standard terms and objective means of evaluating efficacy. One article, for example, noted the importance of having a standard definition of the terms recidivism and sex offender, and that offense type and length of follow-up differences could affect cross-studies comparisons. These studies strive to be scientifically sound because studies on recidivism rates play a large role in creating policy dealing with sanctions for sexual offenders.

How anecdotal is the evaluation of programs or treatments?

Reports that carefully and scientifically compare different treatments are rare, as are those that actually use control groups, and include follow-up data. Most of the evaluations are merely case reports that do not follow single case design standards.

What is the balance between research and clinical evidence concerning programs or treatments?

Although there is minimal research on the effectiveness of different treatments including group therapy, group therapy continues to be the most widely used form of treatment. Clinical evidence suggests that it may be effective, but more research needs to be conducted. There have been no studies comparing group therapy to other forms of treatment, and only a small set of data supporting the idea that changes occur within a group setting.

What changes have taken place in the treatment of homosexuality?

Up until 1973, homosexuality was considered a sexual disorder, along with pedophilia, necrophilia, bestiality, and other atypical sexual practices. One course of treatment for patients with atypical sexual disorders consisted of reparative therapy, which attempted to change a person's sexual orientation from homosexual to heterosexual, to socialize homosexuals to develop sexual urges for the opposite sex. This included reconditioning and aversive therapy, and these reparative therapies were essential in treatment of both homosexuals and sexual offenders. One form of such reparative therapy included psychologically-based behavior change aversive therapy. In one form, an electric shock was often administered to the patient's leg while the patient watched depictions of homosexual activity. That treatment was generally combined with individual or group psychotherapy, and on occasion with sex therapists who would guide a patient through increasing opposite-sex sexual activity. Non-scientific-based therapies have included attempts by Christian and other clergy to change homosexual orientation through prayer, religious conversion therapy, and individual and group counseling. The reparative therapy movement developed from 1960s psychological professionals Irving Bieber and Charles Socarides, who suggested that homosexuality was a disorder and that it was possible to change one's sexual orientation. In the 1980s, Elizabeth Moberly further promoted the reparative therapy movement by suggesting that homosexuality developed from a developmental deficit. Using theories of Sigmund Freud, Lawrence Hatterer, and Bieber, Moberly theorized that homosexuality developed when an individual was rejected by his or her same-sex parent during childhood. The individual's insecurities were then eroticized and projected onto same-sex individuals. Even though homosexuality has been declassified as a disorder, sexual orientation conversion therapy remains available. The general sense of the psychological community is that reparative therapy does not work for homosexuals. Several studies have noted that these behavior change therapies succeed only in suppressing homosexual urges and not in developing attraction for the opposite sex. These therapies, therefore, diminish sexual desire in general in same-sex oriented individuals. Treatment has shifted from trying to alter the homosexual's sexual preference to affirmative therapy, which seeks to support the patient emotionally in coming to terms with his or her own homosexuality. These gay-affirmative therapies are available to help same-sex oriented people adjust to their awareness of their orientation. These therapies rely on the assumption that homosexuality is intrinsic and unchangeable. Through counseling, therapists inform patients of the issues involved with living as a homosexual in society, and help patients develop emotional, physical, and social wellbeing.

Reparative therapy has been used in treating sexual offenders. At the same time, there has been some acknowledgment that atypical sexual preferences, such as pedophilia and necrophilia, are beyond the individual's control, similar to the psychological community's view of homosexuality. Pharmacological treatment and castration are now available for sexual offenders. These treatment options lower the patient's sex drive and sexual fantasies, decreasing the individual's desire to act on his sexual impulses. While affirmative therapy used for homosexuals has not been extended to sexual offenders, the idea that sexual preferences are inborn has been extended to some extent to the treatment of sexual offenders.

Should evidence of treatment effectiveness be a prerequisite to the commitment of an individual as sexually dangerous?

Some argue that treatment effectiveness for the individual should be a prerequisite of commitment of a sex offender. For example, treatment programs should be catered to patients, keeping in mind which treatment type will most help the patient overcome his sexual impulses. In this way, treatment programs will not be punitive, but rather rehabilitative. Advocates argue against simply corralling sexual offenders into an ineffective treatment facility with the guise of helping the patient, when in fact the patient will emerge years later with the same risk to the community. Others argue that treatment effectiveness is not a necessary prerequisite to commitment of a sex offender. This has been the mode of thought up until recently, as offenders were given many different treatment programs when there either had been no demonstration of effectiveness, or the efficacy rate was very low. Furthermore, evaluation studies do not follow up on patients; therefore, the efficacy rate is oftentimes unknown. However, sex offenders are still offered treatment for punitive reasons—the community and the victim will be somewhat appeased knowing that the system has done its best to ensure that the sex offender will not reoffend.

Should lack of treatment availability be a deterrent to the commitment of an individual as sexually dangerous?

Courts, legislatures, the public, and the mental health professions have grappled with the worrisome issue of whether lack of treatment availability should prevent or deter commitment of an individual as sexually dangerous. Those arguing for protection of the public contend that the sexually dangerous need to be confined. If they cannot be confined or retained under the criminal justice system, because their sentence has run its course or because they were dealt with more leniently in the past than the present circumstances would seem to warrant, then they should be eligible for commitment to an institution whether or not treatment is available there. Treatment, this view argues, is only a distant second goal to protection of the public. Lack of treatment, therefore, should not be a deterrent to the commitment of a sexually dangerous individual since the current goal of confinement would be to prevent recidivism. By detaining sexually dangerous people, the community would be safer. A secondary argument would advance the idea that treatment aimed at preventing future sexually deviant acts is often combined with other forms of treatment that address other cognitive or physical dependency issues. Sex offenders, who often suffer from comorbid psychological and dependency issues such as depression and substance abuse, could finally be treated when they are committed for sexual dangerousness, whether or not their sexual problems were addressed.

Some argue that it is illegal and immoral to civilly confine a sex offender without providing treatment because they believe the detention is a form of punishment imposed outside the criminal justice system. They contend that the purpose of hospitals and other similar facilities is to provide treatment, not to serve as incarcerative locations for punishment. Further, as release is dependent upon recovery in most such detainment centers, recovery, when treatment is not provided, proves impractical.

5. *MEDIA, POLITICAL, SOCIAL, AND RELIGIOUS REACTION TO THE SEXUALLY DANGEROUS*

What are media responses to the sexually dangerous?

The media have never shied away from coverage of the sexually dangerous, especially when the scenarios involved are more lurid or unusual, presumably in response to public interest. Allegations involving celebrities, such as Mike Tyson or Pee Wee Herman, have garnered press not only because of the figures involved, but because the media is aware of the public's obsession with celebrity and its exaggerated features, which is not limited to either worship or vilification. While child sex has and likely always will be taboo, the media circus that has surrounded Michael Jackson's molestation charges in 1993 and 2005, and the relationship between schoolteacher Mary Kay Letourneau and her high school lover, reveal a simultaneous public fascination and disgust. Further to this issue, the media provided significant publicity to the North American Man/Boy Love Association, or NAMBLA, upon its founding, well aware of the predictable public reaction of inquisitive outrage. More atypical scenarios such as those involving claims of ritual satanic abuse, as in the case of Paul Ingram, also generate considerable interest surrounding such feared and mysterious practices.

Violent crime and abuse, however, are dealt with in more sensitive terms, given the significant trauma of the crimes and also the similarities between the victims and the news audience. When serial rapists, especially those involving homicides, and child abuse are reported, the focus generally occupies the purpose of public safety rather than entertainment. When Dennis Rader, known as BTK for Bind Torture Kill, of Kansas was finally captured in 2005, his violent acts were reported with minimal or vague references to the sexual component of those crimes.

Child pornography, in particular, has been approached as an issue with the expected negativity but also with a sense of paranoia. News reports of apparently normal individuals caught with such materials in police stings and surprise raids are widespread, and the resulting paranoia seems to some to stem from the invisible threat to one's own sexual preference, rather than from any actual crime against a child. As a result of legal responses to parental fears over this hidden and pernicious threat to their children, the past decade has seen a significant rise in legislation addressing this issue, such as the Child Protection Restoration and

Penalties Enhancement Act of 1988 and the Child Pornography Protection Act of 1996.

What are political responses to the sexually dangerous?

The political responses to the sexually dangerous are complex and have played a significant role in shaping the social history of many societies. For centuries, political leaders have been particularly adept at using psychological fear of the sexually dangerous to arouse public action and social solidarity. In contemporary American politics, sexual dangerousness in the political realm appears to be divided between those who pose immediate, physical sexual danger and those whose actions are seen as dangerous to the moral fabric or values of a given society. In the first category, one finds sexual predators such as rapists and pedophiles, fear of whom has managed to fuel political momentum around large-scale restructuring of laws as a reaction to the idea that the current laws are insufficiently punitive. Interestingly enough, these kinds of reforms have been pursued from both ends of the political spectrum, demonstrating the political infeasibility of appearing soft on sexual predators. The other group of sexually dangerous people includes those who pose a moral threat to society. Groups such as homosexuals, prostitutes, the bondage and discipline, sadomasochism community, and sexually promiscuous women have often been categorized in this way. Fear of these groups is often harnessed by politicians to create the impression that only certain politicians can sustain the morals of a society. Even as late as the recent American presidential election, some contend that this technique of political exploitation was used with remarkable success by the reelected administration of President Bush. That campaign, they argue, capitalized on growing public anxiety around the issue of gay marriage, and as gay marriage was legalized in Massachusetts and the opposing candidate was from Massachusetts, the winning campaign provided a neat political answer to this new wave of concern about homosexuality in the Federal Marriage Amendment. That campaign, some analysts argue strongly, rallied its base constituency by painting the integration of sexually dangerous peoples into the traditional family as a threat to that family, and as a result, enjoyed a high turnout and recaptured the Presidency.

What are social responses to the sexually dangerous?

Because the news and general word-of-mouth focus so heavily on the sexually dangerous and present them as more prevalent than they are, there are two distinct reactions through which to examine social responses to what are perceived as the ubiquitous sexually dangerous. The first is a preemptive measure, a consequence of the rooted belief that there are certain efforts which, through education, may possibly prevent any sort of future interaction with the sexually dangerous. Beginning early, new parents are strongly encouraged by social pressures to instruct their children to be wary of strangers and never to either go with them or accept anything from them. As the child grows, these instructions are often amplified by preschool and kindergarten teachers, reinforcing the understanding that there is a potential for danger lurking almost everywhere in the world. While parents may avoid giving these lessons an edge of sexual predation to their youngest children, the warnings nevertheless feed the goals of fear and of prevention regardless of the particular explanation which is given. In later years, parents, teachers and peers alike form interlacing webworks of pressure and reaffirmation. Party-going teens are frequently forewarned never to allow someone else to pour or retrieve their drink for them, and never to leave a drink unattended, due to the possibility that it might be spiked or drugged. Horror stories of rape and abuse at such parties often proliferate on high school and college campuses in order to further impress upon young people that there exists a real and imposing danger in lessening one's guard. Parents frequently set curfews in order to deter their children from being beyond their scope of influence for too long, and few leave home without being reminded to remain aware of their surrounds, and to avoid poorly lit areas. Thus, one of the strongest social responses to the existence of sexual dangerousness is the force of preventive measures.

The other social reaction to the sexually dangerous is one which exists for the sake of those who have been victimized. Rather than preemptive measures, it is one of post hoc consolation and support for those who experienced the sexually dangerous firsthand. More generally, society strives strongly to create a lasting and significant impression that the victim should never be blamed for what she or he has gone through, be it date rape or abuse for example. Beyond this, peer help and counseling groups flourish within most major cities, and on the majority of college campuses across the country. Society comes to stress the importance of these safe spaces in order for victims to find a healthy outlet within which they can speak of what they have gone through, and overcome the horrors of the experience.

What are religious responses to the sexually dangerous?

Most Western religions maintain an extremely strong view concerning sexual dangerousness, as much of sex in particular has been seen as the root of moral evil. Because dangerousness inherently involves natural sin, the sexually dangerous subject themselves not only to the law, but to an even higher power, God. However, there are typically two different reactions coming from the same religious group. Because committing a sex crime is such a sin against God and His people, some believe that the sexually dangerous will be sent to eternal damnation. Others believe that if the perpetrator repents for his sins he will be forgiven. In the case of the Catholic Church crisis, the initial response of the church was to cover up the scandal and try to dissociate itself from the crimes. However, that response proved detrimental to the reputation of the church, since the public placed most of the blame on the church and its officials. The church was criticized for hypocrisy, as it attempted to set a stern moral tone concerning homosexuality and sex outside marriage while at the same time dealing leniently with those priests who engaged in sex, whether homosexual or heterosexual, with parishioners. With some other Eastern religions, the sex offenders are excommunicated from society or are imprisoned and castigated by the society with no chance of redemption.

In the American context, religious responses often combine with political responses. Since the rise of religious social conservatism in the 1980s, Protestant evangelicals have led many of the responses to a wide variety of what they consider to be sexual danger. These responses have included harsher punishments against sex offenders, as well as the promotion of the idea that the damage done to the moral fabric of society during the social changes of the 1960s and 1970s were responsible for an increase in sex crimes. In Buddhism, sexuality and sexual danger are seen as impediments to enlightenment. The third precept of Buddha advises individuals not to engage in adultery, rape, pedophilia, or bestiality. Buddhism, however, does not feature the same preoccupation with sexual danger that its counterparts such as Christianity and Islam do.

6. LEGISLATIVE, JUDICIAL, AND OTHER LEGAL RESPONSES TO THE SEXUALLY DANGEROUS

What are legislative responses to the sexually dangerous?

The legislative responses to the sexually dangerous happen at both the national level in Congress and at the state level in state legislatures. State legislatures have passed dozens of sex offender-related pieces of legislation in the last decade and states have historically determined their own rules regarding the regulation of sex and the organization of the family. Prostitution laws, age of consent laws, same-sex marriage laws, and sex offender treatment laws, among other important measures regarding sexual dangerousness, are all determined at the state level.

Congress has passed several influential pieces of legislation regarding sex offenders in recent years, including the Wetterling Act of 1994, Megan's Law, and laws designed to help the Department of Justice prosecute the creators and disseminators of child pornography. Congress's recent boldness in dealing with questions of sex offenders and sexual morality such as those mentioned above represents something of a departure for the federal government and reflects the political viability of rallying against the actual or perceived sexually dangerous. In fact, rallying against what legislators perceived as a disjunction between common sense and morality concerning the sexually dangerous, and an article published in 1998 in an American Psychological Association official publication, Psychological Bulletin, caused Congress to formally condemn, for the first time ever, a scientific article. That article, a meta-analysis by Bruce Rind and colleagues, examined fifty-nine studies and found that the associations between child sexual abuse and later psychopathology in college students were often weaker than generally thought. The American Psychological Association subsequently apologized for having published the study and was itself then criticized by academics and others supporting freedom for scientific inquiry even when its conclusions challenge prevailing views.

What are judicial responses to the sexually dangerous?

The distinction between immediate physical sexual danger and the more general moral sexual danger is important in discussing judicial responses to sexual dangerousness. In regards to individuals and groups who pose immediate physical sexual danger, including rapists, pedophiles, and other sex offenders, the court system has provided a diverse array of opinions, varying from what some call convoluted justifications for greatly punitive laws passed by legislatures to what others call opinions that seem overly protective of the defendant.

In regards to moral sexual danger, the American court system has been at the center of the morality debate involving the sexual freedoms between two consenting adults. In 1986, for example, the U.S. Supreme Court in *Bowers v. Hardwick* found Georgia's laws criminalizing homosexual sodomy constitutional. The Georgia legislature had concluded that such behavior, even if consensual, was so dangerous as to be criminal, and the U.S. Supreme Court found no reason to declare the Georgia statute unconstitutional. Interestingly enough, during deliberations, Justice Powell, who changed his view from dissent to the majority, told justices and a clerk, an unacknowledged gay man, that he had never met a homosexual. Some commentators wondered what might have happened if the clerk had spoken up. And in 1990, in response to discussion after a talk he had given, he said he then had concluded that he had made a mistake by changing his view. He said he had thought the case was frivolous because Hardwick was never prosecuted and that it would have been a different matter if he had been, for then Eighth Amendment issues of cruel and unusual punishment would have been involved.

In 2003, the U.S. Supreme Court reversed itself. The influential *Lawrence v. Texas* case essentially created a right to privacy among adults regarding their sex lives, nullifying hundreds of state and local laws around the country that had criminalized as dangerous sodomy, oral sex, and other common sex practices. Though *Lawrence v. Texas* concerned two gay men who were arrested for sodomy, the logic of the decision extends itself to other groups whose sexual practices are often conceived of as dangerous, including the bondage and discipline and sadomasochism community. The Supreme Court, by defining a right to privacy, appears to have dismissed the potential moral dangerousness of a given sexual act as a reason for its regulation. Further the *Lawrence v. Texas* case formed at least part of the basis for the decision of the Massachusetts Supreme Judicial Court's finding in 2003 in *Goodridge v. Department of Public Health* that the Massachu-setts constitution permitted same-sex marriage.

Courts have also played a central role in defining the dangerousness of obscene materials. *Stanley v. Georgia* found in 1969 that laws against the mere possession of obscene materials were unconstitutional. Four years later, *Miller v. California* set forth the oft-cited community standard definition of obscene materials. The court found that for a material to be obscene it must be considered obscene by the average person applying community standards. Later court cases regarding obscenity have battled over the definitions of the average person and which com-munities are in question in any given instance of obscenity.

What major cases have focused on confining the sexually dangerous?

The major cases that have focused on confining the sexually dangerous include *Kansas v. Hendricks,* 1997; *Kansas v. Crane,* 2002; *Smith et al. v. Doe et al.,* 2003; *Connecticut Department of Public Safety v. Doe,* 2003; and *U.S. v. Morrison,* 2000.

In *Kansas v. Hendricks,* the U.S. Supreme Court upheld the Kansas statute allowing Leroy Hendricks to be involuntarily civilly committed following com-pletion of his prison term. The court ruled that the statute's requirement of a mental abnormality, rather than the psychological specification of a mental ill-ness, in order to commit did not violate Hendricks's rights to due process under the law. In addition, the court ruled that double jeopardy and *ex post facto* laws did not apply to this case because it was a civil, not criminal proceeding, and therefore the issue of punishment was a moot point.

The *Kansas v. Crane* case revisited and clarified Kansas's *Sexually Violent Pred-ator Act* upheld in the *Kansas v. Hendricks* ruling. Justice Breyer wrote in his majority opinion that no demonstration of total or complete lack of control is necessary for civil commitment of a sexual offender to take place; only some determination of inability to control behavior as well as some type of mental ill-ness, abnormality, or personality disorder must be present. This ruling served to greatly increase the number of sexual offenders meeting the necessary criteria to be civilly committed by the state.

Smith et al. v. Doe et al. and *Connecticut Department of Public Safety v. Doe* were two cases in which the Supreme Court upheld Alaska's and Connecticut's particularly stringent statutes involving the registration of sex offenders. The Alaskan statute requires aggravated or repeat sex offenders to register for life and one time non-aggravated sex offenders to register for a minimum of fifteen years, both with quarterly information verification. Both Alaska's and Connecticut's registration laws included internet posting provisions, making once convicted sex offenders' information accessible well beyond the community in which they reside. The Court's decision to uphold these laws suggests a continued trend in providing the states with significant scope in the construction and enforcement of laws confining sex offenders.

U.S. v. Morrison is one example of a Supreme Court decision that actually limited the state's latitude in their confinement of the sexually dangerous, by striking down a more radical provision of the Violence Against Women Act, or VAWA. This decision went against the trend toward ever harsher punishment of the country's sex offenders. The Court ruled that women would not be allowed to sue their aggressors for damages through the federal court system, a provision that the law originally included. The rest of VAWA was left intact, requiring increased penalties for sex offenders and domestic abusers by doubling the maximum prison term for repeat offenders.

What does Kansas v. Hendricks conclude?

Kansas v. Hendricks was a 1997 U.S. Supreme Court ruling that concluded that Kansas's Sexually Violent Predator Act was constitutional. The Kansas law allowed the involuntary civil commitment of sex offenders after they had completed their prison sentences. One sex offender complained that the law was *ex post facto* because it extended his confinement after he had already been sentenced for his crimes. He also complained that his constitutional right to be free from double jeopardy was violated because he had to appear at the separate civil commitment proceedings for his crime. The Supreme Court found that Kansas's law was civil, rather than criminal, and that the sex offender's *ex post facto* and double jeopardy rights applied only to criminal proceedings. Therefore, Kansas's law was constitutional. The ruling opened the door for other states to pass similar laws.

What is the Wetterling Act?

The Jacob Wetterling Crimes Against Children and Sexually Violent Offender Registration Act, also known as the Wetterling Act, enacted in 1994, served as one of Congress's earlier attempts to enforce stricter regulation on protection children from dangerous criminals. In 1989, an eleven-year-old Minnesota boy, Jacob Wetterling, was abducted at gunpoint by a masked man while he, his brother, and a friend were riding their bicycles near the Wetterling residence.

Jacob's body was never found. The Wetterling Act requires convicted child molesters and sexually violent offenders to notify authorities of their whereabouts for ten years after release from prison, parole, or community supervision.

What is Megan's Law?

The law is named in memory of Megan Nicole Kanka, a seven-year-old girl who was raped and murdered by a neighbor and convicted sex offender, Jesse Timmedequas, in a New Jersey suburb during 1994. Megan's Law is an amendment to its preceding statute, the Wetterling Act, and requires law enforcement to notify communities of the presence of a registered sex offender. Each state establishes its own discretionary criteria for disclosing information about registered sex offenders, but must make the information publicly accessible under the national enactment of Megan's Law in 1996 by President Clinton. Some states have implemented a three-tiered system for categorizing sex offenders through low, medium, or high risk of recommitting crimes. More than half the states have also implemented a sex offender registry online.

What is the Lychner Act?

The Pam Lychner Sexual Offender Tracking and Identification Act of 1996 was one of three statutes passed by the United States Congress in the 1990s that required states to strengthen their methods of registering sexual offenders. This act, along with the Wetterling Act and Megan's Law, required states to establish local law enforcement registration programs and enforce public notification programs, following the growing trend toward a more severe confinement of sexually deviant predators in order to keep the community safe. This act was named after Pam Lychner, a Houston real estate agent, who was brutally assaulted by a twice-convicted felon. The attack was interrupted by her husband, and, consequently, her life was saved. The attacker was sentenced to twenty years in prison, but was paroled after only two years. After his release, he sued Lychner for ruining his life. This hypocritical act led Lychner to dedicate her time to encouraging tougher laws against violent crimes.

The Lychner Act, amending the Violent Crime Control and Law Enforcement Act of 1994, sought to make the sex offender registry more powerful by drawing more stringent registration requirements for those once convicted living in a community. Sexually violent predators deemed most dangerous to public under the act would be required to register for life. The act sought to clean up older laws and also bring about organized efforts of the entire country. The law required the FBI to maintain a national sex offender database, known as the National Sex Offender Registry, or NSOR, that would allow authorities to track the movements of registered sex offenders across all fifty states. The FBI was also delegated the responsibility of handling the registration of sex offenders in states that had not yet met the minimum compliance standards, unable to carry out the registration programs on their own. By establishing the NSOR, increasing fines and prison times for registered offenders who move and fail to notify authorities, requiring states to meet minimum registration requirements or face penalties, and officially defining the term sexually dangerous predator, the Lychner Act greatly toughened the registry laws for sexual offenders.

What is the Violence Against Women Act?

The first Violence Against Women Act, or VAWA, was authorized in 1994. It was a landmark piece of legislation in both its scope and its mission. It raised awareness of and subsequently transformed the nation's response to dating and domestic violence, sexual assault, and stalking by officially defining these terms, acknowledging their devastating impact on women's lives, and granting funding to take action. Funds sanctioned by the VAWA were used to support enforcement of protection orders, legal assistance, intensive training, community education, and local community efforts in regards to dating and domestic violence. In 1995, the Office on Violence Against Women, or OVW, was created. Its purpose was to implement the VAWA and provide national leadership to help deal with domestic violence, dating violence, sexual assault, and stalking.

Since the first passage of the VAWA, a shift has occurred in the response to and approach of violence against women. More emphasis is currently placed on local coordinated community response. It is now believed that justice is better served and victims are safer when criminal justice officials, victim advocates, community leaders, elected officials, and health workers all work together to deal with violence against women. Consequently, the more recent Violence Against Women Acts have dealt more specifically with these issues. The VAWA has made a great deal of progress and has had wide reaching effects; in just one of the grant programs, over a six month period, 50,000 victims were served, over 120,000 services were provided to victims, almost 24,000 individuals were trained regarding violence against women, and more than 2,600 individuals were arrested for violation of protection orders. However there is still a great deal of work to be done in regards to domestic violence and sexual assault.

What are the roles of defense and prosecution lawyers in cases of the sexually dangerous?

A defense lawyer assists the defendant in collecting evidence for exoneration throughout the entire case. He investigates the facts and evidence, cross-examines government witnesses, objects to improper questions and evidence against his defendant, and represents the legal defense of his client. A defense lawyer advises the defendant of his or her rights and assures that his client understands the criminal procedure. The lawyer ensures that a defendant's constitutional rights are not violated by law enforcement personnel or during court proceedings and may negotiate a plea bargain with the government on behalf of his client.

Prosecution lawyers in criminal trials are the chief legal representatives responsible for presenting a case against a defendant charged with breaking the law. Prosecution lawyers, unlike defense attorneys, possess the primary role of seeking justice rather than victory in the form of a trial conviction. Prosecuting attorneys, therefore, will often try to settle, foregoing the risks and costs of a trial, through a plea agreement. The agreement usually involves a plea of guilty to a lesser charge or a more lenient sentence than would have resulted in an outright guilty verdict in a trial.

How much evidence is required in cases of the sexually dangerous?

In the United States, criminal defendants are strictly protected by legal standards and are found guilty only if the evidence or proof presented is beyond the reasonable doubt. Many experts believe that this standard amounts to certainty of between ninety-five and ninety-nine percent. This helps to assure that innocent suspects are not incarcerated or punished for a crime they did not commit. A lack of legal proof is considered to be a consequence of insufficient evidence. Sufficient evidence is required for proof to convict or persuade an arbiter, namely a judge or a jury.

What are the roles of psychologists in cases of the sexually dangerous?

Psychologists often play important roles in individual cases. Their opinions and evaluations are relied upon for expert testimonies which can be one of the determining factors in the final verdict of a case. Psychologists are generally called in to give their opinions, officially labeled an expert testimony because of their qualifications, of an individual's sanity prior to the crime, at the time of the crime, and currently. Their diagnoses are important because they often play a role in deciding how to deal with the defendant in such issues as whether the defendant is capable of standing trial and whether the criminal's current or past sanity should be taken into account when determining the verdict. However, psychologists have no final decision making power and their role is often undermined by the fact that psychological diagnoses are somewhat subjective. Often both the prosecution and the defense bring in different psychologists who each have their own opinions of the past or current mental state of the defendant. In the case where expert testimonies conflict, which they often do, the psychological decision is left to the judge or the jury who most likely have minimal experience with psychological disorders.

To what extent does the view of confinement as non-punitive conform to the reality of confinement?

The confinement of sexually violent predators following the completion of a prison sentence is often referred to as a civil commitment. Because the confinement is civil, rather than criminal, it is legally considered non-punitive in nature. Therefore, the official purpose of the confinement statutes is not to inflict further punishment. When sexual psychopath statutes, as they were originally termed, first appeared in the mid-twentieth century calling for the special commitment of sexual offenders, they were aimed at rehabilitation through an indeterminate involuntary psychiatric hospitalization in place of incarceration. The statues were based on the belief that sex offenders had clearly recognizable mental illnesses and were therefore good candidates for treatment. When treatment proved largely unsuccessful, the therapeutic and rehabilitative nature of confinement began to lose favor with the public and the criminal justice system. Today, the existence of a mental abnormality is still necessary in order to confine a sexual offender through civil commitment, but the law does not guarantee treatment to those committed. Because the law considers confinement neither punitive nor rehabilitative, its purpose is that of preventive detention and the protection of society.

The legal system regards this type of confinement as non-punitive, as indicated by the U.S. Supreme Court's ruling in *Kansas v. Hendricks* that the sexually violent predator statutes, calling for the special commitment of sexual offenders, do not violate double jeopardy, *ex post facto* laws, or substantive due process.

However, many critics of civil commitment feel that the constitutionality of the sexually violent predator statutes is highly questionable because the statutes themselves are ambiguous and in fact do serve a punitive purpose because their very nature is marked by extended incapacitation without any prerequisite of treatment.

What should the balance be between civil liberties and public safety?

The balance between civil liberties and public safety is a tension that has existed since the drafting of the Constitution and remains today. Though outside the scope of this book, that tension permeates the discussion of the war on terror and of persons considered dangerous who are suspected of, accused of, or found responsible for terrorist acts. As that tension and that balancing applies to sexual dangerousness, the distinction between immediate sexual danger to individuals and long-term danger to the social and moral fabric of society becomes important again and asks the question as to who and what is really physically at risk when it comes to sexual dangerousness. The idea of civil liberties is inherent in American political discourse as the Bill of Rights and the subsequent amendments to the Constitution have made guarantees to the individual citizen regarding the sovereignty of his or her actions. The notion that an individual has a near-absolute right to control a particular sphere of one's life, such as thought and faith, is derived from the thinkers of the Enlightenment such as John Locke. Civil liberties and civil rights exist for the benefit of the individual at the expense of the state. This notion is contrasted against the idea of utilitarianism, which holds that whatever action will benefit the most people in society should be pursued.

The tension between civil liberties and public safety is a conflict between these two schools of thought, both of which imagine themselves to be the fundamental element of a free democracy. Contemporary advocates from the civil liberties perspective include the American Civil Liberties Union, civil libertarians, and other rights-based advocacy groups, most of which fall to the left of the political spectrum. Generally, these groups consider civil rights and civil liberties to be inalienable and that conditions in which a government may encroach on these rights should be either non-existent or minimal. Moreover, some of these groups, including the ACLU, advocate a broader interpretation of what qualifies as civil rights to reflect a changing society. On the other side of the debate are those who claim that the positions taken by the ACLU and its allies are too extreme and do more harm than good to American democracy. Many on this side of the debate advocate that there must be conditions in which civil liberties are sacrificed for the public good. Among these conditions is the threat of sexual harm. Is sexual harm such an egregious violation of public safety that preventing it should supercede the civil liberties of those deemed sexually dangerous?

This issue has the most resonance regarding convicted sex offenders and the special restrictions placed on them after their release from prison. Proponents of these laws claims that sex offenders are the most likely to reoffend, that treatment rarely works, and the only recourse for protecting people from sexual predators are these restrictions. Opponents, however, claim that the criminal justice system should ask offenders to pay for their crimes in a given prison sentence, not as a lifetime category, and these special restrictions turn sex offenders into second class citizens. The debate between proponents and opponents continues, as the answers to the frequently asked questions and the cases in this book illustrate. Whether with regard to the dangerous by means of terrorism or to the sexually dangerous, the specific issues and the general considerations detailed in this book will continue to be at the forefront of society's concerns. Balancing will remain a difficult task for all who undertake it.

Case Examples

7. CASE STUDIES

Bernard Baran
Child rape and a day-care center

Abstract

On January 30, 1985, Bernard Baran, then nineteen years old, was convicted of three counts of rape and five counts of indecent assault and battery on children aged three to five. Baran worked at the Early Child Development Center in Pittsfield, Massachusetts as a teacher's aide. The Baran case was one in a series of accusations of day care sexual abuse in the 1980s, which have been challenged legally and psychologically in recent years. Baran has spent twenty years in prison for a crime, which much of the evidence suggests he did not commit. Recently, attorney John Swomley, along with others, has been fighting for a new trial for Baran. This case has raised many legal and psychological issues that impact cases of the sexual abuse of children.

His early life

Bernard Baran was born on May 26, 1965, in Pittsfield, MA. He was the youngest of three children. His father abandoned the family when Bernard was three. His mother, Bertha, caring and hard working, loved her children very much. In his early teens, Bernard realized he was gay. Although his mother understood, empathized, and still loved him, Bernard was victimized at school where his classmates were routinely cruel and frequently violent toward him. When Bernard turned sixteen and completed ninth grade, he left school. At this time Baran entered the Comprehensive Employment and Training Act, or CETA. In this program he was assigned to the Early Child Development Center, or ECDC, a Pittsfield daycare center. This was a good job for Baran since he had a lot of experience babysitting and liked children. Baran did well in the program and at ECDC, and in August 1981 ECDC hired him directly to work as a teacher's aide. His performance at ECDC was excellent, the children liked him, and no parent ever complained. All of that changed on October 4, 1984.

The accusations

Baran's life was tragically altered when a boy, named Peter Hanes, a pseudonym, as are all other names of children and their families, accused Baran of molesting him. Peter's life at home was profoundly difficult. His father, James, left his wife, Julie, when Peter was a newborn. James' brother, David became romantically involved with Julie and soon moved in with her and her two sons. Both Julie and David had serious problems with drugs. They used cocaine as well as barbiturates and opiates. Julie often overdosed. David was both deceitful and abusive toward Julie and the children. He stole the prescriptions for the children's medications for himself. Peter often showed up at ECDC with large bruises. Julie showed signs of abuse as well, and was once dangled by her ankle from a second story window while David threatened her with death. Because of the major problems in the Hanes household Peter was briefly put into foster care.

Not surprisingly, Peter had major personal and behavioral problems at ECDC. He suffered intense mood swings, injured other children and often screamed obscenities. He threw objects at teachers and children, defecated in the play area, and wet himself nearly every day at naptime. His mother was told to send a change of clothes with him every day, but she usually forgot.

In the fall of 1984, David Hanes complained to ECDC that he did not want Baran around Peter because Baran was a homosexual. Because of Baran's sexual orientation, David Hanes believed he should not be permitted to work at ECDC. On October 1, 1984 Peter Hanes was taken out of daycare at ECDC. On October 5, David Hanes called the police to say that Peter had come home from school the day before, a day on which he had not in fact even at been at ECDC, with blood on or coming out of his penis. The blood was allegedly discovered while Peter was taking a bath on the night of October 4 when he complained that he was in pain. Peter was then asked if anyone had touched him there and he allegedly said that Baran had done so.

The investigation

This allegation launched an investigation and caused widespread panic among many of the parents at ECDC. When the police spoke with the staff at ECDC they were told that it was ECDC's policy never to leave any one adult alone with children. In every room there was a head teacher, an assistant teacher, and a teacher's aide. There were also CETA workers and volunteers continually around. Bathroom doors were kept open in case children needed help. There was little chance that a person could get away with molesting a child without someone seeing or hearing it. Regardless of this fact there was alarm, although at this point Baran did not even know he was being investigated.

After this initial investigation, the ECDC Coordinator, Carol Bixby, called her friend, Judith Smith, to tell her about the allegations. Smith had a three-year-old daughter, Gina, who had attended ECDC. She had been in Baran's room from April to July but only for about five hours a week. After Smith spoke to her, Bixby began grilling Gina, asking her leading questions about whether Baran had ever touched her in an inappropriate manner. Gina at first said nothing untoward had happened, but then revealed that she and Baran had played the Bird's Nest Game and that Baran had touched her privates. Mrs. Smith was shocked and called the police because she believed that Gina could not have fabricated such a story. The police later interviewed Gina. Although she initially would not talk, after much prodding and questioning by the detectives and a social worker, she told a bizarre story of physical and mental abuse.

After this, Baran was arrested. Jane Satullo of the Rape Crisis Center completed further interrogations of Peter and Gina. She videotaped her interviews, which used anatomically correct dolls so that the children could show where they had allegedly been abused. A young pediatrician named Dr. Jean Sheely, examined Gina and Peter. Gina had been seen by Dr. Sheely in July after leaving ECDC, at which time no anomalies or problems had been found. Now, however, on closer examination, Dr. Sheely noted a one to two millimeter tear in her hymen. Studies have shown that hymeneal flaws are common among all children, not only those who have suffered abuse; small hymeneal tears actually occur in fifty to sixty percent of non-abused children. In spite of this, Dr. Sheely noted the damage as proof that Gina had suffered abuse. During the examination Gina added to her story, claiming that she had blood on her privates and that Baran cleaned it up. She maintained that the assistant teacher, Eileen, had witnessed this. She also later said that Stephanie, the head teacher, had witnessed it as well.

A throat culture performed on Peter Hanes was positive for gonorrhea, which was also entered into evidence as proof of abuse by Baran, even though Baran's gonorrhea test was negative. In a 1988 study by the federal Centers for Disease Control, it was found in over one third of the cases where children tested positive for gonorrhea, the organism was actually something else. At the trial, Prosecutor Daniel Ford would bring in a physician to testify that gonorrhea was most common in prostitutes and male homosexuals, which reinforced the biased view that gay men are likely to carry the disease.

Subsequent to Baran's arrest, a meeting was held for the panicked ECDC parents. Social workers distributed a list of symptoms for sexually abused children, which included bedwetting, nightmares, fear of the dark, and genital curiosity, among other things. Though any three to five year old child could innocently exhibit these indicators, the ECDC parents presumed their children had been abused by Baran based on having observed some or all of these symptoms in their children. The children were also shown a puppet show in which good and bad ways of touching were demonstrated. This type of display has subsequently been shown to be highly suggestive for young children, and indeed, after this meeting, four more accusers came forward.

Two of the new allegations appear to be objectively baseless, yet they were taken completely seriously and entered into evidence against Baran. Two boys accused Baran of abusing them in a shed while on a winter field trip. The two boys, however, had only been in Baran's room in the summer, and the shed was kept locked. Baran had no key and more significantly, Baran had never been on such a field trip.

Another accuser was Virginia Stone. Virginia's mother, Marsha Stone Lopez, was a close friend of Julie Hanes, and Marsha was a prostitute. Virginia initially denied any incident, but came later forward with a story of abuse. An insurance company report stated that Virginia told a therapist that nothing really happened but her mother had ordered her to tell a story of abuse so they could get money and toys.

The last accuser was a girl who had just turned three who, when pressed to describe how Baran had touched her, told an investigator from the Department of Social Services that Bernie had touched her in a place she referred to as her tuku.

The trial

After the allegations, Baran was offered a plea deal to serve five years in prison. If he had accepted, he would have been out of jail for the past fifteen years. However, Baran would not admit to something he insisted he had never done. When the case went to trial, Baran had only five hundred dollars to spend on his own defense and so could not afford a private attorney. The public defender did little to discredit the testimony of the children and their advocates, and the defense's case lasted only one day. Baran's homosexuality played a central role in the prosecutor's case against him.

Before the trial the children were rehearsed many times by social workers, police, and their parents. A psychiatrist, Suzanne King, was also hired to see Gina Smith once a week. During these meetings, Gina's story became more and more bizarre and implausible. Her final story was that Baran scooped blood from her vagina with scissors and then stabbed her in the foot with the scissors. All of this, according to her, had occurred in a doorless bathroom adjacent to a classroom filled with teachers and other children who testified that they had never heard or seen anything.

At trial, Baran was denied the right to confront his accusers. The children were seated so they did not have to see Baran and he could not see them. Because of this, Baran had a hard time following what was occurring at his trial.

In spite of all their rehearsals with parents and social workers, the children were poor witnesses. They had trouble responding and often did so nonverbally, nodding or shaking their heads in reply to questions. Prosecutor Daniel Ford was allowed to ask leading questions, and was even permitted to repeat questions until the children came up with what he considered the right answer that they had previously forgotten or incorrectly expressed. In an interesting turn of events that the judge and jury ignored, Peter Hanes was brought into the courtroom and ran over to Baran to greet him happily. When Peter was taken away from Baran he protested loudly, then complained that he did not like the attorneys. When questioned by Ford, he responded either with silence or by screaming curse words.

When Gina Smith was asked if she bled, she answered that she forgot it. Ford followed up with a barrage of leading questions, including asking her what Bernie had done when the blood came out. Finally, she repeated her story that he had scooped it out with scissors. However, she went on to state that this had been done in the classroom, which was inconsistent with her prior statements. At this point Ford reminded her that it had happened in the bathroom.

When other children testified they often gave answers that differed from previous versions, and Ford repeatedly questioned them as he had Gina, suggesting that they were simply too frightened to tell the truth. One boy admitted under cross-examination that he had been telling fake stories, while another girl insisted that she liked Baran and that he was a good boy.

The majority of the parents seemed to believe sincerely that their children had been abused and so were good witnesses for the prosecution. The teachers, on the other hand, were solid witnesses for the defense. They testified that there was a complete lack of privacy at ECDC and therefore no opportunity for abuse to occur unnoticed, and they testified that they had never witnessed any suspicious behavior whatsoever. The therapists, King and Satullo, testified that children were not suggestible and dismissed all the inconsistencies in the children's stories. They asserted unequivocally that there had never been cases of children falsely accusing anyone, an assertion now known to be false. King also stated that the parents' anxiety was not transferable to the child, a claim that has likewise since been proven false. Research by Loftus, Bruck, Ceci and others has shown that children are highly susceptible to suggestion and anxiety is, in fact, transferable.

Baran then took the stand. He answered all questions and continually denied that he had done anything improper with any child. Dan Ford repeatedly asked Baran about his relationship with his boyfriend and whether he liked children. Ford was unable to establish a motive, but did establish the fact that Baran was a gay man who liked children.

Daniel Ford's closing argument wove a web of innuendo, making connections between homosexuality and pedophilia that were insupportable by research and not even suggested by anecdotal evidence. Stating that Baran had many opportunities to abuse the children at ECDC, Ford implied that because Baran was a homosexual, he was also a pedophile. In his summation, Ford equated being a homosexual with being a child molester, suggesting that at ECDC, Baran was like a chocoholic in a candy store.

The jury spent a little more than three hours deliberating. They found Baran guilty on all counts: three of rape and five of indecent assault and battery. He was sentenced to two concurrent life sentences.

Not all the parents believed that Baran was guilty. One mother equated Baran with a miracle worker who had helped her son overcome his problems and start on a path of normal childhood. She pleaded for Baran before sentencing, but to no avail. A 1986 appeal of Baran's case was denied. Now, twenty years after his conviction, Baran remains in prison. Because he continues to maintain his innocence, he does not show the requisite remorse, and so parole is not a possibility for him.

Life in jail and hope for the future

During the two decades that Baran has spent in jail he has suffered physical and mental abuse, both from other inmates and from the prison staff. He claims he has been repeatedly raped and abused, and has been given insufficient medical treatment. He wrote letters in which he stated that he often has no hope, because he has been fighting for justice and freedom, and neither has been achieved. He has said he does not know how much longer he can go on. In his letters he wrote that he is regarded as the lowest of the low: a sexual predator who preys on children. For his own safety, Baran has been held at the Bridgewater Treatment Center, where he was committed as a sexually dangerous person.

In the past few years Boston attorney John Swomley has become aware of Baran's case, and has been working diligently to get Baran a new trial. Swomley stated that he never asks his clients about their guilt or innocence, but believes that Baran is an innocent man, based not only upon the evidence, but also upon his demeanor. Other inmates, including one who has been incarcerated for twenty-three years and is a self-described sexual abuser, have stated that they are certain that Baran is an innocent man. Corrections officers have noted that they, too, believe that Baran is an innocent man. Three of the six child accusers recanted their stories after Baran's conviction; two told their therapists within a few months of the convictions, and a third did so in front of a high school class.

Among the reasons militating for a new trial, one is particularly notable: the law firm Cain, Hibbard, Myers & Cook had a conflict of interest that may have affected the quality of the 1986 appeal that the firm prepared for Baran. More specifically, the firm represented the family of a girl who attended ECDC and who was one of Baran's accusers. The family wished to prepare a civil suit against ECDC seeking financial retribution. Swomley has suggested that the firm's interest in the Baran criminal case predated even the start of Baran's trial. David O. Burbank, a former Cain, Hibbard associate testified that he represented the girl and her family, and that he helped to prepare Baran's criminal appeal. This conflict appeared to have played a part in the declination of Baran's first appeal.

Swomley filed a motion for a new trial on June 17, 2004, and later a supplement to that initial motion, including more documentation alleging the unfairness of the initial trial and citing evidence for Baran's innocence. An evidentiary hearing on March 21, 2005 was held at the Worcester County Courthouse and Judge Francis Fecteau presided. The hearing presented the most current research concerning the use of anatomically correct dolls in cases of child sexual abuse, including the fact that this approach was discontinued due to the high incidence of false confessions obtained by their use. Swomley has also maintained that the prosecutor in the case, Daniel Ford, now a Superior Court judge, buried evidence to secure a high-profile conviction and fame for himself in prosecuting and convicting a sexual predator who preyed on children, an accomplishment that made him popular with the public.

Further hearings were held on April 21, 2005 and June 16, 2005. Swomley presented additional evidence of prosecutorial misconduct, including the withholding of exculpatory evidence and ineffective assistance of counsel. He also presented newly discovered evidence. At the end of the hearing Judge Fecteau stated that he would reach a ruling as quickly as possible, but he also warned everyone that he had a voluminous amount of material to read and evaluate, and he was very busy with other commitments. Baran still awaits the final ruling.

The 1980s sexual abuse accusation epidemic and psychological lessons

In the 1980s there was an escalation of accusations of sexual abuse against day care workers. The Baran case was the first conviction in a string of day care child molestation cases, which also included the Amirault and McMartin cases. Baran's case did not draw as much immediate or long-term media attention as the other two.

The Fells Acres Day Care Center case also took place in Massachusetts. Gerald Amirault, his sister, Cheryl, and their mother, Violet, were convicted by juries and received long sentences for sexually abusing students at their day care center. The evidence strongly suggested that the abuse could not and did not happen. This case included many fantastical stories of abuse which included space ships, children naked and bound to trees on a busy urban street in the daytime, as well as the characterization of Gerald Amirault as a magic clown. The judge and jury did not seem to think rationally about the evidence. Amirault was convicted and sentenced to prison. He was released on parole on April 30, 2004 after serving eighteen years.

The McMartin Case, which took place in California, was another well-known and sensational example of 1980s child sexual abuse hysteria. In this case the first accusation came from an alcoholic, paranoid schizophrenic woman who insisted that her son had been sexually abused. It was suggested by many who knew her that the accusations were no more than hallucinations on her part. After the first accusation more children came forward claiming to have suffered sadistic, ritual sexual abuse, which almost certainly could not have occurred under the actual circumstances. The case took over six years to make its way through the courts, and ended with no convictions. It was the most expensive trial in history, costing California over ten million dollars. The McMartins were bankrupted, their lives and livelihood destroyed.

There were many other cases of a similar nature that were prosecuted in the 1980s. The hysteria associated with these trials, with their questionable court proceedings and faulty psychological data, brought about still more accusations and prosecutions during this time period. One thing many of these cases have in common is that they were built around improper interviewing techniques employed with young children. Since those cases in the 1980s, it has been proven that children can, indeed, fabricate complex and detailed stories of sexual abuse, given enough prodding from parents, social workers, and psychologists. The use of anatomically correct dolls has also been shown to promote false stories of abuse.

The psychologist Dr. Maggie Bruck is an expert on child testimony. She has published over forty articles in peer-reviewed journals. She and Stephen Ceci published the book *Jeopardy in the Courtroom*, a book about child testimony. Bruck and Ceci's research shows that nearly every technique used in the Baran case was flawed, and that many of the assumptions psychologists used in the case were incorrect. Bruck's research has shown that children may be reluctant to reveal sexual abuse, but when questioned about the abuse, there is very little evidence that the children will ever deny that it occurred. Bruck has also found that recantations are extremely rare. Studies conducted by Bruck, as well as by many others, have also shown that children come to believe the statements of interviewers: children are, in fact, very vulnerable to suggestion. Another major point that Bruck brings up regarding the unfairness of child interviews is the fact that videotapes of child interviews rarely depict the first interview, as was the case in the Baran trial. This is a problem, because early interviews tend to contaminate subsequent interviews.

Bruck has outlined the proper way to interview children, so that they are less likely to invent stories. The correct way to interview a child is to use open-ended questions and to have children say things in their own words. Interviewers should not guide children along their own preconceived path. The interviewer must stress to children the necessity of only talking about things that actually happened. Most importantly the interviewer must be neutral on the subject and must think about the child's story and whether it makes sense. The child psychiatrist Dr. Suzanne King who interviewed Gina and the counselor Jane Satullo in the Baran case seemed to have violated all of these rules and procedures.

Bruck demonstrated that the major problem afflicting improper interviewing is interviewer bias. Another hallmark of poor interviewing is atmospherics. Atmospherics occur when the interviewer sets a specific tone, making emotionally charged statements such as telling the child that he knows he is scared. The interviewers of the children in the Baran case were routinely guilty of this, as was Daniel Ford.

One more major problem with the Baran interviews was that they all used anatomically correct dolls. The children saw and treated the dolls as play objects, not as symbols of themselves or Baran. The children also used them suggestively. Bruck points up in her research that three- and four-year-old children do not yet have the cognitive apparatus to use these dolls properly. Children this young do not understand that the dolls are supposed to represent them or other people; they react to the dolls as dolls, not as symbols.

A major psychological lesson to be learned from these cases is the importance of skillful, objective, careful conduct by a professional in the interview of children about sexual abuse. It is obvious that suggestive techniques cause the children to assert things that may never have happened. Rewarding children for admitting things that never occurred will encourage them to do so. The extent to which stereotypes and bias against certain groups can influence a case is another important lesson to be learned from the child abuse cases of the 1980s. For example, in the Baran case there were many examples of how significantly homophobia influenced the parents', prosecutors', investigators', and jurors' views of the case.

This case raises several critical questions, not the least of which is how we are to view child testimony and accusations about sexual abuse. The Baran case forces us to consider how seriously child testimony about and accusations of sexual abuse are taken and how seriously they should be taken. Although child accusations of sexual abuse must be investigated and taken seriously, fantastical stories of abuse with little or no physical or logical substantiation need to be scrutinized much more carefully and examined with appropriate skepticism. At the same time, children's claims of abuse that have even the tiniest bit of actual evidence need to be pursued and prosecuted vigorously.

The Baran case, along with other false accusations of sexual abuse, raises concerns about the manipulation of children; the unquestioning belief of children's stories of abuse that have often been fabricated or embellished with the help of parents and/or psychologists. The major lesson of this case is the necessity to fully investigate claims of sexual abuse and to substantiate those claims with actual evidence. Additionally, those charged with carrying out the law must guard against allowing prejudices against homosexuals or other minority groups to affect how a case is handled. It seems clear that in the Baran case, many people involved presumed the fact that Baran was gay was evidence that he was therefore sexually dangerous. It is clear that a constellation of biases warped this case, causing an innocent man to sit in prison for over twenty years. Baran's only hope is that he can receive a new trial in which the facts can be presented and objectively viewed.

Notes about sources

The website www.freebaran.org was an invaluable resource in researching this case. The site includes detailed accounts of the case along with letters from Baran about his ordeal and links to nearly every Baran source on the internet. A short video entitled *The Bernie Baran Story*, by The Choirboy Regime, was also used. The articles *Lost Innocents* and *Subject to Debate* by Katha Pollitt from the *Nation* were helpful sources. The motions filed by John Swomley and the transcripts from the hearings to aid in the procurement of a new trial for Baran were consulted as well. I used the police reports and the transcripts of the testimony of all the witnesses at the trial. The book *Jeopardy in the Courtroom* was also very helpful for information on proper and improper child testimony and interviewing techniques.

Benjamin Davis and Stefany Reed
Consensual sadomasochism

Abstract

In July 2000, a police raid in Attleboro, Massachusetts resulted in the arrest of the host and one guest at a sadomasochistic party. Called the Attleboro Raid, or Paddleboro by those who challenged the police action, the occurrence sparked a series of court battles as well as substantial inter-community discussion on what was perceived to be dangerous, abusive sexual inclinations, and the law's stance in respect to such practices. This case study examines both the nature of the community which fosters such activities, as well as the legal and psychological debates which were catalyzed during and in the aftermath of the court case.

Bondage and discipline, domination and submission, sadism and masochism

The Bondage/Discipline, Domination/Submission, and Sadism/Masochism lifestyle, otherwise known as BDSM, is marginalized in American society. It resides at the fringe of sexuality that, as those of the lifestyle like to claim, was once occupied by homosexuals. Each of the three dualities has evolved into its own distinct interpretation of the lifestyle and brings into the picture varying materials and conceptions. Generally speaking, however, they each share an ambience of give and take, of pleasure and pain, of the dominating force and the dominated force. Sadism/Masochism, one of the more proliferating relationships within the BDSM community as a whole, involves the sadist inflicting harm upon a consenting masochist, a two way relationship in which the former gains pleasure from harming another, and the masochist gains pleasure from the pain being inflicted upon them.

Those in the scene, however, are quick to point out that what takes place is far from abuse. Those who take BDSM into a dangerous extreme are rejected from the community in a firm and consistently self-screened monitoring that is ever ongoing. If a submissive reports ill of a dominant, word often spreads throughout the community, a process of social scrutiny that discourages going too far into their chosen roles. A pair will often employ what are known as safe words, which can be spoken by the submissive or masochist in order to gain an immediate end to whatever activities are occurring.

In a reflection of its strong concern for protection and personal wellbeing, the community adopted a maxim: Safe, sane, and consensual. Most community

BDSM groups have provided information on safe practices to the curious, and have hosted selective events for those in the lifestyle to meet and interact in a safe and private environment. While outsiders have tended to focus on the use of props in BDSM, such as floggers, rope, handcuffs, and whips, those who have lived the life claimed that they have paid far more attention to ensuring the safety of those involved. One submissive remarked that no matter what might have been done to her or how scared she became, she always knew at the back of her mind that she would never have been truly hurt beyond reason. Her dominant was quick to chime in, asserting that while fear was often an important aspect of BDSM play, it was always intended to be superficial. As soon as the submissive was in a position to be genuinely hurt, the allure of the moment was gone. It was what happened when the fantastic and misunderstood met the eyes of the media, he said, that gave this open-minded community its bad reputation.

The Attleboro raid

On Saturday, July 8, 2000, in Attleboro, Massachusetts, local police broke up a private sadomasochism party. The guests, all known well by the host, were all over twenty-one years of age. A donation at the door was requested but not required, and the host later claimed that all monies collected were donations to cover food, drink, and rent charges for the space. The party, like many of its kind, was intended to provide private space for consenting adults to engage in alternative sexual activities involved in the BDSM lifestyle. As the BDSM communities were concerned with educating their members about technical skills and safety issues relating to their activities, these parties permitted members of the community the opportunity to observe, learn, and practice a variety of activities under the tutelage of more experienced members. In this way, the parties often functioned as educational workshops where novices could safely learn new techniques and receive assistance when necessary.

At the time the police arrived on the scene, thirty-five to forty people were in attendance. Despite repeated requests from the host and a few other guests to see a warrant, one was never produced. Benjamin O. Davis, the host of the party, told the detectives that they could not enter without a warrant. One of the policemen later claimed that Davis shoved another officer as they crossed the threshold of the house, and he arrested Davis on an assault charge and handcuffed him. Along with a printed copy of the guest list, upon which all those in attendance were identified by their online screen name or handle, the host had his wallet, Palm Pilot, and employer-issued laptop computer seized by the Attleboro police.

Likewise, equipment bags belonging to the host and many guests were also confiscated, some without property receipts from the police.

Two people were arrested. The first, Benjamin Davis, was the host of the party and was arraigned on twelve separate charges, including operating a business without a license, keeping a house of prostitution, possession of an item of "self-abuse," assault and battery of a police officer, accessory to assault and battery before the fact for facilitating consensual acts of S&M being performed at the party, and eight counts of possession of a dangerous weapon for possessing BDSM accessories.

The second individual was Stefany L. Reed, a guest who was charged with one count of assault and battery for spanking another scantily clad female partygoer with a wooden spoon despite the claimed consensual nature of the act, and possession of that dangerous weapon. The Attleboro case of Benjamin Davis, or Paddleboro as the BDSM community rallied behind it, was taken up by defense attorney David Duncan, a partner in Zalkind, Rodriguez, Lunt, and Duncan. The prominent firm was well known in Massachusetts for its successful defense in several high-profile criminal and civil cases. Richard M. Egbert was Stefany Reed's attorney.

General legal issues

The Attleboro raid created a series of ripples, both in the BDSM and legal communities, by raising several distinct legal issues regarding civil liberties and sexual privacy, particularly in an aspect of sexuality which is arguably more widespread than most believe. The 1990 Kinsey Institute Report on Sex claimed that between five and ten percent of the U.S. population engaged in sadomasochism for sexual pleasure on at least an occasional basis. Further, a later research survey in 1998 found that forty-nine percent of the men and thirty-eight percent of the women surveyed have spanked or have been spanked as part of their sexual foreplay. The law in Massachusetts, however, clearly indicated that spanking your sexual partner, even with his or her consent, was illegal.

The BDSM community has been quick to point out both the puritanical and archaic nature of the applicable laws. Especially with such sexual practices on the rise according to the previous studies, it has been contended that these laws were being selectively applied against a community who composed too small a minority to have had a sufficient voice. Further, as evidenced by on site testimony and complaints from the Boston leather and fetish community, all that was transpiring over the course of the Attleboro party was consensual. Those involved were adults all well over age, and the woman who had been spanked with the spatula insisted that nothing had been done against her will or without her knowledge.

Other legal issues which this case raised included the right to sexual privacy and the freedom of alternative sexual expression among consenting adults, indulging in a parallelism with gay and lesbian rights ten to twenty years ago that lifestylists had been quick to point out. It raised the question about the right of people to participate in consensual sex of any sort, in private, without necessarily fearing that the police would arrest them. In Massachusetts, as in many states, it was illegal to own an instrument for "self-abuse," which included sex toys as well as more traditional BDSM paraphernalia such as whips, crops, chains, etc. The host was charged with running a house of prostitution simply for requesting donations. According to one source, this created a problem because of a lack of public spaces suitable for holding parties and conducting educational seminars about alternative forms of sexual expression. The costs of these gatherings also posed an impediment to hosts. When even the privacy of their own homes could not offer protection, given the actions of the Attleboro police, many community members were wondering where to go.

But the Attleboro police remained firm despite the outcry from the BDSM community as well as the media at the manner in which police handled the situation. Egbert maintained that law enforcement illegally entered the private party and wrongly arrested his client. He contended that the police had no probable cause to enter the private room and that Reed was not properly read her Miranda rights after being charged with assault. Prosecutor Roger Ferris, in an interview in late November 2000 with the *Providence Journal,* defended the arrests, contending that Davis had struck one of two police officers who discovered the party while on a routine patrol of the building, which Ferris claimed gave the officers the right to enter and make a search of the premises.

The fetish community viewed Ferris's comment as less an adequate explanation and more as a cover up for the fact that once the police had entered the party, they used their presence in order to actively pursue people whose conception of a good time simply did not match with the officers' view of mainstream norms. Numerous news reports made mention of this strong discrimination, as well as the fact that the club, located across the street from the Attleboro police station, had long been the site of many parties without the police noticing. This, one editor remarked, suggested that the S&M enthusiasts were clearly not bothering anyone or disturbing the general public.

The defendants were nevertheless left facing charges that cut to the core question of whether sadomasochist practices should be allowed at all. Massachusetts, like many other states, still had laws against unconventional sexual practices, such as the use of self-pleasuring devices like dildos and vibrators, and engaging in sodomy, even for consenting adults acting behind closed doors in the private of their homes. The numerous stores in Boston that sold sex toys indicated that the police generally did not enforce these regulations, but the BDSM cases such as Attleboro seemed to signal a revival of the laws. This selective application unearthed the problematic case of whether it was appropriate to apply the law in a discriminatory manner which seemed, thus, to revolve around law enforcement and the judicial system's opinions rather than unbiased law.

The case of Benjamin Davis

When the case of Benjamin Davis was originally brought to trial, defense attorneys continued to argue that the police had violated the U.S. Constitution by entering the party's premises without a warrant and failing to read the partygoers their Miranda rights before they were questioned. District Court Judge Francis T. Crimmins threw out any evidence collected after the officers had entered the party, although he did not cite constitutional violations as the reason for doing so. As a result, a variety of charges against Davis, including possession of a dangerous weapon and objects for masturbation, were dismissed by prosecutors in June 2001.

In the aftermath of this ruling, Stefany Reed's case was also dismissed. Reed was charged with assault and battery as well as possession of a dangerous weapon. The case against her was based on one officer's report of having seen her strike a Worcester woman with a wooden spoon. According to state law, a person could not consent to be abused, even for sexual pleasure. Reed eventually maintained that she had not struck the woman and further claimed to have passed a polygraph lie detector test. The woman she had allegedly struck corroborated her story. With all evidence within the party thrown out, there was no case remaining, and prosecutors dropped the charges.

Davis was left facing the two remaining charges of assault and battery on a police officer and keeping a house of prostitution. In September 2001, Judge Crimmins denied Davis's motion to throw out the charge of keeping a house of prostitution. Davis's attorney had argued that the police evidence against Davis did not in fact support such a charge, yet Prosecutor Roger Ferris continued to claim that records now in police custody, confiscated from a woman outside the party at a table that had been set up at the entrance, were sufficient to pursue the prostitution charge against Davis.

On Wednesday, October 10, 2001, in the Attleboro District Courthouse, the criminal phase of the Attleboro case finally reached a conclusion at a bench trial with the disposition of both remaining charges. Davis was found not guilty of the charge of keeping a house of prostitution after the Assistant District Attorney (ADA) Roger Ferris rested his case after a short half hour of testimony from one of the detectives, whose testimony came under question more than once as he recollected events. After the not guilty ruling, the ADA offered a continuance without a finding for the police assault charge. There would be no criminal record, and while the case was pursued, it was also dropped after six months. As there was only one additional witness to the interaction between Davis and the officer, and Davis continued to persist in claiming there was never contact of any kind between himself and the officer before the police entered the rented party space, this seemed the best course of action for both the defense and prosecution. Thus, after a little over one year and four months of proceedings, the Attleboro Raid Case was brought to a close.

Psychological issues

Sadism and masochism both appear in the Diagnostic and Statistical Manual of Mental Disorders Fourth Edition, or DSM-IV, as paraphilias. Sadism is defined by the DSM-IV as the act of deriving pleasure, often sexual, from mistreating others, and therefore these people will seek out others whom they can victimize with their behavior. Notably, the DSM-IV claims that this must create clinically important distress or impair work, social and/or personal functioning.

Sexual masochism, on the other hand, involves the act of being humiliated, bound, beaten, or otherwise made to physically suffer for purposes of sexual stimulation. In order to possess the disorder, one must gain some sort or enjoyment from the harm being dealt. While the fantasy of such things is not unusual, actually acting upon these fantasies creates a risk, according to the DSM-IV. As with sadism, however, this must cause what the DSM-IV refers to as clinically important distress, or must impair work, social, or personal functioning.

One woman who has pursued the BDSM lifestyle noted that the public views BDSM as some sort of abuse, and believes that submissives or bottoms have something wrong with them. To the contrary, she insisted, BDSM could be a healthy and important aspect of people's lives when taken safely and in moderation. People, she claimed, only think of BDSM the way the media or poor jokes have portrayed it, with men and women in leather and latex wielding whips and asking if you have been bad.

It is in question, then, whether either member of those in a functioning domination and submission, or D&S, relationship truly suffers from these respective disorders, as it is likely that neither would claim any personal upset in their lives. To the contrary, many members of the BDSM scene insist that it is a source of social and personal support and a strong community, as well as an outlet for their sexual desires. For some, BDSM is only an occasional indulgence, but for others it is a personal identity and social circle, something they construct their habits and lives around. As one scene member pointed out, what is the difference between consensual flogging and running a thirty mile marathon, or going into a boxing ring, knowing that a broken nose or worse might be the result? If, he claims, police and the government suggest that those in the BDSM lifestyle are psychologically flawed and incapable of assessing the danger of their activities, what is to be said for stuntmen and skydivers, or those who frequently take their thrills on the ends of bungee cords?

This penchant for bondage, dominance, submission, and sadomasochism seems to fall somewhere in the gap between a sexual fetish, which is defined by the DSM-IV as requiring a particular object, body part, or behavior in order to become sexually aroused, and a sexual orientation. As one member of the Boston Dungeon Society claimed, it is not unlike a form of sensory exploration, suggestive of the same delving into emotion and personal essence that more acceptable sports often encompass.

Some sadomasochists have further suggested that BDSM leads toward an even closer relationship than most normal sexual couples, called vanilla by those in the scene, can develop. One dominant remarked that he must always know how his submissive is feeling, what sort of mood she is in, and to know her well enough to predict how she might respond to certain events or stimulations. Due to the nature of BDSM, it is common for those involved to discuss a scene, a word that encompasses the BDSM-related practices of a single sitting or occurrence, in detail. This lifestyle, he claimed, requires open communication for it to work, and open discussion both before and afterward.

He contrasted this with regular relationships, in which sex and foreplay were givens occurring with little or no talk before, during or after. In those there would be less sensitivity to what each partner was experiencing, and neither bothers with what he termed mental anticipation. The BDSM partners, in contrast, would have concocted the fantasy days or even weeks before the scene, letting it build as the time counted down. One would be more likely to make suggestions, to generate ideas for making a scene more special, unique, and exciting for both partners. Vanilla couples, he remarked rather dismissively, were far more likely to watch television together before sex. A BDSM couple might make a trip to the mall, supermarket, or other venue to collect what they will use that night. Far from a psychological disease, he claimed, it tends to bring people together more closely than most other relationships comfortably allow.

Sexual dangerousness

This case raised two issues pertaining to dangerousness. On the one hand, there are the two instances of arrest, in which Benjamin Davis and the spatula-wielding Stefany Reed were each charged with counts of assault and battery due to what they were either permitting to occur, or what they themselves were engaged in at the time the police arrived. This relates to the legal issue of whether it is possible to consent to abuse.

The second, broader aspect of dangerousness is that of the BDSM community and interrelationships as a whole, rather than the actions of these two individuals. It is the dangerousness of harm dealt to a masochist by the sadist, by a dominant tying up a submissive. Such interplays in the BDSM community can often involve anything from simple spankings, to floggings and whippings with paddles, crops, whips, chains, and other instruments. It is difficult for the law to find a clear manner of differentiating between consensual abuse, if such a thing exists at all, and nonconsensual battery and abuse in a poor relationship.

The law makes no effort to differentiate between the two in Massachusetts, or in many of the states where laws permit the state to prosecute on behalf of the abused irrespective of whether the person wishes to proceed with the suit or not. This aims to protect those who would otherwise be intimidated out of pressing charges. The dangerousness is therefore that of physical harm involved in sexual activity on a larger scale, which makes the circumstances of the abuse all the more perverse in society's eyes.

Nevertheless, in setting rules as to when one can consent to violence, the law is often either broadly under-inclusive or over-inclusive. Some argue that it becomes a matter of deciding upon the lesser evil, or greater good, rather than producing some overreaching solution which can address all the issues raised, and protect the safety of the people in all cases. Others argue that good, sane people can and should be capable of consenting freely to what society may deem bad things, under the theory that no third party is hurt. Yet the law in practice, they conclude, should never be used as a vehicle to permit any consensual violence which results in serious physical injury.

By holding someone strictly liable for actual lasting harm, the law constrains what is admittedly mostly male violence, be it against women or men. While in rare cases some accuse this doctrine of over-inclusiveness in holding culpable those defendants who claim to have played by the rules of S/M. Even though there are rules, in the vast majority of cases which turn up in the criminal justice system such issues of consent are questionable at best. Pure cases such as Paddleboro are admittedly rare in the legal sphere, although the issues they raise are not. Experience has shown that the doctrine of strict liability more often has been invoked to protect those most at risk of dehumanizing abuse, rather than to persecute those who are humane in their sexual encounters.

Another claim advanced by some is that the law should treat sex as it does sport and allow involved parties to consent to physical injury as long as all involved are aware a priori of the involved risks. If it is possible for someone to consent to play hockey, or to enter a boxing ring, why they ask is it not possible for them to consent to private sexual activity which is arguably no more dangerous? Yet some caution that it is important not to permit those involved in such encounters to avoid culpability under a theory of consent if truly dangerous physical violence beyond the anticipated sphere should occur. The argument that sex is a sport may thus have the unintended consequences of allowing those in the BDSM lifestyle, or who would claim to be, to utilize violence to satiate sexual desires which do in fact result in serious harm.

A further argument maintains that the doctrine of consent failed to recognize that rough sex is not always victimizing to the masochist, who is generally the woman in the paradigmatic heterosexual ritual. Some have even argued that sadomasochism can create avenues of empowerment for the masochist as she becomes paradoxically stronger and the sadist weaker. Thus, the difficulty of the law in distinguishing between situations which are consensual and empowering and those which are humiliating and victimizing can present an unresolved and irresolvable dilemma.

It has also been contended that the effort to distinguish permitted from prohibited force can pull the law into a hopeless quagmire, with under-enforcement the inevitable result, but that this problem cannot be solved by moving the line between the two kinds of force to a slightly different place. What is perhaps more surprising, and certainly more frustrating many conclude, is that this problem cannot be solved by prohibiting all uses of force. That approach will not avoid the vagaries of distinguishing permitted from impermissible force, because physical activity, some of it forcible, is inherent in intercourse. And many of the other physical aspects of sexuality, though not inherent in intercourse, are expected and pleasurable provided that there is consent.

In no way should this argument be construed as a moral judgment of those who practice safe and consensual S/M and are careful and communicative with their partners. Many who engage in S/M, according to various interviews and an excess of research on the subject, follow clear rules and guidelines, some of which include the demand that neither alcoholic drink, drugs, or anything else that could impair one's judgment be consumed prior to a scene. Ironically, many questions surrounding violation of sexual autonomy in the course of an acquaintance or date rape situation would be far more easily answered if everyone engaged in similar negotiations, made clear when yes meant no and no meant yes, and refrained from the excessive use of drugs and alcohol which might contort desires or intentions. Thus, safe, sane, and consensual BDSM in its purest form truly does not seem likely to trouble the law.

Inevitably, it seems necessary that the law and criminal system address BDSM cases of violence and consent on a case by case basis, rather than attempting either to redraw the line of what amount of force constitutes excess, or to establish a blanket policy for addressing such alternative lifestyle issues. It is impossible to know how many of those who practice BDSM truly follow the rules, and thus the ultimate interest of the law must lie in protecting the people not from the self-governing, self-selective middleground of the BDSM community, but from those who the community itself would castigate and reject.

Notes about sources

I frequently referred to updates in the *Boston Phoenix* and *Providence Journal* for information on the legal proceedings of the case as well as the raid itself. Interviews were conducted with multiple members of the BDSM community who chose to use aliases in order to accurately depict how such relationships should and do function without the intervention of the law or truly threatening violence. I also referred to other articles from the National Coalition for Sexual Freedom and the Massachusetts State Legislature which addressed BDSM, Paddleboro, consent, and the law.

Free Speech Coalition et al.
Object and speech as sexually dangerous

Abstract

The case of *Ashcroft, Attorney General, et al. v. Free Speech Coalition et al.*, concerned the ability of artists or others who want to depict, in any sort of obscene or sexually explicit situation, people who are children under the law. For over one hundred fifty years, lawmakers have been attempting to define obscenity and pornography; the 2001 case has led to the establishment of far more specific limits concerning what is legally acceptable in the visual, performance, film, and digital art world. This specific case was brought by the Free Speech Coalition, a California-based trade organization for the adult entertainment industry, and similar organizations. The central legal question in this case was whether it is constitutional to outlaw sexually explicit art that depicts someone legally underage, but not a real child, such as an actor playing a younger person or a digitally-created child. There have been myriad other obscenity cases, but this case in particular brought up two important philosophical and other issues: artistic freedom and the location of dangerousness of sexually explicit art.

Facts of the case

Ashcroft, Attorney General, et al. v. Free Speech Coalition et al. was brought before the United States Supreme Court in 2001. The case was begun by the Free Speech Coalition, an adult entertainment trade association, in conjunction with a number of other, similar organizations, because these organizations felt that their First Amendment rights were being suppressed by the broadness and vagueness in the language of the 1996 Child Pornography Protection Act, or CPPA. The Free Speech Coalition and its fellow organizations risked being severely punished under the CPPA for doing the same things they had been doing before 1996: producing and distributing adult entertainment. The CPPA was broad, sweeping legislation that prohibited any depiction of obscene or sexually explicit activity or behavior by minors or people that appeared to be minors. The CPPA did not acknowledge any importance of content, the real or virtual nature of the people depicted, or the potential for this speech to be valuable. The CPPA also made it illegal for any product, from film to magazine, to suggest that speech within may contain obscene or sexually explicit depictions of apparent minors, regardless of whether the product actually contained these depictions. For example, a magazine that claimed it had photos of underage girl, but in fact used youthful, legal models, would still be liable under the CPPA. Additionally, the CPPA made possession of any of these materials illegal. The violation of the CPPA was a felony, and suggested punishment for offenders was severe. Under this law, owning a copy of Vladimir Nabokov's *Lolita,* or for that matter, a copy of William Shakespeare's *Romeo and Juliet,* was illegal and punishable by up to fifteen years in prison by first-time offenders.

Historical background of obscenity law

Obscenity laws have changed a great deal in the past two hundred years in the United States. Obscenity laws are used to control a great range of behaviors; however, the most important application to this case study is how these laws have applied to sexually dangerous art. In the past few hundred years, books have been the art form most frequently affected by obscenity laws, given that many other media, such as film, television, digital photography, and the internet, are relatively recent inventions.

In the 1800s, the Comstock Laws controlled what was obscene; under these laws, many books that we now view as classics were censored. These books include John Cleland's *Fanny Hill*, Aristophanes' *Lysistrata*, Chaucer's *Canterbury Tales*, Daniel Defoe's *Moll Flanders*, Voltaire's *Candide*, James Joyce's *Ulysses*, Walt Whitman's *Leaves of Grass*, and the story collection *Arabian Nights*. Comstock Laws, of which the Federal Anti-Obscenity Act of 1873 was one, kept these books from being exported to the United States and banned their printing and distribution within the United States. Many of the Comstock Laws are still on the legal books, though they are less often enforced today. The legacy of these laws is seen in various modern-day legislation, from the 1996 Telecommunications Reform Bill which applied to material available on computer networks and over the internet, and the CPPA, in whose language and message the antiquated ideas of the Comstock Laws can be most easily identified.

It is important to examine how these laws have been upheld. On the one hand, government agencies, from the U.S. Postal Service to the local police, have aided in the enforcement of obscenity laws. For example, the U.S. Postal Service seized the copies it found of Joyce's *Ulysses*, and continued to seize them until 1933, when it became legal to publish the book. On a more local level, a Georgia high school required that students have permission slips to read plays such as *Hamlet*, *Macbeth*, and *King Lear*, given that the school board believed these plays to contain sexual and violent situations. On a more global scale, the Catholic Church has an Index of Prohibited Books which is continually updated. Thus even when books are no longer prevented from being shipped and distributed or banned in libraries and classrooms, many books remain categorized as obscene and morally banned because of religious restrictions. The rules concerning prohibited books in the Catholic Church stem from the decisions made at the Council of Trent close to five hundred years ago. While some of these rules have been updated by various popes throughout the centuries, the same basic principles of morality still guide which pieces of art the Catholic Church chooses to deem obscene. Thus someone living in the very modern world may still be following rules concerning obscenity which were established half a millennium ago. Given the variety of ways in which obscenity laws are upheld and, for that matter, created, from political to religious to distributional authorities, it is easy to see how obscenity laws are incredibly important to how art is viewed in society. Additionally, this long history of banning what is thought to be obscene art gives credence to the idea that sexual and sexually explicit art has always been thought of as dangerous in and of itself, for a variety of reasons and in a variety of contexts.

Important Supreme Court cases for obscenity law

Obscenity concerns and laws came to the fore in two 1957 cases: *Roth v. United States* and *Alberts v. California*. Those cases tightened the obscenity laws a great deal, essentially saying that any material with a prurient theme could be considered obscene and banned. Additionally, those cases specifically addressed whether the First Amendment protected the speech of those who created explicit words or images; the decisions in both of these cases stated that the First Amendment only covered ideas with social value, and that obscene images lacked any social value. The stage was thus set for the difficult battle ahead: would the explicit work of artists, which clearly the artists themselves believe has social value, be rejected as valueless by the law?

After these two cases and before the establishment of the CPPA, there were two key cases that set the basic standards for deciding if speech, the general term used to apply to any material threatened or protected by the First Amendment, was both obscene and dangerous, and therefore not protected under the First Amendment. These two cases were *Miller v. California* and *New York v. Ferber*, both described below.

Miller v. California established three important criteria for speech not to be protected under the First Amendment: it had to appeal to prurient interest, it had to be unquestionably offensive by general standards of the given community, and it had to lack real value, whether that value was artistic, sociopolitical, medical, or any other value category. Thus the works of literature mentioned above, *Lolita* and *Romeo and Juliet*, were protected under *Miller v. California* because they both hold indisputable literary value. Thus any depiction of sexually explicit acts, even those involving children, if seen in the light of art, and not of pornography, were thus protected.

New York v. Ferber limited the production and distribution of sexually explicit speech, also called child pornography, for two central reasons. First, the speech would be a permanent and damaging record of the abuse that occurred, and such a record should not be distributed for the sake of the involved child or children. Second, the government has an active interest in limiting the production and distribution of child pornography because the lucrative nature of this illegal distribution promotes that abuse. Thus those same works of literature, *Lolita* and *Romeo and Juliet*, were protected under *Ferber* because *Ferber* targeted how the speech was created, not its content. No children were abused in the creation of either *Lolita* or *Romeo and Juliet*, nor was the sale of these works in any way profiting people who are abusers. *Ferber* firmly established the reason for any obscenity limits on the First Amendment: to protect the children who might be harmed in the creation of the speech, and to discourage and make illegal any economic benefit that might rise from recording and distributing records of such abuse.

Thus the two cases described above firmly established the reasons why there needed to be legal restrictions on free speech when it came to sexual explicit depiction: if the speech had no intrinsic value to society, and the production and distribution of the material directly harmed children. The restrictions were not designed to prevent any sexually explicit material from being created; far from it. As one Supreme Court Justice remarked, it would be greatly detrimental to society to restrict adults solely to materials also suitable for children. The government could not legally restrict material simply because said material might indirectly fall into the hands of children, or influence behaviors towards children; these two cases firmly established this precedent.

Ashcroft v. Free Speech Coalition: facts and implications

Ashcroft v. Free Speech Coalition was particularly important because it tested the CPPA, and it was found that the CPPA was indeed too overreaching and vague. During the 1990s, as the CPPA and other attendant laws came to the forefront of social and political discourse, many artists had their work censored by a number of different parties. Sometimes, their local law enforcement agents would enforce obscenity laws, often by shutting down or threatening to arrest anyone who entered into a particular gallery. Artistic expression was also frequently suppressed by morality groups and churches, many of whom attempted to get books banned, art destroyed, and museums closed. Finally, the National Endowment for the Arts, or the NEA, under pressure from the legislative branch of the government, decided to revoke certain grants to sexually explicit artists. Many of these strategies backfired, giving infamy and international exposure to the artists and work that was censored. For example, Tim Miller was a relatively unknown performance artist receiving small grants from the NEA for his gay-themed work until one of his grants was rejected, due to the new decency clause that Congress had amended to the NEA's standards. From relative obscurity Miller became internationally famous, and the issues that he cared about and worked on became better known because of the censorship than had he never been censored. Similarly, the many attempts to censor Nabokov's *Lolita* or John Cleland's *Memoirs of a Woman of Pleasure* had, instead of reducing the book to the obscurity that banning it would desire, brought the book repeatedly into the view of the public, ensuring immortality and fame for these sexually charged, but objectively masterful, works of literature. Regardless of the fickleness and effects of the media and the public, the important issue at stake was the effects that *Ashcroft v. Free Speech Coalition* had on the CPPA. The CPPA demanded that any sexually explicit depiction be censored; *Ashcroft v. Free Speech Coalition* said that such blanket censorship is unconstitutional, and that there were ways in which sexually explicit images appear in our culture that are not prurient, and which have social value as art, literature, and ideas. *Ashcroft v. Free Speech Coalition* states, importantly, that motives, not just content, also matter when it comes to what should be censored: an image that was created for economic benefit and not in a purely artistic bent should be censored, but an image that was sexually explicit but created as art should not be uniformly censored.

Whether sexually explicit speech is dangerous: Lolita as case example

The major question here concerned whether the existence of sexually explicit art that depicted children was dangerous to society in general, or whether such art was merely dangerous to the specific children who had the potential to get exploited in the creation of such art. This was an important legal question: do obscenity laws protect the people who might be offended or influenced by the obscene material, or protect those specific persons who might be exploited in the creation of that obscene material?

Obscenity legislation and these issues affect the creation of art. This section examines how obscenity laws influenced a piece of art by Vladimir Nabokov: his seminal novel, *Lolita*. Can art such as Nabokov's *Lolita* and its 1997 film adaptation be made illegal if that art does not actually exploit children? *Lolita* did not harm any children; it was simply a book. But there was something in the book's subject matter, its sexually explicit nature and its relationship in particular to children and what we view as sexual perversity, that can be argued made the book in and of itself dangerous.

Lolita's publication was fraught with issues from the beginning. Given the obscenity laws at the time, no American publisher wanted to, or really could, take on the publication of such a novel. It was published in Europe, and when copies reached American audiences, reaction was so varied that the book divided the literary world into those that thought it was a masterpiece and those who thought it was a filthy and crude disgrace. The book was banned all over, and it took until 1958 for an American publisher to bring the book officially to the United States. Once it was published here, the book was a best-seller; whether this success was due to the incredible literary and artistic value of the novel or because of prurient interest in an infamous text has remained a topic for debate. Regardless, *Lolita* did not die because American publishers and American audiences were squeamish or scared. Instead the incredible controversy about the book kept it distinctly in the public eye.

The 1997 film version of *Lolita* was, unfortunately for the director, produced in the first year after the CPPA passed. Given the ambiguity surrounding the CPPA and its powers, the film was forced to make a number of uncomfortable decisions. First, the director had to hire an actress to play the titular role who was older than the character was written to be; Nabokov's Dolores was twelve and thirteen, and the actresses who played Lolita on screen have been at least fifteen. The decision to use older girls was fraught with issues. The integrity of the story demanded that we examine the love of a pedophile for a child, or in his terms, nymphet, and not for a young woman or teenager. Thus casting a girl of fifteen who would be mistaken for sixteen or seventeen further confused the story: was it about a pedophile, or about an older man who liked his women to be younger? Did it accomplish anything to have made *Lolita* about ephebophilia instead of pedophilia? Did obfuscating Nabokov's true story ameliorate the supposed moral problems, or did it create further difficulties by placing the story somewhere between truly illegal and yet profoundly fascinating, as in Nabokov's original, and somewhat illegal but with a more run-of-the-mill set of sexual issues? But leaving these artistic issues aside, there was another serious and uncomfortable situation that the film's creative team had to handle: the constant presence of a lawyer in every part of the film-making process. From the casting to shooting to the last minute of editing, an entertainment lawyer was present and had an active voice. Several accounts of the process made it clear that while the lawyer was uncomfortable vetoing directorial ideas, he in the end had no choice: it was a decision between having a shot or scene in the film and having the film be finished and distributed. It is difficult to imagine having to take the opinion of a lawyer more seriously than the desire of a director in creating a film, but the legal restrictions on free speech, particularly the CPPA, changed the landscape of the boundaries between artistic license and protecting against dangerousness.

The case results and implications

In the end, the Supreme Court ruled in favor of the Free Speech Coalition and its brethren. In the written opinions of the justices, most adamantly disagreed with the proposition that the law should restrict or suppress all sexually related speech. The spirit of intellectual, personal, and creative freedom was dear to the founders and upholders of America's ideals. At the same time, much was made both popularly and legally of the current conception of America, and indeed the world, as filled with new and dynamic dangers. Given these two ideological poles, the outcome of *Ashcroft v. Free Speech Coalition* was far from sure. However, it appears that the court has caught up with technology. One of the most difficult aspects of law has been keeping up with current trends; fifteen years ago, virtual pornography or digitally enhanced or changed photographs would not have been an issue. More than anything, the notion that motive, intention, and value made no difference in the banning of speech was rejected by the judges and the law overall.

Ashcroft v. Free Speech Coalition found that it was indeed unconstitutional to make sexually explicit art that in its conception did not exploit or use any children illegal. This finding thus clarified, it would seem, to whom such depictions were dangerous: to the children who might get exploited, and not the public in general. This conception of the dangerousness of sexually explicit art was different from a generally understood notion of why this type of material was illegal or banned: because it was somehow dangerous in and of itself, and should generally not be around to influence, pollute, or otherwise enter the thoughts of individuals in society. One must also examine how sexually explicit art may, in general, be considered dangerous to people other than those that it may directly exploit, and not merely in the context of whether it was categorically obscene.

Since obscenity laws began, it has been difficult to create a comprehensive and yet constitutional law governing what is obscene and therefore sexually dangerous. Because obscenity laws do not make illegal all depiction of sex or sexual acts, the law has had to further subdivide the category of depictions of sex into condoned depictions and condemned depictions. Additionally, this case drew attention to one of the most important issues when discussing sexual dangerousness: the intersection of law and morality.

Whose morality should guide the creation of law? There are certain universal truths that society has agreed upon, and on which our laws seem to be based: a Judeo-Christian tradition wherein rules like not taking away other people's rights to their life, their property, and their personal happiness, broadly interpreted, are most important. But when we get into issues of sex, and especially into issues of sex and art and freedom of expression, the law gets very tricky. Do we base our laws on what the most widely available moral text, the Bible, says about sex, ignoring the separation of church and state and the fact that not all people in this country believe in that text? Do we attempt instead to ignore the Bible and create laws based on a secular morality? If so, on what do we base out judgments? Art that appears to be the nexus of freedom of expression and the avant garde to a group of intellectuals or other artists may seem obscene and even dangerous to people who are not of that ilk, people who disapprove of such art because of moral or personal beliefs. Whom should the law protect? The artist, or those who are offended or feel that their rights are encroached upon by that art?

The law and art: philosophy and politics of interdisciplinary relations

The law has, for a long time, had many difficulties in attempting to understand, accept, and legislate fairly when it comes to issues of sex and particularly sexually explicit art. In 1988, on the Senate floor, Senator Jesse Helms actually destroyed the catalogue for a show of photographer Robert Mapplethorpe's work, because the senator found the work to be too dangerous and offensive to his sensibilities. This action brought to light one of the key issues in attempting to legislate the difference between art and pornography: what role should personal taste and morals have, and if they should be kept out of the decision altogether, what sort of rubric should be used to define sexually dangerous art? This particular case aided in understanding how to define how we view sex and sexual issues as a society. Do we believe that the depiction of all sexual acts is categorically obscene? If so, what implication does this have for art? What sorts of things can be considered sexual, sexually dangerous, and in which situation or situations? Can only people be considered sexually dangerous? For example, in the case of Holly Hughes, an artist whose work focused on sexually explicit stories and on lesbians, would the artist herself be considered sexually dangerous, or just her work? Similarly, how do we separate Nabokov from *Lolita*, and should there be a separation? Can a thing, such as a book or movie, actually have qualities that make it empirically sexually dangerous?

This particular case addressed one of the central issues in the intersection of art, psychology, and law. That is to say, the question of what is pornography, what is art, and why and when and to whom are these things harmful. This case's finding indicated that the court believed that sexually explicit art was only dangerous to children when they might get involved in it. This conception was vastly different from the general conception of what may be sexually dangerous about art. Few parents who shield their children's eyes from what they view as lewd imagery do so because they worry that their own children will become the victims of child pornographers. Instead, they cover their children's eyes because they believe that there is something inherently dangerous in exposing one's children to this sort of imagery. Is this really the case? If kids are exposed to sexually explicit art, do they somehow grow up abnormally? Will such art, not even pornography but the type of art shown in galleries and museums across the country, twist their children's minds? This question drives many of the obscenity and banning law-suits across the country. This case's outcome seemed to say, however, that the court's primary concern was the welfare of children who were directly exploited by this art or pornography, not the nebulous effect that sexually explicit art may have on the minds of children and adults alike. Attempting to tease apart what was sexually dangerous about being involved in such art, and what was simply sexually dangerous about the art itself, was one of the most important psychological puzzles around which this case centers.

Lessons taught by the case

In this case, the legal lessons are myriad. First, that the higher courts may refine their previous decisions and permit people more freedoms and the government fewer, a finding that many cynics might believe impossible. But more impor-tantly, an important lesson to learn from this case is that the law has to keep up with society, and that this is often a difficult process. After all, the question of whether the digital age has the same rules as all previous eras. Can one say that a piece of art is obscene and dangerous if no real people are depicted? To whom, then, is such art dangerous? The law has had, in recent years, to create entirely new categories for the digital age, and new legislation will continue to pour out in response to how society itself is adjusting to this new paradigm. Additionally, this case continues the work of redefining what, more than who, is sexually danger-ous, and putting stopping places on the slippery slope that is legislating danger-ousness.

Notes about sources

The primary source used for this case study was the U.S. Supreme Court case of *Ashcroft, Attorney General, et al. v. Free Speech Coalition et al.*, particularly the affirming and dissenting opinions of the various Justices. Additionally, the legal documentation of the various cases mentioned in the above study, particularly the opinions in the *Miller v. California* and *New York v. Ferber* cases. Much of the information about the National Endowment for the Arts and its attendant issues came from such newspapers as the Washington Post and the New York Times at the time of the events, and from information provided by the American Civil Liberties Union on their website. Vladimir Nabokov's novel *Lolita* and articles in the New York Times concerning *Lolita's* publication were the sources for that section of the above case study. Finally, such legal websites as findlaw.com and oyez.org, the Supreme Court website, provided background on obscenity law, the Bill of Rights, and other important documents.

John J. Geoghan
Pedophilia and the Catholic Church

Abstract

The sex abuse scandal in the Catholic Church was first made widely public in January 2002, and involved abuse by priests and the cover-ups by the cardinals and bishops. Since the 1980s, more than fifteen hundred priests have been accused of sexual misconduct, including, but not limited to, pedophilia, defined as sex abuse of prepubescent children, and ephebophelia, or sex abuse of post-pubescent adolescents. Father John J. Geoghan was the man behind the first church scandal case published by the *Boston Globe*. The public revelation of this scandal incited national and international attention towards even more scandals within the American Catholic Church. Geoghan was a pedophile who preferred prepubescent boys of lower socioeconomic status, typically with single mothers. These boys did not have a father figure to look up to, and so Geoghan's acts of kindness and thoughtfulness were seen as a blessing by the single mothers, especially coming from a holy father figure. For more than three decades, the man who was viewed as a role model and spiritual leader in the church sexually abused prepubescent boys. For a while, the scandal was kept a secret from the public and the members of Geoghan's parish, while church officials, like Cardinal Bernard Law, strove to conceal Geoghan's mistakes by transferring Geoghan to different churches and covertly paying off victims and their families. After the scandals were recognized, trials and sentencing occurred, placing Geoghan in prison where he would be killed by an inflamed inmate.

Early years of John J. Geoghan

When he was five years old, Geoghan's life was shaken by his father's death. Though the experience was painful, it ended up serving as a very spiritually uplifting time in his life as his mother directing him toward a lifelong relationship with God. The rest of his childhood and early adolescence was considered a pleasant experience. His mother's brother invested love and interest into the young boy's life and looked out for Geoghan as if he were his own son. Geoghan's uncle played a very large role in Geoghan's relations with the church, introducing him into the priesthood and helping him when he needed recommendations, advice, or other assistance whenever he got into serious trouble.

Throughout seminary school, Geoghan struggled emotionally from an anxiety condition. He typically blamed this disorder for his occasional lack of obedience and unexcused absences from school. After attending seminary school for a short while, Geoghan transferred to Holy Cross, a Jesuit college in Massachusetts. After two years at Holy Cross, he returned to the seminary before eventually taking his vows to become a priest in 1962.

At the beginning of his career, he was noted by the other priests and teachers to be a very effeminate, immature, and intellectually unmotivated young man. This was at first thought to be a problem, but everyone assumed he would soon grow out of this stage in his life. His problems during his time in the seminary were reported later by some of Geoghan's therapists to be the result of his lack of maturity and inability to have sex. Though he grew up claiming to be interested in women, sporadically dating in his teenage years, he abstained from any sexual contact, even avoiding masturbation. This sexual repression was very likely responsible for his desire for relations with boys in his years of priesthood.

Pedophilia in the church

After Geoghan entered into his first parish as a priest at Blessed Sacrament in Saugus, Massachusetts, he first realized that he was beginning to be sexually attracted to the altar boys and other young males in the church. During his time at that church, he sexually abused boys of different ages reportedly ranging from ages seven to eleven.

When he was transferred to St. Paul's Church in Hingham, Massachusetts, he befriended a family and became the father figure whom four boys had lost, taking them out for ice cream, babysitting them, bathing them, and tucking them into bed after reading a bedtime story. Their mother, seeking out a role model for her four sons, did not have any suspicions towards Geoghan. In fact, she saw the priest as a great man to fulfill that role, and felt lucky to have Geoghan spending so much time with her sons. It did not seem odd that he would disappear into the boys' bedrooms every now and then. But when one of her sons came up to her one night, asking her not to allow Father Geoghan back into their house, she became suspicious. When she asked why, her son told her that he did not like his private parts being touched. She then asked all four of her sons why they had not told her of this before, and they replied that Geoghan had told them to keep it a secret and that the sexual behavior was somewhat like confession in their home, as he forced the boys to recite aloud the Hail Mary and Our Father prayers as Geoghan practiced oral sex on them.

After the news of the sex abuse in St. Paul's, Geoghan was again transferred, this time to St. Andrew's in Jamaica Plain, Massacusetts, where he served for six years. Here he helped with the local Boy Scout troop and was a supervisor of the church's altar boys. He next targeted a family there, composed of a single mother caring for her three sons, a daughter, and her niece's four sons. As with the earlier boys, he also spent much time with these boys and took them out for ice cream. Later, the mother found out that while he was spending time with the boys in their bedrooms, he was performing oral sex on them and would pet their genitals and the boys were instructed to reciprocate.

This sexual abuse continued with many different families and hundreds of other boys over the years as Geoghan was moved from church to church to prey on new children. He never understood the abuse to be an emotional or pastoral problem, and was continuously irresponsible with his moral conduct. With no intent on changing his ways, he would always be a risk for any church community with young boys. Even with therapy and treatment, pedophiles generally have a very high recidivism rate. Geoghan himself made it clear that the therapy was basically useless.

During his career, Geoghan sexually abused at last two hundred pre-pubescent males, committing abuses at every church in which he resided. The estimate of victims would probably be much higher, perhaps around seven hundred, if it included the ones who have not publicly come out. His abuse was not the typical violent rape in the other cases in the Catholic Church, but still highly traumatic to the victims and their families. Often Geoghan would bring these boys back to his bedroom or to shower in the rectory, or even abuse them in their own homes. Sometimes he would wrestle with the boys and have them dress up in priest's clothing. He also always enjoyed the company, and benefits, of the altar boys and other boys who spent lots of time at the church preparing for their First Communion. These boys among the accusers were mostly from poor families with single mothers. Geoghan stated that the poor children had always been more affectionate to him because they did not have a father figure in their lives, and thus he devoted more time to them.

Web of secrets

The scandals were marked by constant lies to protect the church. In the situation with the earlier family, the mother went to another priest who knew Geoghan and told him about what happened with Geoghan. That priest suggested she try to forget about everything and understand that it would never happen again, for if it did Geoghan would immediately lose his priesthood. Such was not the case. In fact, that priest testified in court that he had never even heard her name, nor had any such conversation about sexual abuse with the first mother.

The second mother approached the bishop at the archdiocesan headquarters, who asked Geoghan if the accusations were true, and when Geoghan affirmed, the bishop ordered the troubled priest to go home. Even though Geoghan never showed much emotion, he was always very honest and straightforward about any circumstances or accusations. After spending a year at home, he was reassigned to another church, St. Brendan's in Dorchester, Massachusetts.

While more young boys were being abused, the Archbishop of Boston, Cardinal Bernard Law, and other church officials kept Geoghan's pedophilia a secret and continued to move him around from parish to parish in order to minimize conflict. The church became even more secretive about the problems, trying to elude the inquisitions and threats by paying off victims as they came.

Throughout all the decades of Geoghan's child abuse, the church knew about his problems, compiled reports, and took detailed notes on his treatments, yet still kept everything from the public eye and ear. They were putting the church members in danger to try to uphold their reputation.

Attempts for treatment

The attempts to treat Geoghan were certainly numerous, but were never substantially effective. By the end of the 1960s, he had already begun to see several therapists in different hospitals and institutes. Most of these psychiatric institutions held very close ties to the Catholic Church and were resources of many of the priests involved with the abuse scandals. During Geoghan's treatment time, he focused most of his energy on reevaluating his problems, and visiting different doctors for their advice. But even after he had completed entire treatment programs, the abuse continued every time he returned to a church.

After the first accusation of child sex abuse in 1968 at St. Paul's, he was treated in Maryland at the Seton Institute by psychotherapist A.W. Richard Sipe, a former priest himself, and returned to the church shortly after. In 1980, again he had to leave the church under the status of a sick leave, and participated in psychoanalysis and psychotherapy with Dr. Robert Mullins and Dr. John H. Brennan. Four years later, Cardinal Law saw the need to remove Geoghan from St. Brendan's in Dorchester and then reassigned him to St. Julia's in Weston, Massachusetts, after more molestation complaints. By this time, Dr. Mullins found Geoghan to be fully recovered and Dr. Brennan said that Geoghan should not have any restrictions on where he could work as a priest.

The therapy Geoghan had encountered in these years was very much focused on trying to treat Geoghan's homosexual tendencies and his pedophilia through both cognitive and behavioral bases. One cognitive technique in the treatment of homosexuality is the directive-suggestive approach in which the therapist openly discourages homosexual behavior to the patient and makes clear the idea that homosexuality is not genetic or biological, but rather entirely pathological. A behavioral technique for homosexuality and pedophilia involved exposure therapy, which is meant to condition a patient to correlate his maladaptive behaviors to an aversive stimuli. However, that technique seemingly was not widely used in the cases of the offending priests. Another treatment plan for pedophilia was cognitive-behavioral therapy which involved focusing on the pedophilic behaviors as wrong, with an emphasis on respectful criticism and specificity of the effects pedophilia has on the victims. This therapy also included group therapy based upon ways to control behaviors and empathize with others.

In April 1989, he went to another treatment program at St. Luke's Institute in Maryland where he was officially diagnosed with homosexual pedophilia. Treatment there typically consisted of one-on-one cognitive-behavioral therapy, sex addiction support groups, and physiological measurement techniques of arousal factors. After this episode, Geoghan was told to leave the ministry by Bishop Robert J. Banks and was again placed on sick leave. He returned to treatment, this time at the Institute of Living in Hartford, Connecticut, and was there diagnosed as moderately improved and able to continue parish work at St. Julia's. Dr. Brennan also agreed that Geoghan was ready to be back in the church.

But as the years went on, more molestation charges arose with more frequency and finally Geoghan himself decided to leave the parish from 1993 to 1996 in order to spend time at the Regina Clari Residence for Retired Priests. During this time, he was accused of molestation again, but the case was dropped in 1994. In 1995, he was advised to avoid contact completely with young males when unsupervised. After his stay at the residence, he sought more therapy in Ontario for six months in the Southdown Institute. This institute is specifically prominent in the church abuse crisis, as the center to which the most troubling priests were sent. Therapy here was very intensive over a longer period of in-patient time and included the cognitive-behavioral therapy techniques listed above as well as psychiatric evaluation and risk assessment for relapse.

Yet even with therapy and treatment, Geoghan continued to abuse, as was typical for most of the abusive priests who generally had a high recidivism rate. All the while, Geoghan denied the effectiveness and necessity of the different treatments. After therapy or sick leave, he was placed into new parishes and each time became a sexually dangerous threat to an entirely new church community, especially because they were uninformed of his past history of sexual abuse. After numerous treatments, he was released and deemed not be a threat to society. However, despite these diagnoses, when he came back into churches, he continued to abuse boys.

The overall results of the treatment raise suspicion of the effectiveness and efficiency of Geoghan's therapy and reassignment. With multiple different treatment periods in different institutes, the entire endeavor became very costly and not worthwhile for the church. It was not until his diagnosis of pedophilia in remission turned into a final diagnosis of terminal pedophilia, meaning he would never recover, that Geoghan's case finally persuaded the church to not let him enter any new parishes.

Trials and sentencing

When the clergy was first approached by the victims, there were no serious immediate consequences for Geoghan. At first the victims always followed the advice of Geoghan and kept quiet about the situation. Yet as soon as the victims began to come forward, the church made sure to take care of the situation and keep the problems out of the public eye through pay-offs in civil suits which were kept secret. Also to quiet the victims and keep a peaceful and safe-appearing environment within the church, the clergy chose to constantly shuffle Geoghan among parishes.

But when the abuse was made public by the *Boston Globe*, the victims and their families were finally able to seek legal relief from the church through the court system. In total, over one hundred fifty families filed abuse claims against Geoghan. When the incidents became public, he was finally convicted for indecent touching of a ten-year-old boy's buttocks at a Boy's and Girl's Club swimming pool many years before. He was sentenced to the maximum of nine to ten years in prison, of which six had to be served, because he was at high risk for recidivism and considered explicitly by the Judge Sandra Hamlin to be sexually dangerous to any young boy with whom he might come into contact. He was set to be tried for many other cases victims had raised against him, but the long-term outcome of the cases ended after he was killed in prison by another inmate.

Death in prison

When Geoghan was first convicted, officials in the prison qualified his level of dangerousness as extremely high. In the maximum security prison, the Souza-Baranowski Correctional Center, he was placed in the same area as the other prisoners who were also considered to be very dangerous. In his immediate cell was Joseph L. Druce, an inmate who decided to enforce his own conception of justice for the abused boys by killing Geoghan. Further punishment is a typical result for sex offenders at the hands of violent inmates in prison.

A voided conviction

After a death in the prison system, the Supreme Judicial Court has in some situations in the past voided convictions on appeals that are pending, but only if the attorney requests the voiding process. In the case of Geoghan, his attorney, David M. Skeels, worked with the appeals court and filed a death certificate of Geoghan, after which the judges decided to void the conviction and to drop all other charges upon Geoghan.

To some of Geoghan's victims, this decision was outrageous. They had taken the emotionally difficult steps of coming out and revealing everything that had been a secret for so long. Of course Geoghan was now dead and that should be their retribution, but for some reason, many victims felt as if all the mental stress they had endured through the personal revelations and time consuming court claims felt like nothing. Others were thrilled that Geoghan's life was taken. After so many years of suffering, they could rest assured that Geoghan was no longer able to enjoy life. Also, he would never again be able to commit the same crimes after getting out of prison.

Yet, considering this crisis took place in a religious environment, there were also those victims that regretted the death of Geoghan not because they felt they had not been justly and adequately compensated, but rather because they believed that Geoghan might have taken that time in prison to repent and grow in his faith. One of the main tenets in the Catholic Church is that nobody is so far gone in sin that they are unable to be forgiven.

In the end, it was the decision of the appeals court, and not the feelings of the victims, that had the impact on voiding the conviction. Geoghan, deceased, officially had his record cleared.

Notes about sources

The primary source of this case study was the book *Betrayal*, written by the investigative staff of the *Boston Globe*. Because the book was written before the imprisonment and killing of Geoghan, additional sources provided information about his trial and death. Because knowledge of Geoghan's specific treatments was unavailable, some of the journals provided for a basis on general treatments for pedophilia and homosexuality. The journals included *U.S. Catholic*, the *Australian and New Zealand Journal of Psychiatry*, *Behavioral Science & the Law*, and *Studies in Gender and Sexuality*. Additional newspaper articles were obtained from the *Boston Globe* and *USA Today*.

Leroy Hendricks
Post-sentence civil commitment of sex offenders and Kansas v. Hendricks

Abstract

Leroy Hendricks had a decades-long history of sexually abusing children. At the end of his last prison sentence, Hendricks became the first person to be civilly committed to a mental institution under a new Kansas law. This law allowed for the involuntary, indefinite confinement of certain dangerous sex offenders. Hendricks challenged his confinement in court, claiming that it violated several of his constitutional rights. The U.S. Supreme Court ultimately deemed the law constitutional and opened the door for other states to pass similar laws.

Background

Leroy Hendricks has admitted to a long history of sexually abusing children. In 1955, while a twenty-one-year-old airman at McConnell Air Base in Wichita, Kansas, he exposed himself to two young girls and invited them to play with his penis. He pled guilty to indecent exposure, and was fined $2.90. Two years later, he was convicted of lewdness with a young girl and spent a short time in jail. Then, in 1960, while he was employed at a carnival in Washington State, he fondled two boys, aged seven and eight. For that, Hendricks served two years in prison, after which he was paroled. In 1963, soon after his parole, he was convicted of lewd conduct for playing strip poker with a fourteen-year-old girl. That same year, he was convicted of fondling the genitals of a seven-year-old girl who was a friend of his family in Seattle. He was required to undergo treatment for deviance, and he was found safe for reentry into society in 1965. Two years later, Hendricks performed oral sex on an eight-year-old girl and fondled her eleven-year-old brother, friends of the family with whom he had gone camping. He refused to participate in a treatment program for sex offenders, and was imprisoned until he received parole in 1972. He was diagnosed as a pedophile and entered into a treatment program, which he soon abandoned. Hendricks later admitted to, but was never arrested for, engaging in sexual activity with his step-daughter and palsied stepson from 1972 through 1976. Both were between the ages of nine and fourteen during this period. Both performed and submitted to oral sex in exchange for chewing tobacco, cigarettes, and permission to drive Hendricks's truck. He often used model airplanes, chewing tobacco, and cigarettes to entice children.

In 1984, Hendricks tried to fondle two thirteen-year-old boys who were customers of the Topeka, Kansas, electronics store where he worked. The prosecutor agreed to a plea bargain of a sentence between five and twenty years for Hendricks, and he was convicted of two counts of taking indecent liberties with a minor. The prosecutor decided not to exercise the Habitual Criminals Act, which could have tripled Hendricks's sentence. The prosecutor also recommended the statutory minimum sentence, and to have the sentences run concurrently rather than consecutively. Hendricks was imprisoned until September 1994, when he was expected to be released to a halfway house.

The civil commitment statute

In July 1993, a Kansas college student named Stephanie Schmidt was raped and murdered by a coworker. The murderer had been paroled from a rape sentence. A task force was formed to determine how to prevent future crimes like those perpetrated against Schmidt. The task force proposed the Kansas Sexually Violent Predator Act. This proposed law allowed for the indefinite involuntary civil commitment of sexual predators, a class that included anyone who had been charged with or convicted of a sexually violent offense, and who suffers from a personality disorder or mental abnormality likely to lead to further sexual violence. The task force found that the general civil commitment statutes, which pertain to individuals who are dangerous to themselves or others and who cannot care for themselves, were not adequate for dealing with sex offenders. The special Sexually Violent Predator Act was therefore necessary.

The task force formed in Kansas after the rape and murder of Schmidt followed the lead of Washington State, which passed the Community Protection Act in 1990. Two incidents prompted that law. In 1989, a man with a history of kidnapping and sexual assault abducted a seven-year-old boy in Tacoma, Washington. The man raped the boy, severed his penis, strangled him, and left him to die in the woods. Then a Seattle woman was raped and killed by an inmate who was out of prison on a work release. The Community Protection Act allowed for the civil commitment of sex offenders after they had completed their prison sentences. The law became the model for other states, which shortly thereafter passed similar statutes. By 2001, seventeen states had enacted sexually violent predator commitment statutes and forty-one had at least debated them on the floors of their legislatures.

The Kansas task force submitted a law that drew nearly verbatim from Washington's law. The Kansas state legislature passed the statute in 1994, shortly before Hendricks's release date. He became the first person against whom the state sought to exercise the new law.

After a finding of probable cause and an evaluation by a psychiatric professional, those against whom the state has initiated civil commitment proceedings are entitled to a trial. At this trial, the individual facing commitment also enjoys most of the trial rights available to criminal defendants. The accused sex offender must also be found, by a unanimous jury and beyond a reasonable doubt, to be a sexually violent predator.

The Kansas and Washington type of civil commitment statute is not entirely new. Between 1937 and 1970, twenty-nine states had adopted laws allowing for the commitment and treatment of individuals who were considered sexual psychopaths. These laws differ from today's sexual offender statutes; the sexual psychopath laws sought to address a psychopathy through medical treatment. These people were viewed as too unwell to be released into society. Current sexually violent predator laws also allow for the civil commitment of those who have committed sex crimes, but the commitment does not aim at treatment; it is a response to violent predation and dangerousness. These individuals are viewed as too dangerous to remain at large. The sexual psychopath statutes fell out of popularity in the 1970s, and most states repealed them.

The process of confining Hendricks

On August 19, 1994, exercising a provision in the newly passed law, Hendricks and his attorney requested in court that the petition be dismissed. The judge found that there was probable cause to believe that Hendricks fit the law's definition of a sexually violent predator, and he therefore ordered an evaluation of Hendricks at a secured state hospital. Acting upon his attorney's advice, Hendricks did not submit to this examination.

At his civil commitment trial, Hendricks's extensive criminal history was described to the jury. Several statements made by Hendricks in previous psychiatric evaluations and at his trial proved damning. He had told mental health examiners that treatment was useless, and he said at the trial that when he is extremely inclined to molest children when he is under stress. He agreed that he is a pedophile and that he is not cured of the condition. He also said that his death would be the only assurance that he would never molest children again.

A licensed clinical social worker with expertise in treating male sex offenders testified that Hendricks had been diagnosed with pedophilia, personality trait disturbance, and passive-aggressive personality. A psychiatrist also testified that Hendricks was a pedophile. On Hendricks's behalf, a forensic psychiatrist testified that future dangerousness of sex offenders cannot be predicted accurately. The jury found Hendricks beyond a reasonable doubt to be a sexually violent predator, and he was civilly committed.

The Kansas Supreme Court's decision

After the jury found him to be a sexually violent predator and opened the door to his involuntary civil commitment, Hendricks and his attorney, Thomas Weilert, claimed that the law breached both the Kansas State Constitution and the U.S. Constitution. In support of this claim, Hendricks advanced several arguments. The Kansas Supreme Court only considered one of them. Hendricks contended that his substantive due process was infringed because the Sexually Violent Predator Act allowed for the commitment of an individual with a mental abnormality or personality disorder, whereas the U.S. Supreme Court had previously ruled that involuntary civil commitment could only be imposed upon a finding of both mental illness and dangerousness. Since an abnormality is not the same as an illness, Hendricks argued, an abnormality was insufficient to impose civil commitment. The Kansas Supreme Court agreed and, without considering Hendricks's other claims, ordered his release.

Attorneys for Kansas went to the U.S. Supreme Court and requested an emergency stay of Hendricks's release, pending a determination by the U.S. Supreme Court whether to hear the state's appeal of the Kansas Supreme Court's ruling. The U.S. Supreme Court issued the stay, which one of Kansas's attorneys said was an unusual step in a non-capital case. The stay resulted in Hendricks's continued incarceration. The U.S. Supreme Court eventually granted *certiorari*, and the case was argued before the court six months later, in December 1996. It was yet another six and a half months before the court ruled. Hendricks remained confined in the interim.

The U.S. Supreme Court's decision

In late June 1997, the U.S. Supreme Court overturned the Kansas Supreme Court's decision in a five-to-four ruling. Justice Clarence Thomas wrote the majority opinion, in which he addressed each of Hendricks's constitutional arguments. First, Thomas dealt with Hendricks's substantive due process claim, on which the Kansas Supreme Court based its decision. Thomas wrote that a finding of mental abnormality did not fall short of due process requirements for civil commitment; in other words, the difference between a mental abnormality and a mental illness was irrelevant.

Hendricks's second claim, which the Kansas Supreme Court never addressed, was that Kansas's law established criminal proceedings, and that any confinement resulting from it constituted punishment. Hendricks extended this argument in two ways. First, since the law was not in place when Hendricks committed his crime, any confinement pursuant to that law would be *ex post facto*. And second, since Hendricks served out his criminal sentence, any subsequent proceeding for the same offense would violate the U.S. Constitution's prohibition of double jeopardy, according to his argument. Thomas wrote that the law was civil in nature, not criminal, and thus did not impose punishment. According to Thomas, the civil commitment statute did not implicate retribution or deterrence. Also, Thomas wrote that the requirement of arrest or conviction served only as evidence of dangerousness; the confinement is not punishment for the crime.

Hendricks's third claim focused on the fact that he had not received any treatment during his confinement in Larned State Hospital, where he had been detained during his appeals and where he would remain confined indefinitely if he lost his appeal. Hendricks contended that the state's failure to provide any treatment for his mental abnormality indicated a punitive purpose to the law. The court rejected this argument on two grounds. First, it stated that incapacitation is a valid end on its own. It provided the example of a quarantine of a person with an infectious illness: the quarantine might not provide treatment but it is certainly not punitive. Thomas's second explanation was that the failure to provide treatment resulted from the fact that the civil commitment program had only recently been implemented, rather than from some punitive intent. According to Thomas, the lack of treatment was less important than the fact that the Kansas Department of Social and Rehabilitative Services, rather than the Department of Corrections, supervised Hendricks. The decision concluded that all of these considerations amounted to a civil law, to which Hendricks's *ex post facto* and double jeopardy claims did not apply.

The dissent

Justice Stephen Breyer wrote a dissent in the case, with which three other justices joined. Breyer agreed that Kansas did not violate Hendricks's right to substantive due process by finding that he had a mental abnormality rather than a mental illness. The point where Breyer disagreed with the majority's opinion was on the *ex post facto* and double jeopardy questions, since he felt that the conditions of Hendricks's confinement did in fact constitute punishment.

Breyer began by noting that incapacitation is a purpose of punishment. He then turned his attention to the issue of treatment. Breyer pointed out that the possibility of treatment had been delayed until the end of his prison sentence, which probably hindered any treatment's efficacy and hinted at a desire to keep Hendricks confined as long as possible. Moreover, Breyer noted, Kansas State conceded that Hendricks could be treated, but had not actually received treatment during his post-sentence confinement. Treatment was not even considered a principal objective of the civil commitment. Thus, Kansas State officials withheld the treatment that they agreed could benefit Hendricks. Breyer said that this pointed to the law serving a criminal, rather than a civil, purpose.

Breyer also makes reference to the seven factors that had previously been established by the Supreme Court in order to determine whether a law is punitive and requires criminal procedural protections. He finds that each of those factors indicates that the law represents punishment.

Objections to the ruling

Aside from Breyer's objections, several arguments can be made against the Supreme Court's ruling. One is that the Kansas law requires less proof from the state than the Supreme Court had previously required. The Supreme Court had concluded that in order to civilly commit an individual, the state must provide clear and convincing evidence of the individual's unsoundness and dangerousness. This standard amounts to roughly ninety percent certainty. Although the sex offender law nominally required a jury to determine beyond a reasonable doubt that the individual should be committed, which would amount to about ninety-five percent certainty, the onus borne by the state in practice was not reasonable doubt. That is because in order to commit, the jurors must believe, beyond a reasonable doubt, that the offender would be more likely than not to commit further sex offenses. If a juror says he is at least ninety-five percent certain that a sex offender is fifty-one percent likely to commit another offense, then that is not the same as saying that one is ninety percent sure the sex offender will commit another offense. The reasonable doubt standard did not actually exist in these trials, meaning that Kansas was not adhering to the Supreme Court's requirements for civil commitment.

There is also evidence that some of the people responsible for the law's passage and execution had punishment as their goal. The state attorney general in office when the Kansas Sexually Violent Predator Act was passed told the state legislature that the law could serve both preventive and punitive ends. Carla Stovall, the former Kansas attorney general who argued *Kansas v. Hendricks* on behalf of her state, said while she was serving on the Kansas Parole Board that the goal of the law was to keep sex offenders locked away as long as possible. She also referred to the sex offenders who are affected by the law as animals. Gene Schmidt, the father of the college student whose murder precipitated the Kansas Sexually Violent Predator Act, echoed Stovall's remarks. He served on the task force that drafted the law and sent it to the Kansas legislature for ratification. He said that the members of the task force expected few committed sex offenders ever to be released.

Commentary on the case

In the national media, the case received limited attention, with several newspapers mentioning the high court's ruling. The *New York Times* provided extensive coverage, which was unusual for national media outlets. Editorial boards that wrote about the case expressed mostly negative opinions of the decision, though this sentiment was far from unanimous.

While the general media did not write very much about the decision, legal periodicals did. In the immediate wake of the *Hendricks* decision, dozens of law journals published articles criticizing the decision. Many commentators, particularly law students who authored notes about the case, focused on the perceived possibility that the state might use civil commitment in an abusive manner.

The effects of the decision

The Supreme Court's ruling in *Kansas v. Hendricks* remains valid and controlling precedent. It has been cited nearly eight hundred times by state and federal appellate courts. It set the stage for another Supreme Court ruling in 2002, about the same Kansas law. In that decision, *Kansas v. Crane*, the court stated that sex offenders may not be civilly committed without a finding that they suffer from some severe inability to control their behavior.

The *Hendricks* ruling provided encouragement for other states to adopt similar civil commitment statutes for sex offenders. Seven states passed laws within the two years following the Supreme Court's ruling.

In Kansas, the number of civilly committed sex offenders has steadily increased since the court's ruling in 1997. Kansas has civilly committed one hundred thirty sex offenders. The state attorney general initiates civil commitment proceedings against, on average, twelve percent of sex offenders who are about to be released from prison. These individuals appear before a judge to determine whether there is probable cause to evaluate them as candidates for commitment. The judge finds probable cause about ninety-five percent of the time. From there, the individuals undergo a psychiatric analysis. In 2000 and 2001, fewer than forty-seven percent of the examined individuals were deemed sexual predators who should be committed. Since then, however, a new lead psychiatric examiner has taken over the responsibility, and the rates between 2002 and 2004 were eighty-one percent, seventy-nine percent, and ninety-four percent. It is now more likely than ever that released sex offenders in Kansas will be civilly committed. The cost of the sex offender program is expected to increase by thirteen percent between 2005 and 2006.

Hendricks's release

In June 2005, Hendricks was released from Larned State Hospital. He had suffered a stroke in 2001 that limited the use of his hands. He was originally expected to live in Lawrence, Kansas, after his release, but a petition drive to keep him out forced state officials to change plans. He was instead released to Leavenworth County. The conditions of his release included constant supervision by state-employed professionals, and surveillance equipment in his house. His house was also located in a remote area. Leavenworth County objected to Hendricks, however, and filed a motion for a restraining order against him. A judge issued the order and Hendricks was forced back into a state hospital. As of July 2005, Kansas had still not found a permanent home for him. Hendricks is the only civilly committed sex offender that Kansas has allowed to be released; every other one remains confined.

Notes about sources

My main sources were the Kansas Supreme Court decision, *In re Hendricks*, and the U.S. Supreme Court decision, *Kansas v. Hendricks*; news reports from the Associated Press, the *Lawrence Journal-World*, and *Legal Times*; the text of the

Kansas Sexually Violent Predator Act; and an article by Eli M. Rollman in the *Journal of Criminal Law & Criminology*.

Additional sources included *Civil Commitment of Sexual Predators: A Study in Policy Implementation*, by Andrew J. Harris; recordings of the oral arguments in the U.S. Supreme Court case, available at www.oyez.org; and a telephone interview with Austin desLauriers, clinical director of the Sexual Predator Treatment Program at Larned State Hospital, among other sources.

In order to gauge the media response at the time, I referred to articles that ran in 1996 and 1997 in the *New York Times, Washington Post, Wall Street Journal, Los Angeles Times*, and other newspapers. I also referred to an array of law journal articles to determine commentators' perspectives of the decision.

Francine Hughes
Spousal rape and abuse

Abstract

Francine and Mickey Hughes got married in 1963 in Mason, Michigan. Despite a later sham divorce, Mickey continued to live with Francine and emotionally, physically, and sexually abused her for fourteen years. Francine was what is now termed a battered woman due to the countless beatings, unwanted sex, and emotional battering that she suffered at the hands of Mickey. In 1977, after Mickey beat Francine and forced her to have sex with him, Francine killed Mickey by setting fire to the room in which he was sleeping. She was tried for murder in the state of Michigan. Francine was found not guilty by reason of temporary insanity and was set free. The trial of *People v. Francine Hughes* was groundbreaking in that it was the first trial to free the defendant based on a horrendous history of abuse and questionable mental state at the time of the killing.

Francine's early life

Francine Moran was born in 1947 to a family living on a farm outside Stockbridge, Kentucky. Francine's family was very poor, and they moved around often. Her father had difficulty with money and gambled. His drinking habits got out of control as Francine grew older, and he died in 1966 when he was fifty-three and Francine was nineteen. Francine rarely saw her parents fight, though she learned from her sister that her father beat her mother after Francine had left home and his drinking had escalated.

When Francine was fifteen, she met Mickey Hughes, who was then eighteen. They dated for a while. After she gave in to his demands to have sex, she felt she had no other choice but to marry him even though she did not love him. Francine and Mickey got married in 1963 when Francine was sixteen and Mickey was eighteen. They moved in with the Hughes family in Dansville, Kentucky. Neither Francine nor Mickey finished high school, and Mickey had a difficult time finding and holding a job. Thus Francine and Mickey were very poor, always struggling to make ends meet, and constantly moving around because they could not afford to pay the rent.

Spousal violence

The first incidence of spousal violence occurred just a few weeks after their wedding. Mickey claimed that Francine's clothes were too provocative and sexy and gave her strict guidelines regarding what clothes she could wear and how she could wear them. One day when she rebelled against these rules, Mickey, in an act of sexual aggression, ripped off her pants and tore them to pieces. Mickey apologized for his outburst and said that he loved her, but this was only the beginning of a long cycle of abuse and sexual control that would come to dominate Francine's life.

Mickey was an overly controlling, selfish, and jealous man. He would not allow Francine to work but was unable to hold a job for any sustained amount of time. Francine was not allowed to go anywhere without his permission, and Mickey would get furious when he discovered that she went to visit a friend. Francine was expected to clean the house compulsively and prepare whatever food Mickey wanted at the risk of being beaten if she did otherwise. Thus Mickey forced Francine into conforming to the stereotypical gender role of a subservient and powerless woman.

In the beginning, the abuse followed a standard pattern: Mickey would get angry and yell and curse at Francine. Mickey's anger would escalate and he would beat her. Once he was satisfied and Francine was crying, he would stop and leave the room. Then, according to typical batterer behavior, he would apologize and affirm that he loved her. Francine would try not to repeat what had provoked him, and she would hope that the situation would get better. However, Mickey's violent rages and sexual aggression only got worse. As Mickey began to drink more frequently, he abused Francine more and more often and the beating intensified in severity, often leaving Francine with split lips, black eyes, and severe bruises all over her body. Francine was also sexually abused by Mickey. Due to social norms regarding sexuality and the roles of women during the time of Francine's abuse, Francine was reluctant, even after Mickey's death, to discuss the sexual abuse she experienced. However, she relayed that she had sex with Mickey even though she did not want to because she feared his abuse if she refused.

Francine gave birth to their first child, Christy, in 1964 when she was seventeen. Though she loved Christy very much and devoted her existence to raising Christy, she felt that it was unfair to have more children when their lives were so unstable and they were so young and poor. However, Mickey, in an act of sexual dangerousness considering the context of his abusive behavior, refused to use condoms. Despite her various efforts to use different contraceptive devices, in six years Francine gave birth to four children, Christy, Jimmy, Dana, and Nicky. Raising four young children with no help from her abusive husband and very little money for food and rent proved to be extremely difficult for Francine.

A divorce

By the time Francine was pregnant with her fourth child, Mickey often slept elsewhere, drank regularly, cheated on her repeatedly, and refused to hold a job, thus providing no money for the family. Because Mickey also refused to sign a welfare application, Francine was forced to divorce him so that she could sign it herself and thus be able to afford to buy food for her children. The divorce, however, had little effect; Mickey continued to stay at her house when he felt like doing so despite her pleas to stay away. Francine felt she had little power to stop him because she knew that refusing him continuously would only bring more abuse. Soon after the divorce, Mickey got into a bad car accident and from then on his violent outbursts become even more horrific then they were before. After the accident, Mickey would become enraged by the smallest things. Not only did he no longer apologize, but often it would take the police's arrival to get him to stop beating Francine.

No help

Francine and Mickey lived next door to Mickey's parents, but even they were powerless in the face of Mickey's rage. Everyone in Mickey's family and many of the people living in their small town knew about the abuse that tortured Francine, but nobody stepped in. After a particularly bad beating in which Mickey was so violent that Francine had to run away for fear that he would kill her, Francine discussed with Mickey's family the possibility of having him institutionalized. Mickey's family, while aware of his troubling violent tendencies, refused to acknowledge what a severe problem he had and thus refused to take any role in its correction. Francine was left on her own to deal with the abuse she confronted on a regular basis. Considering the lack of concern even Francine's own family expressed in response to her husband's abuse and the restrictive social norms regarding sexuality at the time, it was clear to Francine that nobody would understand or be receptive to saving her from the sexual abuse she also endured.

Law enforcement was also ineffective at helping Francine. When the police came after being called by one of Francine's family members, Mickey's rage would subside, and he would not beat Francine in their presence. The only times Mickey was arrested was when he acted violently toward the police. In those instances he would be arrested and detained for no more then a night after which he would return home to Francine even more enraged than when he had left. The police could do nothing unless Francine went to the prosecutor's office and signed a complaint. However, with none of her own assets, nobody who could help support her and the children, and no job experience, Francine did not think she was capable of supporting their four children on her own. In addition, Francine feared Mickey's wrath should she take an active role in punishing him for his behavior.

The events of March 9, 1977

On the day that Francine finally took action, Mickey got angry because Francine arrived home ten minutes late from school where she had just begun taking classes. Mickey's anger escalated as he realized that he did not like the dinner Francine was cooking for him. Mickey sent the hungry kids outside while he proceeded to beat Francine as she made dinner. Mickey beat Francine mercilessly, threw all the food on the floor, forced her to clean it all up, threw it all on the floor again, and then beat her some more. He forced her to burn all of her school books and to say that she would never attend school again. In the midst of his abusive outburst, the police came. Mickey threatened the police and told them he was going to kill Francine, but the police did nothing since they never saw him physically harm her. After the police left, Mickey continued to abuse Francine as before. Once he was finished, he ordered Francine to bring some food to his room. After he finished eating, Mickey wanted to have sex. The thought of having sex with Mickey made Francine nauseous, but she knew that if she resisted, his violent rage might never end. Francine had sex with Mickey so that he would stop hurting her and go to bed. She hated having sex with him, and this was the final act that drove her to committing her desperate act.

Francine realized that her situation was never going to get better and that no matter what she did, Mickey would ruin the life that she made for her family. She realized how awful her life was and what terrible lives she was making for her children, and she decided that she must take them away. Francine hated her life and wanted to forget about it entirely. Francine decided that she would burn the house down, with Mickey inside, so that she would not have anything to return to and thus could truly escape the pain she endured. Francine brought all of the kids to the car. She went into the cellar, got a gas can, and unscrewed the lid. She went into the bedroom where Mickey was sleeping, poured gas onto the floor, and threw a lit match on the floor. As the gas caught fire, she ran for her life and drove away with the children.

Spousal rape

While this case seemed to be only a matter of physical abuse, there was also a significant sexual element to Mickey's abuse. On the night that Francine killed Mickey, he forced her to have sex with him even after torturing her. Mickey did not physically hold Francine down while he was having sex with her nor did he state what would happen if she refused his requests. However, considering Mickey's violent history and the raging state he was in at that time, there was no question in Francine's mind that if she refused to have sex with him, he would continue to beat her, possibly to her death. The physical, sexual, and psychological threat that Mickey posed all merged on the night that Francine killed him.

This type of forced sexual intercourse was not something that Francine was unused to. Francine discussed how she was unable to escape Mickey's sexual desires. She referred to sex as one of her duties because, for her, sex was something that she had to schedule into her day along with mowing the lawn and doing the laundry. She described her sexual experiences with Mickey as lacking care and love. While Francine occasionally would experience what she referred to as sexual release, she explained that sex with Mickey never felt good because the whole time she hated for herself for letting him do this to her. Francine would go to the bathroom and put a washcloth over her face so that she could sob without the children hearing her. She hated having sex with Mickey, especially on days when he was especially abusive towards her. After having sex with Mickey, Francine would feel miserable.

The term spousal rape, as now defined, refers to sexual acts committed by a man against his wife without her consent or against her will. According to this definition, sexual acts can be committed using physical force, threats of force against a woman or a third person, or through implied harm based on prior assaults which led the woman to fear physical violence if she resisted. Thus, since rape in this context is defined as a woman submitting to sexual acts because of fear or coercion, it is not necessary that a woman fight back in order for the sexual acts she unwillingly commits with her husband or ex-husband to be considered rape. Sexual acts include but were not limited to penile-vaginal intercourse, the insertion of genitals into the mouth or anus, and the insertion of objects into the vagina or anus.

Until the 1970s, most states did not consider spousal rape a crime, however today all fifty states consider it a crime for a husband to rape his wife. Until 1976, there was a section in the rape laws entitled Marital Rape Exemption which dictated that a husband could not be charged with raping his wife or limited the severity of the offense with which a husband could be charged for marital rape. This exemption was understood as common law in some states but existed as actual legislation in others. As of 1996, seventeen states had completely abolished the marital rape exemption. However, notwithstanding the existence of the marital rape exemption, all states currently have at least one section of their sexual offense codes, which differ from state to state, which dictate that marital rape is a crime. Thus a man can currently be tried in any court in the United States for raping his wife. Women also have the option of suing their husbands in civil court for pain, suffering, and medical and other costs incurred because of sexual battery. Unfortunately Francine did not have this option because spousal rape was not considered an illegal offense during the time she was forced to endure it.

Studies have found that ten to fourteen percent of women who have ever been married have experienced spousal rape at least once. Studies of women staying in battered women's shelters have shown that between one-third to three-quarters of these women reported experiencing spousal rape. Research reports that spousal rape victims are more likely to have been raped more often than stranger and acquaintance rape victims. In a study on spousal rape victims, the majority of victims reported being raped more than once, and one-third of the victims reported being raped more than twenty times over the course of their relationships with their husbands. Contrary to popular belief, women who have experienced spousal rape have long term physical and psychological damages that are as severe or more severe than women who have experienced other types of rape.

The choice of the plea of temporary insanity

Aryon Greydanus, Francine's lawyer, faced a difficult task in defending the unique circumstances of Francine Hughes' act. Pleading simply not guilty was not an option since Francine had already admitted to the act. Pleading guilty to a count of murder in the second degree, which is killing that is not premeditated, planned or executed in a heat of passion, or to voluntary manslaughter, which is killing that is committed with no prior intent to kill, would result in a less severe jail sentence than being found guilty of first degree murder. However, after spending countless hours every week visiting Francine and getting to know her and the abuse she endured, Greydanus felt that even these lesser prison sentences were inappropriate given Francine's circumstances. He was certain that the horrible abuse that Francine endured should be a deciding factor in her sentence, but this type of defense had never been used to excuse a crime.

Greydanus also considered the option of a self-defense plea which justifies an individual's crime if it is committed in the face of direct and immediate threat to that individual's life. Although Francine was not being directly threatened by Mickey when she burned their bedroom, Greydanus felt this plea was still legitimate because of Francine's firm belief that Mickey would have ultimately killed her and that it was just a matter of time. With limited financial and social resources, Francine had tried everything possible to escape from Mickey's abuse including divorce, the welfare office, the police, and a mental-health clinic. Nobody was able to offer Francine a way out that would protect her and her children. Greydanus did not believe it was fair to punish Francine for doing the only thing she could to save her life. However, despite the constant threat that Mickey posed to Francine's life, the self-defense plea was still questionable because, legally, self-defense required that the danger be immediate. This would be difficult to prove since Mickey was sleeping when Francine killed him.

Greydanus decided on a plea of temporary insanity. The temporary insanity defense stated that when the crime was committed, the defendant was mentally ill or mentally incompetent and thus should not be held criminally liable for her actions.

According to the temporary insanity defense, the defendant was legally insane when the criminal actions were committed but returned to a state of sanity after the event. Greydanus felt that this plea was ideal because he believed that Francine's description of her trancelike state as she was burning the house fit the profile of temporary insanity and because a defendant acquitted by reason of temporary insanity served no criminal sentence as long as this defendant could prove a current state of sanity. What was difficult with this plea, however, was that the defendant's state of temporary insanity had to be proved by the defense, such as through the expert testimony of a psychologist or psychiatrist, and then believed by the jury.

The trial: The people v. Francine Hughes

Francine's trial began on October 24, 1977, seven months after being jailed, in a courtroom in the City Hall of Lansing, Michigan. Aryon Greydanus was appointed by the court to defend Francine. Martin Palus conducted the prosecution. Francine was originally charged with two offenses: first degree murder and felony murder. Specifically, the first count stated that Francine deliberately, willfully, and with premeditation murdered Mickey. The second count stated that Francine murdered Mickey while committing the crime of arson. The original judge, Michael Harrison, withdrew from the case before the trial began after rumors emerged of his prejudice against Francine. The newly appointed judge, Ray C. Hotchkiss, dropped the second count at the request of Greydanus on the grounds that it repeated the first count. A panel of fourteen jurors, two men and twelve women, heard the evidence of the trial and decided the verdict.

Palus attempted to present the case as a simple case of a wife murdering her abusive husband, however Greydanus used his extensive research on Francine's situation to present a much more complicated scenario. While the facts regarding Mickey's death were generally agreed upon by both the defense and the prosecution, the degree to which Francine premeditated the killing was widely contested. The issue of premeditation was one of the primary issues of the trial because it largely dictated Francine's sentence.

The prosecution presented the relationship that Francine had with a man named George Walkup as a motive for her criminal actions and thus proof of her premeditation. Using a series of love letters Francine had written to Walkup when she was in jail, Palus tried to prove that Francine killed Mickey so that she could be with Walkup. Greydanus, however, demonstrated that the infatuation that was expressed in these letters was the result of Francine's desperate and lonely state in jail and not something that was on her mind at the time of her criminal actions. Another motive offered by the prosecution was that of revenge. Palus tried to prove that Francine had been planning Mickey's murder as a means of getting back at him for all the pain and misery he had caused her. However Francine's history of non-violence in addition to her testimony that she had never even thought of killing Mickey emerged more credible.

Through the excellent testimonies of important witnesses such as Francine's neighbors and children, Greydanus' cunning cross-examination of Palus' witnesses, and Francine's eloquent four hour long testimony, Greydanus was able to paint a picture for the jury of the horrific atrocities that Francine experienced and the helplessness that encapsulated her life. Once the jurors had an understanding of Mickey's appalling physical, sexual, and emotional abuse, Greydanus brought in the expert witnesses to testify to Francine's temporary state of insanity at the time of the murder. Dr. Arnold Berkman, a clinical psychologist, testified that his examination of Francine revealed that when she committed the crime she was operating under an irresistible impulse and thus was mentally ill and unable to control her behavior. Dr. Berkman diagnosed Francine with Borderline Syndrome with hysterical and narcissistic features. Furthermore, Dr. Berkman stated that he did not believe Francine was capable of planning to commit murder. Dr. Anne Seiden, a staff psychiatrist at a hospital in Chicago, diagnosed Francine's mental state at the time of the murder as acutely psychotic. Dr. Seiden stated that Francine could not control what she was doing because she was in a state of ego fragmentation when she committed the murder. Dr. Blunt, an expert in legal psychiatry called upon by the prosecution, did not find Francine to be legally insane at the time of her murder. However, he stated that he did not believe Francine's criminal actions were the result of premeditated planning.

On the eighth day of the trial, the jury found Francine Hughes not guilty by reason of temporary insanity. On November 4, 1977, Francine was released and held on bond until she underwent a final psychiatric examination. Once her sanity was proved, Francine was freed. Despite suffering from depression and guilt, she worked in factory jobs and moved to a home in Jackson with her four children.

Francine's mental state of temporary insanity

In trying to describe and explain to herself and others what happened on the night of March 9, Francine often said that she did not know what she was doing and that she must have been going crazy. Not yet aware of the fact that she could be diagnosed as legally insane, Francine identified her behavior and thought process at the time of the act as abnormal and incomprehensible. After Mickey forced Francine to have sex with him, Francine described the way she felt as a helpless, frozen fury. Francine had trouble recalling the passage of time and reported that she was not really thinking. After Mickey went to sleep, Francine said she and the children watched the television, though she had no recollection of what they watched or how long they were sitting there. She reported that she was thinking about her life, how awful it was, and how much she was suffering. She said that she suddenly began to feel empowered. From there, her thoughts began racing and she reported that she felt clear-headed as she began to make impulsive, irrational decisions to drive away with their children.

In a frenzy, she excitedly began making plans without paying attention to the consequences of these actions. In this whirl of emotional planning, Francine decided that the only way that she would never return to her horrible life was if she destroyed it all, including Mickey. She then described herself as alternating between states of excitement, panic, and calmness. As Francine walked to

Mickey's room to pour the gas around his bed, she recalled feeling clear, light-headed, and free, as if what she was doing was ordinary and easy. In a moment of hesitation before she poured the gas, she reported that she heard a voice which urged her to do it. Francine claimed that her memory after this was spotty. She remembered having the matches in her hand but not how she got them. She remembered there being a flame but did not remember lighting it. It was only after Francine threw the match into the room that she thought about what she had done. She then ran to the car in utter shock, unable to think straight. Her children reported that she was screaming, but she did not remember this. Francine described her thought process as being fragmentary. Urged by her children, Francine drove to the police station and, by the time they got there, she was in hysterics. She later said that that she could not talk to the police officers and that she felt as if she was in a dream and was paralyzed. Whenever she tried to speak, she just heard herself scream.

While this was indeed a very traumatizing and disturbing event for Francine, a great deal of the emotions and behaviors that she described classified as elements of a disordered emotional state. Specifically, her detachment from herself as if she was watching herself from the outside, her inability to remember certain aspects of the event, the fragmented nature of her memory, her loss of reality and rationality, and her sense of being possessed by an external force were all signs of disordered thinking.

Dr. Berkman diagnosed Francine with Borderline Syndrome which he believed she continued to have at the time of the trial. He explained that people with this syndrome were unable to deal with certain kinds of stress and could fall apart in what was termed psychological decompensation. Borderline Syndrome is a classification which is not easily defined and one which has changed greatly over time. According to the Diagnostic and Statistical Manual of Mental Disorders Fourth Edition, or the DSM-IV, the essential characteristics of Borderline Personality Disorder, as it is now referred to, are adult impulsivity and a pervasive pattern of instability in regards to relationships with others, self-image, and emotions. People with this disorder frantically try to avoid abandonment, are very sensitive to environmental stimuli, and have a pattern of unstable and intense relationships. Individuals diagnosed with Borderline Personality Disorder may also have an identity disturbance that is demonstrated by a distinctively unstable sense of self. In addition, individuals with Borderline Personality Disorder may show emotional instability due to intense mood reactivity. Borderline Personality Disorder is a difficult diagnosis to make and one that cannot be entirely objective. While Francine certainly met some of the criteria for this disorder, such as relationship instability and emotional and identity disturbance, it was not entirely clear that she had Borderline Personality Disorder.

Battered women's syndrome

For years, domestic abuse was something that was not acknowledged or discussed in American society. It was viewed as domestic squabbling that was private and meant to be kept within the home behind closed doors. For ages women were viewed as inferior to men, and laws existed which allowed domestic violence as a means for a man to punish and control his wife. The case of Francine Hughes was viewed as a milestone case in that it acknowledged the struggles of battered women and the lack of support and assistance they received. Francine's testimony on her experience of abuse made a powerful statement that domestic abuse exists and needs to be recognized and addressed. The timing of Francine's case was crucial. During the 1970s, the United States was in the midst of a feminist movement that focused on equality for women and increasing awareness of the prevalence of and difficulties faced by abused women.

While domestic abuse has become much more widely acknowledged, there still remains a great deal of debate surrounding the issue of what standard to apply to abused women when trying to understand how they deal with abuse and, in some cases, defend themselves. Some advocate the use of a sex-neutral standard in which all of the circumstances of the participants in the incident are taken into account equally. Others criticize this standard for reinforcing sexual stereotypes because, though it is termed sex-neutral, it still focuses on the defendant as a woman. The second standard, called the reasonable woman standard, dictates that men and women have different perceptions of danger, harm, and force, and thus men and women have different reactions to the same threat. Consequently, a woman's actions should be judged by a separate standard than a man's actions. The fear of stereotype reinforcement is also a criticism of this standard.

The third standard involves an original concept of self defense based on the standard of the reasonable battered woman. It has been difficult to mainstream a concept of self-defense for women because women are stereotypically viewed as passive and submissive. However, people are beginning to acknowledge that women may need to use force to defend themselves and thus may need to act in non-stereotypical proactive and violent ways. While this type of behavior is generally not looked upon favorably because of these women's deviation from expected gender norms, it is still very important that a standard for women is advanced that depicts women as active and in control. It is simply unfair to assume that women should always act weak and powerless, especially in the face of danger.

The concept of the battered women's syndrome, or BWS, was advanced in 1979 by Leonore Walker in her book *The Battered Woman*. The use of the term syndrome has been criticized because it implies that abused women have a disease. However BWS was intended to refer to the reactions and characteristics of regular women who are caught in dysfunctional relationships yet are surrounded by societal norms that dictate appropriate feminine behavior and render these women incompetent to deal with their relationship. BWS is currently not a legal defense, but an approach to explaining the experiences of battered women. It describes the structure of a battered relationship from a woman's perspective.

BWS identifies a cycle of violence in battered relationships which consists of three stages and involve the concept of learned helplessness that women acquire after living with an abusive man. More specifically, the cycle involves the tension building phase, the acute assault phase, and the contrition phase. In the contrition stage, the abuser is very affectionate toward the victim, and he ensures that his violent outburst will never reoccur. This phase may disappear after a certain amount of time and is then replaced by a pause until the next violent outburst. This cycle leads to the battered woman feeling trapped; she feels that she cannot fight back against her abuser without risking her life. Seligman's concept of learned helplessness presents a theory that can help explain why women stay in such relationships. At first these abused women think that by changing their behavior, they can prevent the violence from occurring. However, no matter what these women do or refrain from doing, their husbands' violence does not stop. These women lose self-confidence and self-efficacy, become passive, and are then unable to find alternatives to the terrible lives they are living.

Battered women's syndrome is often used as a means of explaining the behavior of women who were in abusive relationships and defended themselves by killing their abusers. According to the BWS, a battered woman is not insane, but a regular, reasonable person who is caught in an irrational situation and responded how any rational person would react. This appears to be paradoxical since one would think that a woman conditioned by the concept of learned helplessness would not take such a drastic, proactive measure as killing someone else. This is explained, however, by the dominating force of the survival instinct. The survival instinct is activated when the abuser's threatened violence surpasses prior violence, and this instinct is thought to override the usually dominant passivity of learned helplessness.

The BWS brings an interesting dimension to Francine's case and her plea of temporary insanity. While it was ruled that Francine was indeed temporarily insane, advocates of the BWS assert that a women does not necessarily have to be insane to fight back, possibly violently, against her abusive husband. It certainly was not delusional or irrational for Francine to feel that killing Mickey was her only way out of her terrible situation. Francine faced very real obstructions when trying to escape her battered relationship, including the lack of assistance from the police and courts, the financial crisis her departure would have caused, and the likelihood of increased violence at her attempt at departure.

While an abusive husband presents a real threat to his wife's life, it is still difficult to use self-defense as a defense for women who kill their abusive husbands because the definition of self-defense requires that the abuser's threat be imminent. However, the BWS may make self-defense a more accessible plea for abused women since the term's definition does not dictate a specific time frame. A battered woman's testimony of long-term abuse and an inability to escape a horrendous situation in combination with an expert testimony confirming these circumstances may be able to set the stage for the self-defense plea of battered women some time soon.

BWS, however, remains a very controversial concept. Many claim that BWS does not exist and is merely a creation of feminist politics. Many see BWS as a ploy by women simply trying to evade responsibility for their murderous actions. Critics believe that BWS is a way out of the long established principle that only clear and imminent danger to life justifies murder. BWS critics also contest the fact that a similar defense did not exist for men. Other critiques of BWS include the fact that there is no single profile for battered women; women react to abuse in very different ways and many women who were abused do not fit the BWS profile. Others also disagree with the word syndrome since it is is not a diagnostic term in the DSM-IV. It is important to note that BWS has not been established or accepted by serious empirical researchers in the field of psychology. There has been insufficient empirical evidence demonstrating that this syndrome meets the diagnostic criteria of psychology and the law. In addition, it is very difficult to separate individuals who suffer from BWS from individuals who merely claim it for their legal defense. Although BWS has been used in a wide range of cases, there remains a great deal of questions regarding its validity. Some believe battered women's defenses should be based on self-defense while others believe being abused should have no relevance to the fact that a person killed another human being.

Notes about sources

For my sources, I primarily relied upon Faith McNulty's account of Francine Hughes' experience written in *The Burning Bed* as well as personal communication with McNulty's grandson, Kellan McNulty. I also referred to the Diagnostic Manual of Mental Disorders, Leonore Walker's *The Battered Woman*, and various law websites on the insanity defense and spousal rape, such as the website for the National Center for Victims of Crime.

Paul Ingram
Repressed memory and confession of sexual abuse

Abstract

Paul Ingram was a respected, high-ranking police officer of Thurston County in Olympia, Washington. He was happily married to his wife, and together they had five children. On November 22, 1988, however, Ingram pleaded guilty to sexually abusing his two daughters. He did not initially remember abusing his daughters, but thought that they would never lie about such serious allegations. He was charged and convicted of six counts of third degree statutory rape. He received twenty years in prison, and was released on parole on April 3, 2003.

Background

At forty-three years old, Paul Ingram already had a strong presence in the community. He was a local official in the Republican Party, and was strongly involved in the Protestant denominational church, Church of Living Water. The family went to church three times a week, in addition to participating in various church groups and functions.

With a house on ten acres of land, Paul and his wife were able to raise their five children the way they had always imagined. There was plenty of space to raise their rabbits, chickens, cows, and ducks and for their large garden full of vegetables, fruit trees, and shrubs. The Ingrams were a self-sufficient family. However, many of the children, especially the eldest boys, did not appreciate the rustic life. The children were subject to many chores, under the watch of their stern father. Besides occasionally spanking his younger children, Paul stated that he did not physically abuse his children. A family doctor confirmed that he had never seen any signs of abuse on the children. The older children were grounded for punishments. Paul was a strong disciplinarian with several household rules. He would let little interfere with his children's school and household obligations, so they were not allowed to participate in any sports or other extracurricular activities. His children complained that he showed little love for them. His relationship with his wife, however, was different. They had a stable relationship, and had a regular sex life.

During an annual church retreat, Heart to Heart, the daughters, Erika and Julie, had an opportunity to talk openly about sensitive issues. In 1983, Erika revealed that she had been sexually abused. The counselors quickly alerted authorities. However there was little basis for her claim, since it had only been a married man that touched her knee. The case was dismissed. Two years later, at another retreat, Julie and Erika revealed that they were sexually abused by a neighbor. Paul took the girls to the police department to file a complaint, but the case was dropped with the little evidence and because of the overwhelming inconsistencies in their stories. In 1988, Heart to Heart welcomed Karla Franko to speak to at the retreat. Franko captivated her audience with her performance as God spoke to her by giving her visions of traumas audience members had to endure. She would make strong proclamations about the audience members, describing scenes of childhood insecurities, trauma and abuse. After her speech, Erika stayed after the conference. On record, Erika cried and could not be comforted by the counselors. She finally told them that she had been sexually abused by her father. Karla Franko, on the other hand, has a different story. After the retreat, one of the counselors had her pray over Erika. As she did so, she kept thinking about the word molestation. She told Erika that she had been molested, and with further praying revealed that she had been molested by her father for several years. Erika began to cry, but did not respond to Franko's bold assertions.

After the retreat, both girls left home, to the concern of their parents.

Initial accusations

A few weeks later, Erika met her mother at a local restaurant, where Erika proceeded to admit that Paul had abused her several times when she was a young child. She claimed the molestation ended about ten years before, when Paul had joined a new church. She also claimed that her two older brothers molested her in the past several years. Julie quickly followed suit with accusations that mirrored Erika's, except she claimed the last time she was abused was only five years earlier.

Later that day, however, the story would change when Erika and Julie communicated with the investigators. The detectives were concerned with Erika's allegations because they were beyond the Washington State statute of limitations of seven years. Erika said that her last occurrence of abuse was a year earlier, in

1987, after she caught a sexually transmitted disease from her father, and was treated by a doctor in California. Julie claimed the last time she was abused was three years earlier, not five.

A few days later Erika claimed the last time she was abused was only a month earlier. The detectives attributed the changes in the girls' stories to the fact that many victims make partial disclosures, and only once they are more comfortable do they reveal the entire incident. Julie continued to disclose information, usually through the form of letters because she was unable to handle speaking about her trauma. In one letter, she changed the last time she was abused to only five weeks earlier. A subsequent letter shocked investigators. Julie indicated that some of her father's friends abused her when they gathered at the Ingram house for poker games. Many of those who attended the games were employees at the Thurston County police department.

Paul was confused about the allegations. He could never see himself molesting his daughters, but at the same time he doubted they would lie about such atrocities. He also cited his discomfort in hugging his children or telling them that he loved them as indirect pieces of evidence of abuse. After only a few hours of interrogation, and a week after he had first heard the accusations, Paul had confessed. He was convinced that he did molest his children over a long period of time, but that he had repressed the memories.

Multiplying claims

Over the next several weeks, the claims made by Erika and Julie began to multiply. The police officers listened compassionately and earnestly as they carefully pressed the girls for more details. The isolated incidents transformed into detailed narratives spanning over much of their lives, starting at the age of five and lasting until the week before Paul was taken into custody. Erika and Julie also began to implicate several of Paul's friends as participants in the abuse, alluding to the existence of a sexual cult.

With two emotional victims, and a confession from Paul, the interrogators were certain that he had sexually molested his children. However, after his confession they were not able to obtain any specific information or evidence with respect to the crimes. As a result, the interrogators, the police psychologist, and Ingram's pastor, Pastor Braton, would assist Paul with giving him clues in the question or asked him alluding questions to the answers they had in mind. The questions would lead Paul to give the answers that confirmed Erika and Julie's claims. In addition, Paul's confessions were marked with conditional phrases, stating what he would have done, or what he could see himself doing, rather than what he had done.

Two of Paul's friends who were repeatedly mentioned as participants in the abuse were Jim Rabie and Ray Risch. When they were taken into custody, their reactions were similar to Ingram's. They too believed that they could have committed the crimes, but that they had repressed the memories. They had, after all, been accused by three people, and they were told that there were photos of them committing the acts. Their wives were shocked, and reported few sexual deviations on the parts of their husbands. Risch's ex-wife stated that he never abused his own children.

Furthermore, the victims were involving their mother as a participant in the abuse, although they initially had to inform her of the abuse. Their mother would either watch or prepare the girls before the abuse. These accusations were especially damaging because she did not want to lose her youngest son. The web of stories became more tangled as the other children became involved. Soon Paul was admitting engaging in sexual relationships with all of his children.

Emergence of ritual cult abuse

As more memories began to be uncovered, Paul and his daughters began to connect the sexual abuse to a larger product of satanic cult abuse. They recounted sacrificing babies, drinking blood, and participating in massive orgies. Other adults and children were implicated, including the canine unit at the police department. At this point it was difficult to ignore the inconsistencies and the fantastic nature of the claims. For example, Paul, Erika, and Julie never remembered the same abuse. In addition Erika and Julie never mentioned each other in their memories, although they shared a room. However, the prosecution still had Ingram's confession, and promises of physical evidence by the girls.

Nevertheless the police department requested $750,000 from the state legislature to cover the purchasing of technology that could assist in finding burial grounds. The request was denied.

Expert evaluation

Hoping to iron out the bulging inconsistencies, the prosecution brought in Dr. Richard Ofshe, a professor of social psychology at the University of California at Berkeley. When Dr. Richard Ofshe listened to Paul's detailed accounts he did not believe the memories Paul was describing. He thought he was either lying, or deluded. Ofshe suspected that Paul was highly suggestible and was probably influenced by interrogators' techniques to recover memories. As he discovered the methods the interrogators, and especially Pastor Bratun, were using to elicit memories, Ofshe became more concerned. Usually, Pastor Bratun would describe a scene, and then allow the imagination to take hold to form a new memory. As a result, Ofshe decided to perform his own experiment. He told Paul that Erika and Julie claimed that he had once made them have sex with their brothers while Paul watched. Paul initially denied its occurrence. Ofshe advised Ingram to pray to try to remember and visualize what he could about the event. After all, Ofshe told him, his daughters had already said this had happened.

Ofshe proceeded to interview Erika, who was eager to give him a glimpse into the ritual horrors she remembered. She estimated that she had attended more than eight hundred cult rituals. Ofshe pressed Erika to reveal specifics of the cult rituals. Yet all she could recall was that they would chant during the rituals, but she could not remember any specific words, which she attributed to suffering from traumatic amnesia. He also asked her why she had continued to endure the abuse until the last week that she was home rather than not moving out sooner. She replied that she did not want her standard of living to suffer. Finally he asked Erika whether her father had forced her and her sister to have sex with her brother. She said no.

By the time Ofshe returned to see Paul, Paul had written a three page detailed account of the event he had been told him to merely think about. When Ofshe informed Paul of his experiment he was unable to persuade him that he had never forced his children to have sex. It had already become a part of his memory. Ofshe began to realize that Paul was probably not guilty of anything, except being highly imaginative with a desire to please authority. A series of psychological tests confirmed Ofshe's personality assessment. Paul scored unusually high on need for approval, need to be liked, and compliance to social convention. As for the girls, Ofshe though that Erika was a habitual liar and that Julie followed in the shadow of her more outgoing and attractive sister.

After he left, Ofshe submitted a final report to the prosecution, stating that this case had the potential to convict innocent victims. Ofshe's psychological report, despite the defense attorney's best efforts, was allowed in court. Paul, however, did not read the report, because Pastor Bratun told him that it might confuse him.

The evidence

Ofshe's report did not change the prosecution's stance. Interrogators kept searching for pieces of corroborating evidence among the claims. It seemed as if none of them were remembering the same abuse. Each episode was missing crucial details that linked it to the others. Since the abuse was continual, the interrogators interviewed two deaf girls that were living in the house at the time of the accusations. Both said that they did not see any abuse but did notice that some of the family relations were strained. They also asked the victims and Paul, whether they noticed any conspicuous marks on Rabie and Risch. No one remembered any, despite the thick knotted scar across Rabie's chest.

As for physical evidence, both girls claimed to have had abortions, in addition to scars and knife cuts from the abuse. Both were hesitant to show their scars, but after being pressed by investigators, agreed to undergo the physical examination. When questioned by the doctor, Erika claimed that she had never had an abortion. In fact, she said she was a virgin. Both girls showed no evidence of an abortion, but the results were not conclusive, since detecting abortion scars is difficult. However, the skin, if made to suffer deep cuts, would inevitably scar. Both girls lacked any scars from physical abuse. Investigators were also unable to find any of the documentation for previous doctor visits for abortions, or sexually transmitted diseases.

After doctor visits examining the girls for their claimed scars, exhaustively searching for the satanic burial grounds, and thoroughly combing the Ingram household, the officers were not able to find one shred of physical evidence of any sexual or satanic ritual abuse.

The case

Rabie and Risch initially believed the charges, but as they began to realize the enormity of the accusations, they defended their innocence. Both stated that the interrogators accusing them and assuming their involvement, the implications by others, and the claims of photographs made them doubt their own memory. They thought perhaps they acted inappropriately unintentionally, but now knew the accusations were much more severe. During their imprisonment, Rabie and Risch were kept in solitary confinement. Rabie was charged with seven counts of statutory rape, rape in the second degree, and indecent liberties. Risch was charged for three counts of statutory rape in the second degree, and rape in the second degree. Neither would take deals that would significantly curtail their imprisonment. Finally, due to the lack of evidence and because Erika and Julie were too traumatized to testify, charges against both were dropped. They had spent more than one hundred fifty days in custody.

As for Paul, during the first court hearing he pleaded not guilty. However, this was seen as a routine plea. For the second hearing, Paul was pressured by the prosecution, his wife, his daughters, and his own attorney to plead guilty because of the emotional trauma his daughters would be forced to undergo if they had to testify. Paul decided that he had made them suffer enough. The prosecution, wisely, omitted all claims relating to the satanic ritual abuse, since the public has been skeptical of such claims. Paul pled guilty to six counts of rape in the third degree, and was sentenced to twenty years in prison.

Subsequent developments

Soon after the trial, Paul began to doubt his churning detailed memory. However, by the time he tried to take back his confession, it was too late. He had been charged with a crime, and in Washington State, it is particularly difficult for a defendant to reverse a guilty plea. Several groups were committed to freeing Paul. However, despite the publications of several journal articles and even a book about the Ingram case in 1994, Paul was not granted any appeals. In 1996, the Washington State pardons board agreed to hear the case. There were several psychological experts that testified, including Ofshe. The board rejected Ingram's request. Ingram was released on April 8, 2003 and currently resides in Washington State. He is still classified as a level three offender.

Problems in the investigation

From the outset, the investigation was plagued by several compromising factors. First, Sheriff Gary Edwards, in hopes of fending off criticism, did not defer the case to another county. He wanted to deal with the situation internally. However, many of the officers were uncomfortable with interviewing Paul, because of his reputation and their relationship with him. Not only had he worked at the force for the past seventeen years, but many of the officers had participated in the social poker games at his house.

Information was also freely exchanged among the interrogators, Pastor Bratun, the attorneys, and Paul and his daughters. Ofshe noticed that Julie's confessions were always after her sister's and incorporated many of the same elements. Paul would also use the elements from what his daughters were remembering and incorporate it into his new recovered memories.

In addition, several officers began to from close relationships with the daughters, causing them to become heavily emotionally invested in the case. When the severe distress of the officers became apparent, the sheriff had psychologists evaluate the investigative team. They were all diagnosed with post-traumatic stress disorder. Several were plagued by nightmares. This attachment added to the investigators' unwavering conviction that abuse had occurred to the point that the investigation cost the county three quarters of a million dollars, the most expensive investigation in Thurston County's history.

The role of the media

Over the last couple of decades, there has been an increasing surge in the number of people claiming to have repressed and recovered memories. Self-help books on the subject, usually written by non-professionals without a background in psychology, have been highly influential and widely read. In *The Courage to Heal*, which is known as a self-proclaimed guide of the incest recovery movement, the authors encouraged their readers to thoroughly investigate their feelings, no matter how small they may be. The authors claim that some of the symptoms indicative of sexual abuse include having low self-esteem, depression, or an eating disorder. Another book, *Repressed Memories: A Journey of Recovery from Sexual Abuse*, similarly encourages readers to admit they have been abused. The authors state that one can express repressed memories as truth, and if the allegations turn out to be false, that it will be easy to set the record straight.

Other books have depicted recovered memories of satanic ritual abuse, such as *Michele Remembers* and *Satan's Underground*. In *Satan's Underground*, the experiences the author shares are strangely similar to those reported by Erika and Julie. The author claims she was forced to have sex with members of the cult and participate in the mutilation of animals and babies. The author explains that the satanic cults have sophisticated methods of disposal for the killed babies and animals so that they will never be found. In addition, the cult forces the members to take heavy doses of drugs that erase the horrifying incidents from their memory.

Interestingly enough, Erika read *Satan's Underground* the summer before she accused her father of molestation. She had borrowed the book from a friend and said she had read the entire book. Yet on record, she had only read a few chapters because she could not emotionally handle reading a story that described her abuse. Julie had read a book about incest that same summer. In addition, one month prior to the allegations the Ingram family had watched the Geraldo Rivera special on NBC, *Devil Worship, Exposing Satan's Underground*.

There has yet to be a case where evidence proved the existence of satanic ritual cult abuse. At the time, however, such claims were taken seriously by therapists and investigators alike. Therapists often supported their clients, and urged them to uncover repressed memories. Police stations, the Thurston County police department included, would bring in experts on satanic ritual abuse to train investigators on how to handle these cases. While the total of homicides in the United States hardly reached twenty-five thousand people a year, victims of satanic abuse were claiming that there were at least twice as many people being killed. The Ingram case came at a time where skepticism was only beginning. The case was integral, in that the Thurston police county believed they had found proof, something all of the other cases were lacking. They believed the allegations and thought they would be able to uncover the nationwide conspiracy that had evaded other investigations. They all believed in the allegations, and had attended seminars on uncovering victims of satanic ritual abuse.

It is difficult to understand what kind of role books and the media have on their audience, but it is highly possible that the exposure to the content can influence our memory and our construction of reality. Psychologists have administered studies that demonstrate how we are capable of forgetting where we obtained information, and that this can help generate the details of a false memory. Similarly, the details of Erika, Julie, and Paul's memories could have actually been rooted in books and popular media.

Psychological stance on repressed and recovered memories

Despite the multitude of self-help books, and the upheaval of celebrities and sensational cases resulting from the recovery of childhood abuse, the scientific data supporting the validity of repressed and recovered memories is scarce. While there are cases of recovered memories, psychologists agree that it is unlikely that the human mind could completely repress long term continuous abuse. Studies investigating other traumatic memories, such as children witnessing their parent being murdered, or living in a concentration camp, do not support repression. On the contrary, these traumatic memories endure the fading of time and are vivid, despite repeated attempts to avoid thinking about them. These memories are not only difficult to repress, but are actually more intrusive as the victims suffer from the memories that they would more than anything like to forget.

There are several studies, however, supporting the existence of false memories in a laboratory. For example, researchers have been able to manipulate their subjects into recovering a false memory in a laboratory setting. The methodology and results of these studies are similar to the experiment Ofshe administered to Paul. In addition, research indicated that there is a strong correlation between high scores on the Creative Imagination Scale, or CIS, and a propensity to believe false memories. Paul was also administered personality tests, which revealed he was highly imaginative.

The role of religion

Ingram was a devout man, and confided greatly in his Pastor Bratun. At one point he had Bratun perform a pseudo exorcism that would eradicate the evil spirits inside of Paul. He also continuously encouraged him to trust the veracity of his memories. Often, during his confessions, Paul would pray aloud, and ask for his pastor to be by his side. Then he would begin to produce memories. The investigators knew his religious background, and would use religious language to elicit more confessions, promising that through them he could earn salvation and redemption.

In investigating the patterns among those who claim to have repressed memories, more than half reported to be active or very active in religion. Nearly one-fifth reported being involved in satanic cult activity. Within religious communities, fundamentalist religious leaders often attest to the veracity of underground satanic cults. Ingram and many of the interrogators were members of fundamentalist congregations.

Concluding thoughts

Research indicates that the production of false memories can be precipitated by suggestive questioning and by fostering beliefs of authenticity. Using more sensitive techniques during interrogations and interviews dealing with recovered or repressed memories could minimize the occurrence of false memories and false confessions. In addition, if interrogators and perhaps therapists place more of an emphasis on obtaining physical evidence, unfortunate individuals such as Paul Ingram and his family could have preserved the stable, united family they once had.

Notes about sources

I relied heavily on the book *Remembering Satan* by Lawrence Wright. He conducted extensive interviews and included psychological background relevant to the case. The website of the Ingram Organization, a group dedicated to freeing Ingram, was also especially helpful. It can be accessed at http://members.aol.com/IntramOrg/. There are links to Ofshe's report, results of the medical examination, and links to other sites.

Adam Lack

Sexual assault and acquaintance rape on college campuses

Abstract

Sara Klein, a freshman at Brown University, accused Adam Lack, a junior at Brown, of sexual misconduct after the two engaged in sexual activity when Klein was severely inebriated. Lack found Klein next to a pool of vomit in his fraternity house and invited her back to his room for a glass of water. According to Lack, Klein initiated all sexual activities and the two talked for several hours after they had sex. Klein left in the morning after giving Lack her phone number. Lack was surprised a month later to receive a notice from the university that accusations of rape had been made against him. Lack was found guilty of sexual misconduct and sentenced to one semester of probation and counseling on alcohol's effects on relationships. Upon review, the punishment was increased to one semester suspension. Lack appealed the decision, which was then reduced to two semesters of probation. However, since the case drew national media attention, the damage had already been done to Lack's reputation. Lack felt so uncomfortable that he took a leave of absence from Brown. He filed suit against Klein for libel and against Brown University for breach of contract, negligence, and gender discrimination. Almost two years after the initial incident, Lack agreed to a legal settlement of his claims against both Klein and Brown University. Brown removed Lack from probation stating that they regretted not being able to resolve what they acknowledged as a dispute between the two parties. Klein stated that she regretted her binge drinking and accepted that Lack may not have been aware of the extent to which she was impaired.

History of sexual assault on college campuses

Crime has always been prevalent on college campuses. One hundred fifty years ago, students at Harvard College commented on the high rate of crimes that were seemingly ignored by authorities. In 1937, a sociological review noted that men in college were exploitive of their partners. In 1957, one study showed that twenty percent of college women were victims of attempted or completed rape. It was not until recently that these warning signs were given any significant attention.

History of legislation surrounding sexual assault on college campuses

Research has suggested that women on college campuses are at greater risk of rape and sexual assault than women in the general population. Some research suggested that on a campus with ten thousand women, three hundred fifty rapes or more could be committed each year. In 1990, the federal government enacted the Student Right-to-Know and Campus Security Act, partly in response to these findings. This act required universities participating in federal student aid programs to provide information to applicants, current students, and employees regarding annual security statistics and campus security policies. The act was amended in 1992 when Congress published the Campus Sexual Assault Victims' Bill of Rights, which was more tailored to awareness and prevention of sexual assaults, as well as to providing basic rights to victims of sexual assault on college campuses. In 1998, Congress again amended the act, this time changing the name to the Jeanne Clery Disclosure of Campus Security Policy and Campus Crime Statistics Act, mandating more detailed reporting by universities, including a mandatory daily crime log to be made available to the public. In 1999, over eight million dollars was allocated to twenty-one different colleges and universities in an effort to fund prevention of sexual assault, domestic violence, and stalking. An additional seven million dollars was allocated in 2000 to twenty more colleges and universities.

Facts of the case

Sara Klein, originally from New York City, was a freshman at Brown University. She was a double major in urban studies and public policy. Adam Lack was a junior at Brown University from rural Nora Springs, Iowa. He held a 3.2 GPA and was a member of the Delta Tau fraternity. Lack majored in business economics and organizational behavior and management.

On February 3, 1996, Klein was watching television with her girlfriends. At about 9:30 p.m., Klein began taking shots of vodka. She proceeded to take ten shots over the next hour before heading to a Brown crew party. From there, the girls moved on to a party at the Brown fraternity, Delta Tau. Klein lost consciousness from alcohol intoxication at about 11:30 p.m. Lack found Klein on the floor of a friend's room in a pool of vomit. He invited her next door to his room to get a glass of water. Lack said that she walked unassisted and that Klein remarked on how much she liked Lack's music. He offered her Tylenol and water, and she accepted Lack's offer to let her sleep in his bed. Lack later said that he thought it would be rude to not let her stay since it was already very late. They shared the bed with their backs to one another, both fully clothed. Lack started to fall asleep, but five minutes later he said that Klein began to make sexual advances. Lack said that as they moved to different levels of intimacy, Klein initiated each one. He said that Klein began kissing him, that she removed his shirt, and that she asked him if he had a condom. After they had sex, Lack reported that the two talked for many hours. They talked about their hometowns, music, and what types of careers they were considering. They smoked cigarettes and drank more water before falling asleep. Klein awoke in the morning and admitted to being hazy about the events from the previous night. She said she did not remember having sex and she asked if they had used a condom. When Lack responded, Lack said that she did not seem upset. Before Klein left, she asked Lack to call her, and the two exchanged phone numbers. Lack called Klein several times over the next few days before he finally spoke to her on the phone.

As time passed, Klein became more distraught about the events of that night. A month after the incident, Klein contacted her women's peer counselor who referred her to a support system, Woman on Call, which women can request through the Brown police. Within minutes, Klein was contacted by a dean who referred her to another service that assigns a faculty member trained to advise sexual assault victims. Marylou McMillan, director of health services, was assigned to Klein's case. McMillan advised Klein on her options, which included meeting with a dean; using an outside party who could bring both parties together for a discussion; going to the Providence police; or requesting a hearing before the disciplinary council. Six weeks after the encounter with Lack, Klein filed a complaint with the Office of Student Life in order to obtain a hearing before the disciplinary committee. Two months later, a panel of faculty members, deans, and students heard Klein's case. Toby Simon, associate dean of student life, presented Klein's case. Lack was represented by his lawyer and an adviser assigned by the university to assist him. Klein's argument was that she was too intoxicated to consciously give consent. Lack's response was that he did not realize the extent to which Klein was intoxicated.

Immediate and long-term outcome of the case

In May of 1996, the University Disciplinary Council found Lack guilty of sexual misconduct and sentenced him to one semester of probation and counseling regarding alcohol's effects on relationships. According to Brown, sexual misconduct occurs when a person has sexual contact with someone whom the person was aware or should have been aware was impaired. The council made a community notification statement addressing the decision in the case. However, neither

Lack nor Klein's names were exposed due to a constitutional amendment protecting student privacy. Despite this anonymity, Lack's name was somehow leaked. Brown's daily newspaper resumed publishing after having ended for the year in order to print a special edition. On May 13, Lack's twenty-first birthday, the *Brown Daily Herald* published an article beside a photograph of Lack detailing the facts of the case. Lack was immediately the center of scrutiny and ridicule, although his accuser's name remained anonymous. This article was also the catapult for the surge of media interest that would follow Lack through his case.

Upon review of the case, the penalty was increased from probation to a six-month suspension. Lack appealed the ruling and on September 3, 1996, a few days after returning to school, the punishment was reduced to two semesters of probation by Provost James Pomerantz, who said that although Lack should have known better, there was not enough evidence to prove sexual misconduct. By this point in time, Lack's reputation had been severely damaged, and he no longer felt comfortable on campus. He decided to take a leave of absence from Brown. Lack filed a civil suit in U.S. District Court against Brown University for breach of contract, negligence, and gender discrimination. The suit alleged that the committee's decision was gender-biased, and that the committee's failure to charge or discipline Klein for violating the student code regarding underage drinking showed selective enforcement. Lack also filed suit against Klein for libel, saying that she made statements to the Office of Student Life that she knew were false. Lack's lawyer, David Casey, said that Lack only pursued this action after several attempts to come to a resolution with Brown officials out of court. Lack sought unspecified damages, although his lawyer said that his client would not require a monetary award if the parties would admit to their mistakes openly. The court case began on February 7, 1997, and did not reach its conclusion until December 31 of that year. Lack agreed to a legal settlement of his claims against both Klein and Brown University. Brown removed Lack from probation, stating that they regretted not being able to resolve what then became deemed as a dispute between the two parties. Klein stated that she regretted her binge drinking and accepted that Lack may not have been aware of the extent to which she was impaired. Lack said that he was satisfied with the settlement and that he believed it cleared his name.

Legal and ethical issues raised by the case

This case raised the issue of consent. Klein claimed she was too intoxicated to give conscious consent and Lack took advantage of her. However, even law enforcement officials require training in order to assess a person's level of intoxication. This is especially difficult when the person is only an acquaintance. This case suggested that the only way to protect oneself against allegations of rape would be to have the other person sign a consent form that he or she had not been drinking alcohol and was consciously deciding to partake in each subsequent level of sexual intimacy.

Many argued that Lack was at fault ethically, if not legally. First, Klein had passed out from her alcohol intake and was lying next to a pool of vomit when Lack entered the room. Lack should have been aware that Klein was severely inebriated. Next, although his intentions may have been honorable at first, he took advantage of Klein's reduced inhibitions, and did not resist her advances. Further, since Klein was not in a state to remember the events of the night, Lack was the only person who knew the truth about what took place. This case was unlike other rape cases in that it was not simply one person's word against that of another. Rather, there was only one person's rendition of the events while the other person did not remember what happened.

This case also showed the danger of rape allegations, as a person accused of rape finds it nearly impossible to clear his or her name. Lack was forced to leave campus after his name appeared on the front page of the university's newspaper. He had to file suit against both his accuser and the university. Even after Klein stated that Lack was not at fault and the university stated publicly that it had handled the situation poorly, Lack's reputation had still been severely damaged, and he had suffered major mental distress.

The role of the university in legal proceedings was also brought into question. During his hearing before the University Disciplinary Committee, Lack reported that he was interrupted repeatedly, and that his interrogator had to be warned several times to stop trying to place words in his mouth. Lack's lawyer was not given the opportunity to speak. Also, by steering away from difficult questions, the committee did not confirm the truth in Klein's accusations. Finally, many have noted that universities do not have access to the same investigative tools as police or district attorney's offices, nor do they require the same level of evidence in order to find someone guilty.

The role of the media

Although the actual comments during the disciplinary action meeting were kept confidential, on May 3, 1996, the *Brown Daily Herald* published a special edition with Lack's picture and the accusations against him on the front page. Lack began to receive obscene phone calls and cold stares. Green ribbons symbolizing freedom from sexual assault appeared all over campus. The article in the *Brown*

Daily Herald prompted the surge of media attention that engulfed Brown for months. Articles detailing the case were found in major newspapers all over New England, including the *Boston Globe*. The *Chronicle of Higher Education* published multiple articles surrounding the debates raised by the case, and although the victim's name was initially kept anonymous, Klein's name was soon circulating in news articles as well.

Media attention grew to a national level when a crew from the ABC newsmagazine *20/20* descended on Brown's campus in order to tape a rally organized by members of the Coalition Against Sexual Assault. ABC news reporter John Stossel incensed Brown students with his sensationalistic reporting style. The rally members quickly tried to drown out Stossel's interrogating questions about the definition of rape with chants against television news. The students encircled Stossel, took the microphone from him and told him to wait his turn. Stossel insulted the students who in turn retaliated, leading Stossel to respond with an obscenity he refused to repeat for the camera. The *20/20* special aired on March 28, 1997. It included interviews with Adam Lack whom Stossel painted as the victim of the situation. Stossel accused overzealous rally members of not allowing freedom of speech and drowning out justice, yet his negative comments towards the students regarding the amount of tuition they paid and their lack of intelligence were not included in the report. Klein was criticized for her willingness to fight against sexual assault and her unwillingness to comment for *20/20*, which Stossel said had tried to act as a forum for her to voice her opinion.

Frequency of reporting rape on college campuses

Too often, victims of sexual assault do not report the incident. Reasons have included embarrassment, confusion surrounding the legal definition of sexual assault, not wanting to identify the assailant as a rapist, or fear of being blamed for the sexual assault. Reporting statistics vary, but some estimates showed that fewer than five percent of completed and attempted rapes are ever reported to law enforcement officials.

Characteristics of assailants

In nine out of ten cases, evidence showed victims were acquainted with their assailant. Boyfriends, ex-boyfriends, classmates, friends, acquaintances, or coworkers have been the most frequent offenders. Assailants have also been more likely to have used alcohol prior to the completed or attempted sexual assault.

Prevalence of sexual assault on college campuses

One comprehensive national self-report questionnaire found that fifteen percent of women reported having been the victim of a completed rape, approximately twelve percent were victims of attempted rape, fourteen percent reported unwanted sexual contact, and twelve percent reported being the victim of sexual coercion. Acquaintance rape and date rape are more common than left-handedness or alcoholism.

Prevalence of date rape

One study found that a large percentage of sexual victimization occurred in the context of a date. Thirteen percent of completed rapes, thirty-five percent of attempted rapes, and twenty-three percent of threatened rapes all took place in a date situation.

Reactions and response to sexual assault on college campuses

Despite the large number of cases of sexual victimization on college campuses, few perpetrators are ever dealt a punishment. Critics have found a discrepancy among students and administrators over what actually constitutes sexual victimization. Some argued that these acts have too often been disregarded as pranks, leaving the campus community with a lax sense of enforcement. The *New York Times* has gone so far as to accuse university judiciary committees and administrations of covering up fraternity crimes. Students who have used the college disciplinary system have often been disappointed. Proceedings were almost always confidential, and most universities did not allow lawyers. These committees have been criticized for too easily siding with the alleged victim in an effort to avoid negligence suits. They have also been criticized for having a more vested interest in the university's reputation than in actual justice. Additionally, investigations and decisions carried out in these makeshift courts might actually complicate proceedings later in a court of law.

Where sexual victimization occurs

The vast majority of sexual victimizations occurred in residences including dorms, off-campus housing, and fraternities. Less frequently, incidents occurred in bars, dance clubs or nightclubs, and work settings. Sixty percent of completed rapes occurred in the victim's own residence.

Risk factors for women

Four main factors increased a woman's risk of being the victim of sexual assault: frequent heavy drinking, being unmarried, having been a victim of sexual assault in the past, and living on campus. Living on campus was only a major risk factor for on-campus sexual assault.

The role of male peer support in the sexual victimization of college women

Male peer support referred to the warped sense of power that some males gather from a peer group. It was based on the idea that abusive men tend to be friends with other abusive men. These men feel the need to maintain a certain image for other men. This peer group provided support for treating women abusively by offering encouragement, thereby legitimizing abusive treatment of females.

The role of alcohol use in the sexual victimization of college women

Approximately fifty percent of sexual assaults have been associated with alcohol consumption by the perpetrator, victim, or both parties. Alcohol inhibited people's cognitive processes, causing them to concentrate on only the most apparent cues to them in a situation. Therefore, a perpetrator could focus on his feelings of sexual desire or entitlement rather than the victim's own suffering. Victims who were intoxicated may not have been as quick to realize their perpetrator's intent or the dangerousness of the situation due to cognitive impairment. One study showed that victims who felt drunk to some extent or who perceived their perpetrator to be intoxicated resisted less than women who did not feel inebriated or think that their attacker was drunk. Alcohol consumption could also place potential victims in social situations associated with higher risk of completed rape such as bars or nightclubs. Research also showed that a perpetrator's alcohol consumption was positively correlated to aggressiveness.

Sexual harassment on college campuses

Recently, it has been acknowledged that sexual harassment could occur outside of the workplace. On college campuses, certain professors have used their positions of power in inappropriate ways. These inappropriate behaviors included anything from frequent comments on a student's personal appearance to placing emphasis on sexuality in unsuitable contexts to excessive praise or flattery of a student.

Many universities have found it difficult to address controversy surrounding professor-student relationships. The University of Virginia passed a no-dating policy between professors and students in April 1993. It also increased its sexual harassment codes, an action that has been taken by many universities all over the country in recent years.

Conclusion

The issues raised by the Adam Lack case go far deeper than one college student's word against another. This case shows how the line between consensual and non-consensual sex becomes blurred when alcohol is involved. Can a person who has consumed alcohol give consent? How much alcohol can someone consume before they are unable to give conscious consent? How much responsibility can be placed on the other person when it is often difficult to judge someone else's level of intoxication? This case also shows the seriousness of accusations of rape. Lack was forced to leave campus because of the humiliation other students made him feel. The severe damage to his reputation forced him to file a law suit to try to clear his name of the allegations against him. Lastly, it is important to note that although this case has no definitive villain or victim, many cases of sexual assault on college campuses are unambiguous. Statistics show that women on college campuses have an incredibly high risk of becoming victims of sexual assault or date rape. Yet despite the high numbers of victimizations, many women still are not coming forward with their cases. Changes need to be made to decrease the high rates of sexual assault on college campuses as well as to encourage victimized women to come forward.

Notes about sources

The sources for this case came from Brown University, including the *Brown Daily Herald* and *Brown Alumni Magazine*, as well as major newspapers from Providence and Boston, including the *Boston Globe* and *Providence Journal-Bulletin*. Additional information was obtained from an exposé on the case from ABC's *20/20*. General information on sexual victimization of college women came from a research report conducted by the U.S. Department of Justice, The Sexual Victimization of College Women. General information as well as detailed information on the role of male peer support came from the comprehensive book by Martin D. Schwartz and Walter S. DeKeseredy. Information was also obtained from several general studies on acquaintance rape as well as studies on the prevalence of alcohol use in connection with sexual assault.

Mary Kay Letourneau
Statutory rape

Abstract

In February 1997, Mary Kay Letourneau, a thirty-four year old school teacher, was arrested for having a sexual affair with her twelve year old student, starting a media firestorm that created a new public discourse around definitions of statutory rape, consent, and pedophilia, and also created a new ideal type for the female sexual predator who has been widely imitated in popular media. Acting as both the fulfillment of a popular adolescent fantasy and as the ultimate violation of parents' trust, Letourneau and her case challenged common notions and images of who could be a pedophile and just who could be truly sexually dangerous.

Teacher and student's first interaction

In the early nineties, Mary K. Letourneau was a respected and popular elementary school teacher in the Highline School District outside of Seattle. Her reputation as an educator was so good that families reportedly fought to place their students in her class. Parents and colleagues would later recall her seemingly boundless energy and great ability to generate creative lesson plans for her students. This energy was considered even more incredible given that she also had four children of her own to whom she was devoted at home.

In 1995, a student named Vili Fualauu entered Letourneau's sixth grade class. He had been a student four years earlier in her class as a second grader, where Letourneau had first noticed his talent for art. This connection through his artwork was rekindled when he became her student again. Over the course of the school year, this connection intensified and the bonding process between the two coincided with two traumatic events in Letourneau's life that will be discussed later in this chapter. Other students in the class noticed at the time that Letourneau would give Fualauu special privileges in the class, including allowing him to go start her car for her as school was ending. These other students as well as Letourneau's colleagues would later recall that they acted as flirtatious peers even in public.

The relationship turned romantic before it turned sexual. That spring Fualauu found a silver ring on the street and gave it to Letourneau asking her to become his wife. She reportedly would wear the ring to school every day. The two professed their love for each other and quickly came to see each other as the loves of their lives. In later interviews Letourneau said that she and Fualauu both believed that they had been lovers in past lives and had conceived as many as ten children together over their lifetimes.

The relationship turns sexual

Over the course of the next summer, Fualauu would often visit Letourneau's house and became good friends with her children. It appears that it was in June of this summer that sexual intercourse first occurred between the two. Steve Letourneau would later recall that his wife would receive strange phone calls in the middle of the night from Fualauu who would demand to see her. Fualauu even accompanied the family on a trip to Alaska and would stay at the house with the family along with his older brother to the point at which Steve Letourneau became fed up with the attention his wife was paying to the boy.

Fualauu changed schools in the next school year, but would come often to visit Letourneau in her classroom at Shorewood Elementary where the two would regularly engage in intercourse in the school's parking lot. It has been generally accepted that Fualauu was the sexual aggressor in their relationship and that he enjoyed the sex with Letourneau. The pair would later reveal that they had sex as between three hundred and four hundred times before her arrest in February of 1997.

Letourneau became pregnant with Fualauu's child in the early fall of 1996. In October Letourneau informed a friend of both the affair and her pregnancy and revealed that because her child would be half-Samoan, she would be unable to lead her husband (who, like she, was Caucasian) to believe that the child was his. Letourneau revealed to her husband the truth, which he already had suspected. Upon hearing this news, Steve Letourneau began the process of officially ending their marriage which had been steadily declining in quality for years.

One of Steve's relatives who learned of the situation felt compelled to report the crime and called the Washington State Child Protection Services in February 1997. Letourneau was arrested at her school immediately after a faculty meeting. When news broke, the story quickly became a local and national media sensation. Letourneau gave birth to her child two months after her arrest. The child eventually went to live with Fualauu's mother.

Letourneau immediately entered a plea of not guilty to the court and found legal representation in David Gehrke. Gehrke eventually worked out a plea bargain with the district attorney in July 1997 in which Letourneau agreed to plead guilty to two counts of second degree rape. By agreeing to plead guilty Letourneau managed to avoid the maximum penalty of seven and a half years of prison time. At her sentencing in August, Letourneau expressed great remorse for her actions and admitted that she had done something that was morally reprehensible. Judge Linda Lau suspended her seven year sentence to only six months in prison and ordered Letourneau to enter treatment for sex offenders. Lau also ordered that Letouneau's newborn daughter, Audrey, be removed from her custody and that Letourneau never see Fualauu again. Letourneau was also required to take medication for the bipolar disorder she was diagnosed with while in jail.

Prison and re-arrest

Letourneau served her prison term where she was reportedly resistant to her therapy. She was released from prison in January 1998 to much media fanfare and went to live in a new apartment. Steven Letourneau had since left with their children to live in his native Alaska. It was later revealed that Letourneau began seeing Fualauu almost immediately after her release. During this time Letourneau's friends reported that she rarely slept and spent little time in her apartment. Some even suspected that she had been living out of her car. On March 6, 1998, the two arranged to meet to see a movie and go shopping. Later that night, as the police were searching for a stolen car in an unrelated incident, they came across Letourneau's car parked outside Fualauu's home with the two inside the car. The police found six thousand dollars in cash, several days worth of clothing, and Letourneau's passport in the vehicle. They suspected that she was about to flee the jurisdiction, another violation of her parole.

For such a grievous violation of her plea agreement, Judge Lau threw the book at Letourneau, ordering her to serve the full seven and a half years of her sentence. At this sentencing, Letourneau appeared frazzled and hysterical and she was led away to prison, again to much media scrutiny. Her lawyer pleaded with the judge that Letourneau's bipolar disorder had caused her seek out high-risk situations like reunification with Fualauu, that she was not responsible for her actions, and that this simply suggested that Letourneau needed more treatment, not more prison time. Judge Lau was not receptive to these arguments.

Letourneau's prison term and her release

In the next seven years, the affair remained a story that captured international attention. It was the subject of a cable television movie, *All American Girl*, and countless late-night stand up jokes. Fualauu published an account of the relationship as a book, but it was only released in France because of claims in the book that were disputed by Steve Letourneau. In 2000, Fualauu and his mother, Soona, sued the Highline School District as well as the Des Moines police for one million dollars, claiming that the two organizations had done too little to protect Fualauu from Letourneau. The civil suit painted Letourneau as the sexual aggressor and Fualauu as the victim of rape, standing in stark contrast to their portrayal of their affair as a love story. Ultimately, a jury ruled that the Fualauus were not owed any money.

Letourneau was released in September of 2004 and was ordered not to see Fualauu. Fualauu petitioned the judge contesting the order, claiming that the order violated his right as an adult to associate with whomever he pleases. The order was eventually lifted and the two reunited and married in April of 2005 in Woodinville, Washington, in front of two hundred wedding guests. All six of Letourneau's children participated in the wedding party with her oldest daughter serving as her maid of honor. The couple was able to sell her wedding story to *Entertainment Tonight*. The two have settled in Normandy Park, the neighborhood in which Letourneau lived with Steve Letourneau before the affair began.

Mary Kay Letourneau's psychological background

Understanding the psychological issues in this case has been an arduous task for any investigator. Not only does the case include the psychologies of Letourneau and Fualauu, but the psychology of the public reaction to their affair that made the case such a media sensation.

Letourneau's early life has been the subject of much speculation as journalists and psychologists have attempted to find events in her past that could explain or foreshadow what drove Letourneau to commit statutory rape. The most conspicuous of these events was her father's extramarital affair with a student of his own in 1982. Letourneau's father, John Schmitz, was a college professor and an arch-conservative politician from Southern California who won a Congressional seat in 1970. His far-right views were considered so reactionary that they cost him his support from the Republican Party and after losing the primary in the next election cycle, Schmitz ran for President with the American Independent Party. In 1982, the story broke that Schmitz had had an affair with one of his students at Santa Ana College and was the father of two children with the student. For a devout Catholic politician who had built his name propagating traditional values, the affair effectively ended his political career and embarrassed the prominent California family. In the ensuing family conflict Mary sided with her father against her mother and remained close to him until his death in 2001.

Another childhood event that received attention in the media was Letourneau's supposed responsibility regarding her younger brother's drowning in the family pool. At the age of eleven, Letourneau was told to watch her three year old brother during a party at the family's home. She lost track of her brother during the party and as soon as she realized it he was found drowned in the pool. Her parents declared that it was nobody's fault, but friends later reported that Letourneau never forgave herself for the incident.

The relevance of these events to Letourneau's eventual mental illness and sexual deviancy remained unclear. Attention has focused more heavily on the events that happened in Letourneau's adult life, particularly her marriage to Steve Letourneau.

Mary Kay Schmitz met Steve Letourneau when they were both undergraduates at Arizona State University. While dating, Mary Kay became pregnant with his baby and the two married shortly after. In later interviews, Mary Kay would speak of the marriage as if it were merely a consequence of the pregnancy. The couple had three more children and eventually settled in the Seattle area, where they were plagued by financial problems and regular fighting. Steve Letourneau reportedly began a series of extramarital affairs that contributed to the marriage's deterioration.

Mary Kay Letourneau's later diagnosis with bipolar disorder shed a certain degree of light on her actions during this time. The Diagnostic and Statistical Manual Fourth Edition distinguished the disorder into Bipolar I and Bipolar II. Bipolar I, with which psychologists eventually diagnosed Letourneau, was characterized by combination of both manic episodes and depressive episodes, with the manic episodes lasting for at least a week and interfering with the individual's social and occupational life. Bipolar II was similarly characterized but the manic episodes known as Hypomanic episodes that last less than a week and do not necessarily interfere with an individual's social life. Psychologists have said that as many as three percent of all Americans suffer from some form of bipolar disorder and those with the less severe Bipolar II disorder have a risk of developing Bipolar I.

Letourneau was known as a teacher and as a parent with a seemingly limitless amount of energy. She sustained this energy through her school day as a charismatic teacher and at home where she stayed up late with her children until her husband arrived home, when she would begin working on her lesson plans. She slept for only a few hours a night and had some trouble arriving on time to meetings, but for the most part she accomplished a remarkable amount as a teacher and a parent. This boundless energy would later be understood as symptoms of the manic episodes that characterized Letourneau's bipolar disorder.

In the 1995–1996 school year, during which Letourneau and Fualauu began their affair, Letourneau was apparently dealing with both her disorder and her crumbling marriage. During that year she also miscarried and learned the news that her father had been diagnosed with cancer. Observers of the case speculate that these traumatic events may have pushed Letourneau even deeper into her manic state, which caused her to seek out high-risk, high-gratification situations without regard to the painful consequences.

For some psychologists who speculate on the case, this disorder provides a thorough enough explanation for Letourneau's actions. Others, however, contend that it does not sufficiently explain her attraction to the adolescent Fualauu, and that her bipolar disorder was simply a piece of a much larger puzzle that included a sexual orientation toward children.

Vili Fualauu's psychological background

In most cases of rape, the victim's psychology is not a relevant factor to understanding the case. Vili Faulauu's seemingly willful participation in the rape and his eventual marriage to his rapist, however makes understanding his role in the affair critical to the understanding of all the psychological and legal issues at play in this case.

Fualauu was from White Center, a low-income neighborhood in Des Moines, Washington, that was a part of the Highline School District. Fualauu was one of eighteen children fathered by the same man, with five different women. Fualauu's father was in prison at the time the Letourneau affair began and has never been a significant part of Fualauu's life. He was raised with his siblings by his mother Soona, who has gained some degree of media notoriety herself.

The aspect of Fualauu's psychology that gained the most attention was his supposed emotional maturity. Defenders of Letourneau often claimed that Fualauu was extremely mature for his age, that he had hit puberty at age ten, and thus should have been considered truly older than he was chronologically. This argument was most often used in the spring of 1997 as the story of a thirty-five year old teacher sleeping with a twelve year old student first broke and the public was looking for some kind of explanation. Something about this relationship didn't make sense the way a relationship between an adult male and adolescent female made sense. Fualauu's maturity was touted as a possible explanation.

Definitions of consent and statutory rape

The Letourneau affair provoked many discussions around the issue of consent, statutory rape, and the applicability of these legal concepts. Fualauu consented to the intercourse with Letourneau in every conceivable way with the exception of his age. He initiated the sex, enjoyed the sex, and continued the relationship for nine months. He published a book proclaiming his love for her and married his rapist upon her release from prison.

What obviously prevented him from giving consent to the sex, however, was his age. In the state of Washington, an individual cannot consent to sexual activity with a partner more than four years older than he until the age of sixteen. Every state in the nation has statutory rape laws which vary by age of consent, but for most part the age of consent throughout the United States is between sixteen and eighteen. The roots of these laws occupy a curious place in legal history as they have been championed at different times by different political factions who have seemingly disparate political and social aims: feminists and social conservatives.

American law inherited the concept of statutory rape from English common law and the age of consent hovered around ten or twelve in most states up until the populist progressive movements before the turn of the twentieth century. Statutory rape laws were of course at this time gender specific, functioning as a protection against sexually aggressive older men and sexually vulnerable younger women. At this time, a coalition of feminists, social conservatives, and working-class labor activists banded together to lift the age of consent. Each faction had its own motives in the movement, but nevertheless the coalition had a remarkable degree of political power and managed to secure a place for the raising of legal consent inside the populist reforms of the era.

As a part of the feminist movement of the 1970s, statutory rape laws were modified again, this time to subvert patriarchal notions of female sexual agency. Feminists successfully lobbied to make statutory rape laws gender neutral in an attempt to deconstruct the paradigm of the sexually aggressive man and the sexually passive woman. In a sense, this movement was acknowledging the potential for cases like the Letourneau affair to occur. Additionally, feminists, also in an attempt to provide sexual agency to young women, advocated successfully for age-span limits to be incorporated with statutory rape laws.

Legal issues in the case and their impacts

Letourneau was able to initially serve so little time in prison because of the Special Sex Offender Sentencing Alternative, a Washington State law passed in 1984 designed to encourage reporting by victims of sex crimes. Special Sex Offender Sentencing Alternative allows for the possibility of treatment in lieu of prison time for sex offenders and was instituted because it was feared the victims were not reporting crimes because they did not want the perpetrators, who were often their close acquaintances, to go to prison. Special Sex Offender Sentencing Alternative allowed for the possibility that some sex offenders deemed amenable to treatment by a therapist to be sent to an outpatient treatment facility.

Over time, however, Special Sex Offender Sentencing Alternative began to be applied to a much wider array of sex offenders and was used extensively in plea bargains such as Letourneau's. Any sex offender who was deemed amenable to treatment became eligible for the program. After the high profile use, and apparent failure, of Special Sex Offender Sentencing Alternative in the Letourneau affair, victims-rights activists claimed that Special Sex Offender Sentencing Alternative had lost its original meaning. They claimed that instead of being used to benefit victims and increase response rates, the laws were being used to benefit sex offenders.

The public reaction to this case

The Letourneau affair aroused international intrigue from the moment the story broke in 1997 to the broadcast of the wedding on *Entertainment Tonight* in 2005. In 1997, the older women and younger man phenomenon was atypical of the public's conception of a pedophilic relationship. Today Letourneau is still the most notorious female pedophile in America and her case became the paradigm of a female sexual predator that the news often compares other cases to.

What made this case particularly interesting was the seeming lack of danger that Letourneau presented to the public. She was, before her arrest, perhaps the model of a non-threatening human being: a pretty, young teacher with a great ability to connect to children and a great family life. Perhaps the dangerous part of her was the fact that she represented the kind of figure that the public would naturally trust to protect and work with children and the violation of that that trust makes her somehow more dangerous.

But the truly interesting aspect was that there was no real, palpable fear of Letourneau that a male counterpart sex offenders would inspire. No one feared that she would re-offend or find another boy to seduce. No one screamed that she should be locked up because she was a monster; they screamed that she should be locked up because that is what we would have done if she were a man.

Intrigue around the case also centered partially on the fact that Letourneau was fulfilling a popular adolescent fantasy of the seductive female teacher. An idea popularized in the music and television of American youth, this fantastical figure seemed exactly that: an unrealistic creation of the young men's minds. As an attractive older woman, Letourneau embodied this fantasy to a remarkable extent, which somehow made her the affair inherently less threatening and humorous. In general, this case suggests that female pedophilia is less terrifying, less disgusting, and less punishable than male pedophilia in the public's eye. A grown woman declaring that she loves an adolescent boy inspires far more sympathy than a man doing the same.

This case also had suggestions for the way a young boy's sexuality is conceptualized. Few people feared the Fualauu had been damaged in any way by Letourneau. There seemed to be something less corruptible about a young man than a young woman. Did we consider him to be less vulnerable or less impressionable than a young woman? Or perhaps the corruption was a part of a male's growing up process the way a female's was not.

Notes about sources

The majority of the information of this case study was compiled using the comprehensive coverage on the case by the writers of the *Seattle Times* between 1997 and 2005. *CourtTV* and *Entertainment Tonight* were also helpful sources. Carolyn E. Cocca's book *Jailbait: The Politics of Statutory Rape Laws in the United States* was especially helpful in contextualizing statutory rape laws.

Larry Don McQuay
State sanctioned surgical castration

Abstract

Larry Don McQuay was a San Antonio school bus driver who was convicted in 1990 for sexually molesting a six-year-old boy. He became famous in 1995 when he requested that the state of Texas surgically castrate him. He said that he had sexually abused about two hundred forty children and if were not castrated, he would not only molest again but would also would kill his next victim so that they could not testify against him. He was released in 1995 and was reincarcerated in 1997 for having also molested the nine year old sister of the boy from the first conviction in 1989. The same year that he returned to prison the governor of Texas at the time, George W. Bush, signed into effect a law that allowed for the voluntary surgical castration of sex offenders. McQuay was released from prison in May 2005 and said that he was surgically castrated before his release.

The development of a sexual predator

Larry Don McQuay was born in Edinburg, Texas, on December 24, 1963. His father was in the military, which caused the family to move all over the United

States. His mother suffered from depression and McQuay has said that his mother's psychological problems had a significant effect on him and his younger sister. Despite the difficult conditions of his childhood, McQuay maintained that he was never deliberately abused. However, Vickie Smyer who conducted several counseling sessions with McQuay contradicted his statement and claimed that he had an unusual sexual childhood and that the boundaries of proper sexual conduct were very unclear within his household.

The constant moving and changing of schools due to his father's military career did not make it easy for McQuay to make and maintain friends or strong attachments. He turned his attention to making friends with children younger than he, and at the age of seven he says he committed his first sexual act on a minor. McQuay claims to have convinced his three year old cousin to take off her underpants while they were in a closet together at his aunt and uncle's house. He admitted he then tried to penetrate her but failed. Though he was also very young at the time McQuay said that he had full knowledge of what he was doing, that it was wrong, and why it was wrong.

As McQuay entered puberty his sexual activities with children continued, usually with younger boys. He said that he performed oral sex on younger boys who allowed him to, and with those who were very young he would molest them under the disguise of playful roughhousing. McQuay said that he was also able to touch both girls and boys by taking on the role of an older friend, teaching them about sex while giving demonstrations. He admitted to penetrating girls with his fingers, and masturbating and performing oral sex on boys as an adolescent man. McQuay also claimed that occasionally the children even performed oral sex on him. His tactics evolved over time and when he was in his early twenties, he said that he learned the effectiveness of guilt on children. He was able to get children who had resisted his advances to allow the sexual misconduct by getting angry and making them feel bad. McQuay said that children would allow him to do things to them because they didn't want to make him angry. He openly referred to this as a fear tactic and noted its effectiveness because the children all had a strong desire to please.

Adulthood

After graduating from high school McQuay moved to Beaumont, Texas. A coworker fixed up the nineteen year old McQuay with a twenty year old woman named Pamela who would soon become McQuay's first wife. McQuay had said that he got married because he wanted to be normal and he thought that being married might allow him to satisfy his sexual desires, but he did not find sex with his wife as appealing as the sexual contact he had with children. The marriage fell apart six short months after it began. His wife at the time saw the divorce as a result of their money problems and his infidelity. She stated in an interview that she knew McQuay was cheating on her but had no idea that he fooled around with children as well as other women.

McQuay then started a relationship with his coworker at K.F.C. They were married in 1985 and divorced in less than a year. She had an infant daughter, whom she eventually put up for adoption, from a previous relationship at the time that she and McQuay were married. She said she had no knowledge that McQuay was a pedophile until he sent her a letter from prison in 1990, after his first conviction, telling her that he had fondled her daughter while they were married, and asking her if they could get back together.

During and after his two marriages McQuay continued molesting children. In one interview he remembered an eleven year old neighbor who often visited around the time of his second marriage. McQuay admitted to repeatedly molesting the child and was convinced that the boy enjoyed the sexual acts. It was this belief that children enjoyed these acts and would welcome his advances that eventually led to his first arrest in San Antonio four years later.

The first conviction

McQuay moved to San Antonio and got a job as a school bus driver. This position allowed him access to many new victims, whom he claimed he would touch inappropriately as they boarded the bus. In a prison interview he stated that it was frustrating driving around all those children because he desired to have sex with all of them and could not.

While working for the school he claimed he would sometimes watch over a class when the teachers needed to take a short break. It was during one such time that he met a six year old boy. McQuay apparently noticed a hole in the child's pants that revealed the child was not wearing underwear. In a strange move, McQuay bought the child several pairs of underwear and gave them to the boy's mother. McQuay and the mother soon started a sexual relationship, which he said was primarily to allow him access to the six-year-old.

A few months later McQuay was forced to quit his job as the school bus driver after a thirteen year old boy gave school authorities notes, written by McQuay, propositioning him for sex. While no legal action was taken against McQuay, a fellow bus driver informed the woman McQuay was involved with. McQuay's girlfriend began questioning her children about McQuay. When her six year old son admitted to being forced to have oral sex several times with McQuay she immediately called the police. McQuay was arrested in 1989 and charged with aggravated sexual assault. In 1990 McQuay was offered a plea bargain, since he had no known criminal history or history of pedophilia. He pled guilty to indecent sexual misconduct with a child under the age of fourteen and was given an eight-year sentence.

Requests for castration

McQuay was paroled in 1993 to a halfway house in Houston, but had his parole revoked later that year. Texas officials said his parole was revoked because of an argument he had with a halfway house supervisor but McQuay told a different story. McQuay believed that his parole was revoked because of a letter he wrote to then governor Ann Richards. In the letter McQuay stated that he would molest again and asked for the state to castrate him. McQuay was back in prison, continuing to serve out his sentence when he became nationally known for claiming to have molested over two hundred forty children.

Between the period that his parole was revoked and his mandatory release from prison in 1996, Larry Don McQuay started correspondence with reporters, the governor of Texas George W. Bush, a Texas state senate representative, and a Houston based victims rights group called Justice For All, among others. He stated that he was a child molesting demon, and that if released without first being castrated he would not only re-offend but would also kill his next victim so that they could not testify against him. McQuay said that he got the idea of being surgically castrated after the controversial case of Steve Butler in 1992. Though McQuay's lawyer said that McQuay had asked him about castration and the effects it could have on his sentencing as early as December 1989, it is important to understand the Butler case and how it differed from McQuay's case.

A related case

In 1992 Steve Butler was a twenty-seven year old African American man facing up to thirty-five years in jail for raping a thirteen year old girl. Butler, a man who made his living shining shoes, learned that the presiding Judge Michael McSpadden was an advocate of surgical castration of pedophiles. Butler suggested a punishment of castration and ten years of probation instead of jail. McSpadden agreed to the punishment and doctors who were willing to perform the procedure were found. A plea bargain was set up in which Butler plead guilty to the crime, and was to be sentenced to ten years of probation provided that he went through with the surgical procedure.

An uproar of media coverage followed this controversial decision. African American civil rights leaders including the Reverend Jesse Jackson intervened, saying that the plea bargain was racist. They compared the bargain to the 1855 Kansas law that called for the forced castration of African Americans who raped or attempted to rape white women. The controversy became so intense that the doctors who had originally agreed to perform the surgery backed out and the plea bargain fell through. McSpadden was forced to sentence Butler to jail time rather than probation with castration.

While Steve Butler never underwent surgical castration, McQuay continued to pursue castration as an option because his circumstances were different. McQuay, unlike Butler, was a young white male and a self proclaimed monster, no one seemed to object to his request for the surgery, and although he originally inquired about castration as part of his punishment in hopes it would reduce the amount of prison time he was sentenced for, he now sought castration as a treatment or cure for his criminal pedophilic tendencies. The state repeatedly denied McQuay's requests to castrate him, stating that castration was an elective surgery that he could opt for as a private citizen but which would not be funded or assisted by the state should he choose to go through with it.

In the fall of 1995 McQuay attempted to castrate himself with a razor and failed. He seemed like a man desperate to go through with the procedure no matter what. By the time he was up for mandatory parole in spring of 1996 several private citizens had offered to pay for the procedure, a doctor volunteered to perform the castration free of charge, and the victims rights group Justice For All had collected money to aid in the costs of McQuay's castration. Yet he did not choose to be castrated. It seemed that McQuay was set on the state creating a law or making a special exception that would allow for him to get surgically castrated at the government's expense.

Mandatory release and parole restrictions

Mandatory release, or mandatory supervision as it was officially known in Texas, was the required release of a convicted criminal to parole when the actual time served in prison plus the credit of time earned by good behavior equaled less than the total time the criminal was convicted for. The criminal would then serve out the remainder of his sentence on parole. Because of Texas' mandatory supervision laws McQuay was to be paroled in 1996 after serving six years of an eight year sentence. The public outrage was remarkable. Many found it befuddling that a man who had virtually guaranteed that he would rape and kill a child once released from prison was being released early for good behavior. Governor

George W. Bush was asked how such a thing could be possible; he responded that he would do everything in his power to keep McQuay behind bars.

Just months prior to McQuay's release the Texas state legislature repealed mandatory supervision. Unfortunately this repeal was only effective for all inmates convicted of a crime that took place after September 1, 1996. Thus despite the removal of mandatory supervision laws McQuay was still eligible for release because the crime he was convicted of took place before the 1996 repeal. To deal with criminals who fell under the mandatory release laws but continued to pose a serious threat to society, such as McQuay, the Texas legislature also passed super intensive supervision legislation which allowed for continual electronic monitoring and confinement to locked housing for violent inmates and sex offenders who were mandatorily released.

McQuay's release

Larry Don McQuay was scheduled for mandatory release in late March 1996; his release however, was put on hold because of pleas from victims' rights groups, most notably the Houston-based group Justice For All. The groups demanded that his release be reviewed and submitted numerous letters that McQuay had written to Justice For All while in prison. In the letters he warned that he would hurt more children if released. In some he even referred to himself as a child-molesting demon. According to the group, parole officials requested copies of the letters on the day that McQuay was scheduled for release. Then, just a few hours before McQuay's scheduled release to a halfway house, the chairman of the Texas Board of Pardons and Parole put the release on hold temporarily. A week later McQuay was released from prison to the Bexar County Intermediate Sanctions Facility, a halfway house near San Antonio. According to a Texas Department of Criminal Justice spokesperson, McQuay would remain locked in the facility, under twenty-four hour supervision, and only be allowed to leave the facility accompanied by a security officer. Another department spokesperson called the conditions of McQuay's parole unprecedented and the most restrictive ever issued. Yet the thought that in two short years McQuay would be free of his parole restrictions frightened the citizens of San Antonio.

Very soon after his release Bexar County authorities began reinvestigating the first crime McQuay was convicted of. It soon came to light that McQuay had also molested the six year old boy's nine year old sister. Once more charges were brought against McQuay and in late June of 1997 McQuay was back in prison serving out a twenty year sentence for three charges of child molestation.

Surgical castration legislation

Inspired by the controversy started by McQuay's threats to continue to hurt children if not castrated, State Senator Teel Bivins, the Republican representative from Amarillo, began sponsoring voluntary castration bills in 1995. McQuay wrote letters to Bivins encouraging the effort. In one of the many revisions that Bivins' bill went through, however, voluntary castration became an option only for repeat sex offenders who had been convicted of two or more crimes. At the time, McQuay had only been convicted of one and therefore would not have been eligible for the surgery even if the bill passed. When McQuay learned of the change to the bill he angrily wrote to the senator asking why it had changed. Bivins said in a newspaper interview later that the bill had been changed to apply only to repeat offenders because surgical castration should only be an option for sex offenders who have demonstrated a lack of control and who personally feel that they do not have the power to control themselves. Bivins also felt that this change would make the bill more acceptable to his more liberal colleagues. In 1995 the voluntary surgical castration bill passed the Texas Senate but failed to pass the House of Representatives.

Bivins continued to pursue his bill and in 1997, about a month before McQuay returned to prison on new charges, Governor George W. Bush signed into law a surgical castration bill sponsored by Bivins. The bill had passed the Senate with twenty-five votes for and four votes against, and had passed the House of Representatives with one hundred thirty-eight votes for and seven votes against.

Many aspects of this law need to be considered to understand its purpose. The surgery was only available to offenders who had been convicted at least twice of indecency with a child, sexual assault of a child, or aggravated sexual assault of a child. The inmate had to be at least twenty-one years old, sign a statement admitting to his most recent child molestation offense, and ask for the procedure in writing. The names of the inmates who do get castrated were to be kept confidential. If the inmate was married his wife must also consent to the procedure. The inmate could withdraw his decision to undergo castration at any point up until the surgery, but once he withdrew a request he could no longer be considered for this procedure in the future. Another important section of the law required that the inmate undergo evaluation from both a psychologist and a psychiatrist provided by the state who would ensure that the inmate was mentally fit to undergo the procedure and counsel the inmate to prepare for it. The inmate would additionally be assigned a monitor who would have experience in the mental health field, in law, and in ethics. The monitor's job would be to make sure that the inmate had been provided adequate medical information about the procedure, or provide information if the inmate has not been adequately informed, and to ensure that the inmate had not been coerced into his decision for castration.

Perhaps the most important part of this law was that voluntary surgical castration was purely meant as treatment and not as a form of punishment. This meant that the inmate could not receive a reduced sentence or increased possibility of parole if they decided to be castrated. This was an important condition of the law because both Michigan and South Carolina had castration laws prior to 1997 that were struck down as unconstitutional.

Courts and legislatures

Jack T. Skinner had been convicted of stealing chickens in 1926. Three years later he was convicted of armed robbery and five years after that he was again convicted of armed robbery. In 1935 Oklahoma passed the Habitual Criminal Sterilization Act. The act stated that people who had been convicted of more than one felony could be sterilized. If the Attorney General pursued the sterilization of the criminal than a jury had to decide if the person is an habitual criminal and if the person can be sterilized without causing detriment to the physical health of the individual. The jury in Skinner's case decided that he could undergo sterilization without harm to his general health.

Skinner challenged the decision, and the Oklahoma Supreme Court stood by the law in a split five to four decision. In 1942 the case went to the United States Supreme Court. In *Skinner v. Oklahoma* the Supreme Court ruled that forced sterilization of criminals constituted cruel and unusual punishment and therefore violated the eighth amendment.

Following *Skinner v. Oklahoma*, states like Michigan and South Carolina tried to pass surgical castration laws by calling them voluntary, but because having the procedure could lower prison sentences or be used as a condition of parole or plea bargain, these laws were deemed overly coercive and therefore equivalent to using surgical castration as punishment.

Michigan's court of appeals found that it was unlawful to have voluntary castration as a condition of probation because it was coercive, causing it no longer to be truly voluntary.

The South Carolina law allowed sex offenders to undergo castration in order to have a suspended sentence. The Supreme Court of South Carolina ruled that this law was unconstitutional because it allowed castration as an alternative to prison time demonstrating that the lawmakers in South Carolina viewed castration as equivalent to punishment. Both of these laws were struck down because prisoners were under coercive pressures to undergo castration in order to avoid prison, making it akin to punishment. Texas lawmakers specifically allowed castration as treatment only in order to avoid it being overturned by a high court.

McQuay's castration and release

Because McQuay's second conviction was for crimes that took place before the repeal of mandatory supervision laws, he was eligible for mandatory release from his twenty year sentence in May 2005. Again his release created an uproar in the community. The Texas voluntary castration law kept the names of inmates who chose to get castrated confidential, so the question of whether McQuay actually opted for the surgery was on everyone's mind. When he was released to mandatory supervision his lawyer told reporters that McQuay had undergone surgical castration prior to his release and that McQuay's sexual fantasies had significantly decreased as a result. McQuay also publicly stated that he had been surgically castrated prior to his release to mandatory supervision. However, when the president of Justice For All asked McQuay to release his medical records to prove that he actually had been castrated, he refused.

Though released McQuay will remain supervised under the strictest standards until July 2016. McQuay was once again being monitored twenty-four hours a day at a Bexar County Facility in San Antonio, in accordance with the Texas Super Intensive Supervision Program. He had to wear a global positioning system bracelet around his ankle and could not leave his work release facility unless supervised.

In July 2016 McQuay will be fifty-two years old. Regardless of whether McQuay was castrated the question of whether he will still be a threat to children will remain. Reports have concluded that the implementation of surgical castration of sex offenders in Europe yielded a recidivism rate of only about two percent of the three thousand people castrated. This figure was drastically less than the fifty to eighty percent recidivism rate quoted by Teel Bivins when he pushed for the law in 1997. However, many professionals then believed that while castration does reduce the amount of testosterone the body creates, and therefore leads to decreased sexual desire, it does not address the reason why these sexual predators prey on children. One argument against the effectiveness of castration is that the minds of these criminals remain unaltered and a person like McQuay could still molest children to fulfill mental rather than physical desires.

Notes about sources

This case study relied on numerous articles from Texas newspapers, such as the *Houston Chronicle* and *Houston Press*. It also relied on Texas state statues, the Texas online registry of sex offenders, radio shows, national news sources like CNN, and civil and victim's rights groups websites, and U.S. Supreme Court decisions.

Michael Ross
Serial rape and murder

Abstract

Michael Bruce Ross was a sexually dangerous predator responsible for the rape and murder of eight young women in the early 1980s. He was ultimately confined by the criminal justice system when he was executed on May 13, 2005. During his sentencing at trial, Ross's attorneys argued that his mental state should serve as a mitigating factor. Ross and his attorneys claimed that he was a sexual sadist who was unable to control intense urges to perform sexually violent acts, and, therefore, should be spared death. The jury, however, did not agree, and sentenced Ross to death by lethal injection. Ross refused to appeal his execution and became a death row volunteer. Although his mental competence to make such a rash decision was questioned by his family and lawyers, Ross was granted his wish to accept his fate without further struggle. A disturbing note from Ross arrived for his psychiatrist just days after his execution, which suggested that Ross believed he had tricked the legal system into giving him what he wanted in the form of a state assisted suicide.

His early life: Signs of trouble

From the outside, Ross's childhood, adolescence, and emergence into adulthood seemed representative of the traditional American experience. Ross grew up in a big family that lived on a farm in rural Connecticut. He was a good student interested in agriculture and eventually received an Ivy League education at Cornell University. However, Ross's seemingly quaint upbringing covered up a much darker undercurrent of family dysfunctions and disturbing sexual fantasies.

Ross's dangerous proclivity for sexual carnage may have been caused by a variety of factors, including both biological and environmental influences. Ross's childhood was wrought with distress due to the unhappy shotgun wedding of his parents, Daniel and Patricia Ross. Patricia Ross, angry and resentful about her life, was said to have beaten her four children. Michael, the oldest child, took the brunt of his mother's physical and mental abuse before Patricia ultimately abandoned her family to be with another man. Ross's early, volatile relationship with his mother may have led to his feelings of aggression toward women, as is the case with many serial killers of female victims. It has also been suggested that Ross may have been sexually molested when he was eight by his fourteen year old uncle. Whether or not the abuse actually occurred is unclear due to his uncle's suicide as a young teenager. Ross has very little recollection of the alleged abuse ever taking place.

In addition to these dysfunctional aspects of Ross's early childhood, biological influences may also have been a factor in molding the mind of this sexually dangerous predator. More specifically, genetic influences may also underlie Ross's criminal behavior; Ross's mother was extremely unstable, suffering from her own psychological problems. She was even institutionalized on two occasions at Norwich Hospital for suicidal ideations. A hormonal brain imbalance has also been cited as an explanation for Ross's sexually violent behavior. It is probable that a combination of these factors contributed to his problems.

The first sign suggesting that the young Michael Ross posed a serious threat to society was exhibited at the tender age of eight, when he took on the responsibility of killing the sick and deformed chickens on his parents' Connecticut farm. Ross came to enjoy this duty, killing the chickens by strangulation, the same method he would use to end the lives of his victims years later. Ross's disturbing fantasies about women also began during this time. He imagined bringing women with him to secret hiding places and keeping them there, forcing them to love him. As a teenager he began to act out some of his more mild fantasies by molesting some of the young girls around his neighborhood. Not until college did Ross's increasingly sexual and violent fantasies finally consume him. As a Cornell undergraduate, Ross began following and stalking young women around campus, a behavior which eventually escalated to a series of sexual assaults, rapes, and murders. For the most part, both Ross's sickness and connection to these crimes went undetected by family, friends and police officials. Even two minor brushes with the law did not impede Ross from acting out his deviant sexual fantasies. By the time his three year killing spree was cut short by his arrest, eight women were dead.

His crimes

Michael Ross committed a string of sexual assaults on college co-eds that persisted for two years before escalating to murder. He raped and murdered his first victim, a twenty-five year old Cornell University student, on May 12, 1981 in Ithaca, New York. After her mangled body was discovered at the bottom of a gorge, police initially believed her death to be a suicide. Not until a more thorough inspection of her remains was conducted was the truth revealed. The young woman had been brutally raped and strangled by a dangerous sexual predator. Remarkably, Ross never fell under police suspicion for his earlier sexual assaults or the murder for which he was responsible.

On September 28, 1981, four months after his first killing, Ross proved less competent at evading police detection. While on a business trip in LaSalle City, Illinois, he kidnapped a sixteen year old girl and dragged her into the woods with the intention of raping and probably killing her. Before gagging her with a handkerchief and belt, her screams were heard, and police officers arrived before she could be harmed. Ross pled guilty to a charge of unlawful restraint. His meager punishment consisted of a five hundred dollar fine and two years of probation. Ross was not charged as a sexual offender because police interrupted the transgression before a sexual assault could ensue. During his two years of probation he killed three more times.

His next victim was a seventeen year old girl from Brooklyn, Connecticut. Ross abducted her while she was walking home on January 5, 1982. She was also raped, strangled, and dumped nearby. About two months later, Ross struck again, this time in Wallkill, New York. Ross picked up a sixteen year old as she was hitchhiking home from school on March 1, 1982. Sodomized and strangled, her lifeless body was found eighteen days later. Ross was not suspected in either of these two cases.

Ross's second run-in with the law came in April 1982 in Licking County, Ohio, when he turned up at the home of a pregnant off duty policewoman, claiming that his car had broken down and asking to use her telephone. Once inside the house, Ross attempted to choke her, but instead decided to flee after she successfully fought him off. The woman was able to give a clear description, and Ross was swiftly arrested on charges of assault. However, he only spent one month in prison before he was bailed out by his parents. After returning to Connecticut, Ross was forced to undergo a brief period of psychiatric study. The reports from this study claimed that Ross was suffering from psychological turmoil as a result of his parents' recent divorce, but made little mention of any effort to ensure continued therapy or further psychiatric evaluations. During this time Ross was not under any police surveillance, which allowed him to rape, kill, and dump his fourth victim, a twenty-three year old woman looking for a gas station after her car broke down on June 15, 1982.

On August 4, 1982, shortly following his fourth murder, Ross pled guilty to assaulting the pregnant officer in Ohio, for which he was fined one thousand dollars and sentenced to jail time. He was not confined for long, however, receiving parole after just four short months. Less than a year after he was released, his killing spree continued when a nineteen year old girl of Norwich, Connecticut was reported missing on November 16, 1983. When the girl's body was found raped, strangled, and dumped face down, the police were able to link her murder with that of Ross's two other Connecticut victims. The marked similarities of these three murders put the police on the lookout for a serial killer. However, Ross would strike three more times before investigators would get the lead they needed. On Easter Sunday, April 22, 1984, Ross committed his first double homicide, killing his two youngest victims, fourteen year old neighbors of Griswold, Connecticut. On the day of his final victim's abduction, rape, and murder on June 13, 1984, witnesses recalled a suspicious blue Toyota driven by a white man with glasses that seemed to be following her. This was the break investigators needed to finally catch Ross.

Case process: The trial and sentencing

When Detective Michael Malchik questioned Ross on June 28, 1984, Ross promptly confessed to the murder of his final victim. Later, while in police custody, he also confessed to the murders of his five other Connecticut victims and led police to the bodies of those not yet discovered. On July 5, Ross was charged with the six Connecticut homicides. For the two murders committed in the Windham judicial district, Ross pled guilty and received a sentence of one hundred twenty years imprisonment without parole. For the murders of four other victims, which fell under New London jurisdiction, State Attorney Robert Satti sought the death penalty. Ross also pled guilty to these crimes and was sentenced to death in July 1987. Years later, while on death row in Connecticut, Ross would be charged, convicted, and condemned to additional life sentences without parole for the two murders he committed in New York State.

In July 1994, the Connecticut State Supreme Court upheld Ross's convictions but overturned the death sentences, based on the trial judge's error to exclude psychiatric testimony on Ross's mental state that may have been influential as a mitigating factor in sentencing. However, soon after a new penalty hearing was ordered by the State Supreme Court, Ross experienced a shocking change of heart. He decided that he wanted to forgo the new hearing in order to spare his victims' families additional grief and volunteered to be executed. Ross spent the next four years working side by side with prosecuting attorney Robert Satti drafting a ten page document that requested permission to circumvent the new trial and proceed directly to the death chamber. This so-called death pact was submitted in March 1998 and then dismissed by a Superior Court judge as unconstitutional as well as disturbing. The penalty retrial was ordered to proceed as planned and began in April 1999. After an arduous year-long trial, the jury reached its final verdict on April 6, 2000. Ross received the same death sentence that was handed down over a decade earlier. After multiple appeals, the State Supreme Court upheld the sentence in May 2004. Soon thereafter, Ross decided to abandon all further appeals and accept his fate. Ross's family and defense attorneys made every attempt to halt his execution, claiming his mental state made him incompetent to drop his appeals. All such attempts failed, and Ross was finally put to death by lethal injection on May 13, 2005.

Diagnosis and treatment

The four psychiatrists who testified at Ross's competency trial, Dr. Norko, Dr. Gentile, Dr. Grassian, and Dr. Goldsmith, all agreed that Ross was suffering from depression, anxiety, sexual sadism, and a personality disorder not otherwise specified, or NOS.

Ross was diagnosed with depression or mood disorder NOS while in prison. This is considered an Axis I disorder, according to the American Psychiatric Association's Diagnostic and Statistical Manual of Mental Disorders, or DSM-IV, a consensus guide of mental disorders for psychiatrists nationwide. Since 1995, Ross had attempted suicide on three separate occasions. After receiving medication, psychiatrists agreed that Ross's depression went into full or partial remission. Ross was also believed to suffer from an anxiety disorder NOS, but these symptoms were also successfully relieved by therapy and anti-anxiety medications. The experts also believed Ross showed traits consistent with a diagnosis of a personality disorder NOS, with narcissistic, borderline, and antisocial traits.

Finally, the psychiatrists all agreed that Ross suffered from sexual sadism, which is listed in the DSM-IV, but is only considered a paraphilia, not a mental disorder. Sexual sadism is roughly defined as a preference for violent sexual fantasies or acts in which the victim suffers physical or psychological pain. Sexual sadists derive great pleasure from the domination and humiliation of their victims and like to have complete power and control over them. Although many sexual sadists feel guilty about their recurring sadistic sexual fantasies, they also tend to exhibit a chronic trend toward increasing severity and danger to society. It is obvious from his string of assaults, rapes, and murders that Ross followed this trend, but whether or not he displayed genuine guilt for his crimes is a more subjective matter that the testifying psychiatrists disagreed upon. Dr. Norko and Dr. Gentile both felt that Ross was motivated to forgo his appeals by the deep remorse he felt for his victims and their family. Dr. Grassian and Dr. Goldsmith, however, felt that Ross's display of guilt was a phony act, and, in actuality, he possessed absolutely no empathy for others.

There was ample evidence suggesting that Ross did feel guilty for his crimes. For instance, Ross's prompt confession and admission of guilt seemed to come as a much needed relief. Ross was also quick to lead police to the bodies of his victims in order to bring the families closer in grieving for their lost loved ones. Michael Ross explains what it is like to suffer from this paraphilia in a 1998 article titled It's Time For Me to Die: An inside look at Death Row. In the article Ross writes that living out his fantasies brought him an intense orgasmic pleasure; however, when he finally relieved himself of his sadist urges by acting them out he became disgusted by the very same thoughts and overwhelmed by feelings of shame, self loathing, and hatred. Ross claimed that his own guilt was so overwhelming that he resorted to extreme measures to quell it, including multiple suicide attempts. However, others close to the case are more skeptical of the authenticity of his remorse, suggesting that Ross's overt display of guilt and self-sacrifice may have been clever, self-serving attempts to gain attention, consistent with his narcissistic and antisocial personality traits. Some who worked closely with the case have said that Ross was a smart and manipulative man, who was more interested in attaining publicity and gaming the system than atoning for his crimes.

While in prison, Ross's team of psychiatrists made several attempts to subdue his violent sexual urges that he claimed plagued him. Ross was prescribed the female contraceptive Depo-Provera, which decreased his testosterone levels to below prepubescent levels. Ross praised this medication for significantly reducing his violent sexual fantasies and urges. In the article It's Time For Me to Die, he explained that the Depo-Provera did not completely eliminate his urges, but allowed him to control them. When he was forced to discontinue the hormone medication due to harmful side effects on his liver, he reported that the uncontrollable nature of his urges reemerged. When given an alternative form of the medication, the same positive results occurred. In his writings, Ross also claimed that he asked to be castrated, but the state of Connecticut refused to grant his request. According to Ross, the medication also increased his feelings of guilt leading to his decision to volunteer for execution.

Sex and power

Ross's violence was sexually charged, but also served the purpose of fulfilling a need for domination, power, and control. For Ross, the sex may have been a secondary concern. It is possible that fantasies of domination led his to arousal and the sexual aspect of his crimes. However, it is impossible to know with absolute certainty whether the violence led to sexual arousal or the arousal created the urge to aggress. It is interesting to note that Ross maintained normal sexual relations with various girlfriends while carrying out his sexually sadistic crimes without garnering any suspicions from them. Ross understood that his craving for sexual violence went beyond social norms and was able to live two separate lives in order to fulfill his disturbing fantasies.

Obvious danger

Michael Ross was a danger to society in the very obvious way that many other people and things classified by society as sexually dangerous are not. Some people believe that sexuality in and of itself and anything promoting sexuality is a danger to society. While controversy may exist as to whether or not a female prostitute or work of art should be labeled as sexually dangerous, Michael Ross was an example of an unarguable danger to society.

Ultimate confinement

Michael Ross's execution represents the severest form of confinement of the sexually dangerous that the law offers. However, Ross viewed his execution as a means of ending his confinement by escaping the prospect of growing old in prison. Other ways in which Michael Ross was confined as a sexually dangerous predator was through two decades of imprisonment in which he was separated from society. Ross's sexual dangerousness was also confined through medications and therapy, such as chemical castration.

In other ways, Michael Ross was not confined. Ross committed multiple assaults and rapes in college without ever being suspected. While his rapes and murders continued, Ross was able to live a relatively normal life free of suspicions from family members, employers, and romantic partners. After he was caught by police on two separate occasions for assaulting women, Ross remained free to carry out his crimes almost entirely unsupervised. The criminal justice system did not seem to suspect Ross to be the serious threat to public safety that he in fact was. If law enforcement had more closely monitored Ross during his probations, it is possible that some of his murders could have been prevented and some of his victims' lives spared. Ross was able to circumvent the system as well, obtaining work by falsely denying any criminal convictions. When he was ultimately captured and incarcerated for multiple murders, he was still able to communicate with the outside world through letters, and he conversed regularly with many U.S. citizens interested in his story. Ross wrote poetry and essays that were posted on a website and even published in journal articles in which he attempted to convey his mental processes. In these ways, he remained connected to society and was not confined by it.

Competent to choose death

Michael Ross spent seventeen years on death row before his execution finally came to fruition on May 13, 2005. After the verdict in his second penalty trial called for execution once again, his team of lawyers and family members pushed Ross to appeal his death sentence repeatedly, leading to constant delays, rescheduling, and cancellations of the date. One year prior to his execution, Ross made the decision to renounce further appeals. In order to prevent his execution, Ross's lawyers and family members claimed that he was not mentally competent to make this decision due to his depression.

At the competency hearing, the Court applied the *Rees v. Peyton* standard. The pertinent question addressed was whether Ross was suffering from a mental disease, defect, or disorder that substantially affected his ability to make a rational choice among his legal options. Ross's stated motivations for his decision to accept the death penalty were to act morally, spare the family of his victims the pain of another trial, and accept the inevitability of his execution. Psychiatrists, Dr. Norko and Dr. Gentile, testified in favor of granting Ross competency based on their common belief that his decision was based on rational motivations. They also testified that his depression was in remission and not a factor in his decision. The court dismissed the testimony of three lay witnesses, all close friends or family of Ross, due to their opposition to the death penalty and obvious bias in favor of Ross's life. In the final ruling, the Court agreed with Dr. Norko and Dr. Gentile and found Ross competent to forgo his appeals and accept the death penalty.

Psychological and legal issue: Irresistible impulse?

A compulsion is defined as an irresistible impulse to perform an irrational act. An impulse is weaker in nature than a compulsion, defined by an inclination to perform an irrational act that is difficult but not impossible to resist. As stated earlier, Ross repeatedly claimed that he suffered from the former, a formidable compulsion to sexually aggress. Whether or not sexually dangerous individuals are able to control their impulses to commit sexually violent acts is a highly debated matter currently thought to be beyond psychiatric expertise at the present time.

There is ample evidence to suggest that Ross did indeed feel intense urges to carry out sexually sadistic acts. In the article It's Time For Me to Die, Ross claimed that he was physically unable to control his actions due to his sexually sadistic paraphilia. He wrote that the obsessions plagued him, and not until he would finally submit to them would he feel a transitory sense of relief. For those readers who might have difficulty understanding his suffering, he likened the urges to living with an obnoxious roommate from whom one cannot escape because he is always there.

An examination of Ross's work record provides evidence for the cycle of building tension leading up to and a relief or calm following his crimes. His employer at a Connecticut insurance company reported that Ross exhibited a significant decrease in work productivity directly prior to his fourth, fifth, and sixth murders and an increase after they had been committed. This pattern suggests that his crimes may have been associated with a degree of mental torment. Ross has also stated that when in a bad relationship he was more likely to aggress. Therefore, it is plausible to suggest that Ross's sexually sadistic urges were associated with significant anxiety and acting on them allowed him to temporarily relieve that anxiety and move on with his life's daily functions.

Although it is likely that Ross did experience sexually deviant urges due to his paraphilia, whether these urges were uncontrollable is questionable. Ross claimed that the compulsion to aggress could come over him at any time. He provided one specific example of being escorted to his cell by a female officer when he was suddenly overwhelmed by a powerful desire to sexually attack her. Ross wrote that he ran away and down the hall while she yelled after him. This example is particularly interesting because it actually provides evidence that Ross's urges are able to be controlled even if extraordinary means, such as physically running away, may be necessary.

Whether or not Ross's urges were controllable was an important psychological issue for jurors deciding his ultimate fate. The psychiatric testimony concerning his mental state at the time of his crimes was allowed at Ross's retrial. However, this testimony was unable to convince the jurors that Ross deserved to be spared the death penalty for his crimes.

Concluding Remarks

There are two existing schools of thought on Michael Ross. Some believe that Ross is simply a narcissistic and antisocial personality, whose claims of suffering from overpowering sexually violent cravings were clever, manipulative, and self-serving ploys to gain attention. Others, however, view Michael Ross as a person afflicted and truly plagued by biological drives that have the formidable power of exerting control over human behavior and compromising one's free will. It is impossible to know which of these two opinions holds the truth. Because of American society's abhorrence and fear of sexual predators, desire for revenge, and quest for moral certainty, it is often satisfied by labeling men like Michael Ross evil and sending them to be executed. However, denying the possibility of such mental afflictions poses the greatest risk to society, by retarding much needed scientific progress in the effort to understand the minds of the sexually dangerous.

Notes about sources

The primary sources for information used to write the Michael Ross case included online profiles and biographies from About Crime, crimelibrary.com, and the Canadian Coalition Against the Death Penalty's official Michael Ross webpage, which included some of Michael Ross's own writings. In addition, online newspaper articles from cnn.com, the *Cornell Daily Sun*, *Connecticut Law Tribune*, and *Times Herald-Record* were also used. A first-hand perspective was obtained through correspondence with Peter McShane, the assistant district attorney in the Michael Ross case.

Salvatore Sicari and Charles Jaynes
Child abduction, murder, sexual molestation, and the North American Man/Boy Love Association

Abstract

Jeffrey Curley, age 10, was abducted, killed, and then sexually molested on October 1, 1997, by Salvatore Sicari, aged twenty-one, and Charles Jaynes, aged twenty-two, men whom Jeffrey thought were his friends. Upon further review of the case, it was discovered that Jaynes was a member of the North American Man/Boy Love Association, also known as NAMBLA, an organization advocating the abolition of age of consent sex laws. After Jeffrey's killers were sentenced to prison, NAMBLA came under fire from the media. The sexual aspects involved in this case were homosexuality, pedophilia, and necrophilia. The legal aspects of this case involved pedophilia and murder. Jeffrey's family unsuccessfully tried to sue NAMBLA for wrongful death. Several members of NAMBLA were also sued by Jeffrey's family in a case as yet unresolved.

North American Man/Boy Love Association

NAMBLA, an organization that advocated the abolition of age of consent sex laws, supported intergenerational relationships and sexual freedom for everyone. NAMBLA promoted the non-criminalization of sexual relationships between adults and minors. NAMBLA also sometimes used the abbreviation NAMbLA with the lower case b symbolizing a boy and his connection to a man which is symbolized by the preceding capital M. In a December 1995 NAMBLA bulletin, a male member bragged about seducing and engaging in sex with an eight year old boy he was babysitting. Although NAMBLA had a male homosexual overtone, it supported people of all genders and sexuality preferences. NAMBLA originated in Boston, and has been based in New York City and San Francisco. Their membership was estimated at one thousand members. Membership is very secretive and supposedly open to everyone. There was no building or headquarters for NAMBLA; just a post office box mailing address in New York and San Francisco. NAMBLA offered annual, tri-annual, and lifetime memberships. Ever since its inception it had been carefully watched by the government, special organizations, and local citizens. There were many NAMBLA publications for sale such as books, articles, magazines, and videos. In order to obtain a NAMBLA video, one had to send a letter to an address requesting a list of video titles. The videos were described as man/boy love videos. This suggested that the videos depicted sexual acts between minors and adults or showed naked minors. NAMBLA also sold books on how to deal with the media and people who are anti-NAMBLA.

Jeffrey Curley

Jeffrey Curley was a fun-loving and energetic ten year old boy. He could always be found hanging out on the streets of Cambridge, Massachusetts. Jeffrey was liked by everyone that knew him. The youngest son of Robert and Barbara Curley, Jeffrey had two older brothers, Shaun and Bobby. Jeffrey was athletic and played sports such as baseball, hockey and basketball. Since he was very friendly, he often hung around children and adults of all ages. Jeffrey sometimes got into mischief but usually stayed out of trouble. He was described as a nice and good kid by friends.

Salvatore Sicari and Charles Jaynes

Salvatore Sicari, aged twenty-one, and Charles Jaynes, aged twenty-two, were petty criminals and troubled young men. Sicari had a prior arrest record for selling cocaine in a school district and for assault, battery, theft, and check forgery. He was also arrested for assaulting his son's mother. Jaynes had an even longer petty criminal record that included threatening, assault, battery, and stealing baseball cards from children. Jaynes came from a very affluent family. Both men could barely keep jobs and were regarded as outcasts by those who saw and knew them. For a while, both men worked at Jaynes's father's auto-reconditioning business, but Sicari was fired for incompetence. It was rumored that Jaynes and Sicari were originally heterosexual, but that they became homosexual lovers after meeting each other in 1996.

Child abduction

On October 1, 1997, ten year old Jeffrey Curley was lured and abducted by these two men who had befriended him. Salvatore Sicari and Charles Jaynes were sexually obsessed with Jeffrey. Sicari lived one block from Jeffrey in Cambridge, Massachusetts; Jaynes lived in Brockton, Massachusetts. Jeffrey's previous interactions with the men included dinner and driving around Massachusetts. On the day he was abducted, Jeffrey went for a car ride with Sicari and Jaynes because they promised him a new bicycle and fifty dollars. Prior to abducting Jeffrey, Jaynes and Sicari were at the Boston Public Library where Jaynes accessed the website of the North American Man/Boy Love Association. Jaynes was a member of NAMBLA.

Murder and sexual molestation

After Jeffrey got into the car with Sicari and Jaynes, according to prosecutors, Jaynes demanded to have sex with Jeffrey. When Jeffrey refused, Jaynes suffocated him while putting a gasoline-soaked rag in his mouth. Jeffrey fought off Jaynes for fifteen minutes, but in the end, the nearly three hundred pound Jaynes was too much for the eighty-five pound Jeffrey. As all this was happening, Sicari continued driving around the Boston suburb of Newton and did nothing to stop Jaynes. The men then locked Jeffrey's body in a car trunk and proceeded to clean Sicari's car for a few hours. After that, they bought a lime, some cement, a rubber container and some alcohol, drove to an apartment Jaynes rented in New Hampshire and sexually molested Jeffrey's corpse. They then put Jeffrey's naked body into the rubber container and put lime on his eyes and mouth to speed up decomposition. They poured concrete into the container and then sealed it with duct tape. Later that night, the men drove to Maine and dumped Jeffrey's body into the Great Works River.

The days following the disappearance

Following Jeffrey's disappearance, Sicari showed up at the Curley residence, behaved strangely, hinted that Charles Jaynes was responsible for the disappearance of Jeffrey and was very eager to help find Jeffrey. Sicari claimed he had previously seen Jeffrey riding in Jaynes's Cadillac and that Jaynes had promised to get Jeffrey a new bicycle. Sicari also handed out flyers and told anyone who would listen that he had seen Jeffrey Curley the day he disappeared. Sicari even drove Jeffrey's brothers to Jaynes's workplace, where Jeffrey's brothers confronted Jaynes. Sicari could not stop talking about Jeffrey Curley. Sicari and Jaynes were immediate suspects because their actions were unusual; they were also disliked throughout the community. Under police questioning, Sicari broke down and told the police everything that had happened. Jaynes and Sicari were subsequently arrested.

The trials

Because of disagreements about the facts of the case between the defendants, Jaynes and Sicari had separate trials. Each man claimed that the other was the driving force behind the attack and murder and that he had watched what happened and did not have a similar intention. Charles Jaynes argued that he did not kill Jeffrey and that he did not participate in any of the other events. He also claimed that Sicari lied to police. Conversely, Salvatore Sicari argued that Jaynes killed and molested Jeffrey. He also claimed that he only helped prepare the body for disposal and helped dump it into the Great Works River. Almost a year later, Sicari was charged with first-degree murder and kidnapping, convicted and sentenced to life in prison without parole. The kidnapping charge carried a sentence of nineteen to twenty years. Jaynes was charged with second degree murder and sentenced to life in prison with the possibility of parole after twenty-three years. The Curleys sued both men and were awarded a symbolic three hundred twenty-eight million dollars in a wrongful death lawsuit against Jaynes and Sicari.

At Jaynes's house, police found numerous NAMBLA bulletins with news articles and drawings of nude boys. They also found NAMBLA publications in

Jaynes's car. During the investigation, Jaynes was discovered to be a frequent visitor to the NAMBLA website. In his diary which police found, he wrote how he felt about NAMBLA and said that the organization was psychologically comforting and enabled him to be proud of his sexual desires. Jaynes also credited NAMBLA for giving him the courage to be proud of his actions.

Life without Jeffrey

On the day Jeffrey was abducted, he asked his older brother Bobby if he could go with him to buy a car part. Bobby refused and instead went somewhere with his friends. Jeffrey's mother Barbara told several newspapers she felt that if she had bought Jeffrey a bicycle, this whole incident would not have occurred and that Sicari and Jaynes would have chosen another child to victimize. Bobby also felt that if he had allowed Jeffrey to accompany him that day, Jeffrey would still be alive. Several months after Jeffrey died, Jeffrey's two older brothers, Shaun and Bobby, aged seventeen and twenty years old at the time of Jeffrey's death, were charged with threatening and harassing Salvatore Sicari's sister and swinging a hammer at her. Although his parents were divorced, Jeffrey's family was very close. Jeffrey's father took comfort in knowing that his son fought off Jaynes with every last bit of energy and did not die without a fight.

Curley v. NAMBLA and others

In 2000, the family of Jeffrey Curley sued NAMBLA and some of its members for two hundred million dollars. During this trial, Robert and Barbara Curley claimed Salvatore Sicari and Charles Jaynes had actually stolen their son Jeffrey's bicycle and that this act was a suggestion which had been printed in a NAMBLA manual on how to lure a child into sexual activity. The Curleys also claimed that while in jail, Charles Jaynes was receiving money and recruiting members for NAMBLA. It was reported that Jaynes had been having sex with other prison inmates and bragging about killing Jeffrey Curley.

The Curleys claimed that NAMBLA promoted pedophilia and taught men how to coerce children into engaging in sexual activity with them. However, the American Civil Liberties Union, ACLU, defended NAMBLA at no cost on the basis that it was an organization and not a corporation or group. The case was thrown out. The Curleys also claimed that if not for NAMBLA, Jeffrey would be alive today. As a result of the ACLU defending NAMBLA, many people were outraged at the ACLU and wrote letters to newspapers, radio stations, and television stations protesting the ACLU. Some also called for an end to donations to the ACLU.

Effects of the case

Due to the public outrage caused by this case, Massachusetts considered bringing back capital punishment. Many people wrote to the Massachusetts legislature requesting that the killers be put to death and that the death penalty be reinstated. Newspapers were filled with letters demanding that Sicari and Jaynes be put to death. The death penalty had passed the Massachusetts Senate many times but had never made it past the Massachusetts House. On October 21, 1997, after debating for six hours, the Massachusetts Senate passed a bill that would allow the death penalty by a vote of twenty-two to fourteen. However, the bill was defeated in the House by one vote, when representative John Slattery changed his vote.

Indirectly, the elements of this crime involved the Cambridge community as they read about the incident and formed their own conclusions. Many parents empathized with the Curleys as they thought about how the incident could relate to their own children. The incident served to raise awareness of crimes against minors as well as make people aware of NAMBLA, which was considered by many to be immoral. It spurred people to take a stand against NAMBLA and to protest the actions of the ACLU. Some argued that members of NAMBLA were victims because their organization received much negative publicity after this case became public.

The sexual aspects involved in this case were homosexuality, pedophilia, and necrophilia. The incident involved two male adults who wanted to have sex with a minor boy and then ended up sexually molesting the dead boy's body. Salvatore Sicari and Charles Jaynes, the two men who befriended Jeffrey Curley, had an ulterior motive which was to have sex with Jeffrey. When Jeffrey refused, they killed him and sexually mutilated his body. Salvatore Sicari and Charles Jaynes were sexually dangerous predators. Specifically, they were pedophiles who posed a threat to the community of Cambridge, Massachusetts, where they often hung around and played with neighborhood children. They also posed a threat to any child with whom they came into contact. Apparently Sicari and Jaynes had observed Jeffrey for some time and devised a plan that involved Jeffrey having sex with them. NAMBLA played a role in this case because the organization's beliefs, mission, and written materials promoted the ideology of pedophilia and somewhat condoned Jaynes's actions and intentions, but not the murder itself.

Due to the gruesomeness of this case, it made national headlines all over the country. The immediate outcome of the case was that the two perpetrators were sent to jail and NAMBLA came under fire from people all across the country.

Many of Jeffrey's family members have appeared on radio and talk shows across the country to raise awareness about sexual predators and to criticize NAMBLA.

Jeffrey's father described NAMBLA as an organization of child molesters. The existence of NAMBLA and its ideology became more public, although it still remained a relatively secretive organization. Individual crusades against NAMBLA involved people who shared the same morals and tried to inform others about its immoral beliefs and activities. Individuals have tried to get the group dissolved by informing law enforcement. NAMBLA was mentioned on the *America's Most Wanted* TV show and has even been spoofed in the *South Park* cartoon.

There have not been many long-term outcomes of the case. The main outcome is increased awareness about NAMBLA. This case made many people aware of the dangers of sexual predators and has raised public awareness of NAMBLA by thrusting it into the national limelight. The moral philosophy of NAMBLA is unacceptable by many who know about the organization and do not support its mission. They strongly feel that NAMBLA's purpose is unlawful and immoral and that the more people know about NAMBLA, the better because it will help in its abolishment.

The current lawsuit

The Curleys' current pending suit against some NAMBLA members may also help increase awareness of the organization and promote further investigations into the organization and its members. Depending on what information is discovered, it could also result in more indictments against its members. Increased publicity about NAMBLA could lead to its disintegration; however, it could also ironically lead to an increase in its membership by those who support the abolition of age consent laws.

Notes about sources

Much of the information for this case came from such newspapers as the *Boston Phoenix* and *Boston Herald*, magazines such as *Time*, and documents from talk shows such as CNN and Court TV.

Richard Sorrells
Video voyeurism

Abstract

The advent of new technology has made it possible for voyeurs to record images of their victims, leading to a new category of voyeuristic crimes called video voyeurism. Until recent years, most state voyeurism statutes only had laws outlawing the viewing of individuals but not the recording of individuals, therefore permitting video voyeurs to secretly record others disrobing and engaging in sexual activities. Furthermore, the law protected individuals only while they were in the privacy of their homes, not while they were in public places. The case of Richard Sorrells, who was caught photographing images up Jolene Jang's skirt, addressed relevant legal issues associated with video voyeurism. Sorrells' case and related cases spurred the implementation of legislation that outlawed video voyeurism offenses.

Introduction to the case

In July 2001 in Seattle, Washington, Richard Sorrells was caught photographing up the skirt of Jolene Jang at the Bite of Seattle Festival. Jang had been standing in line at an ice cream booth when she noticed Sorrells standing behind her with his hand in her purse. Jang assumed that he was attempting to steal her purse. When Jang turned around to confront him, Sorrells immediately fled the scene. Police were able to apprehend Sorrells, and they arrested him for attempted robbery. A witness, however, reported that Sorrells had been photographing up girls' skirts at the festival. Police searched through a camera in Sorrells' bag, and discovered images that had been photographed up the skirts of Jang and other women and girls at the festival.

Voyeurism

The fourth edition of the Diagnostic and Statistical Manual of Mental Disorders, or DSM-IV, classifies Sorrells' behavior as voyeurism, a specific type of paraphilia, or atypical sexual interest. Voyeurism is defined as the viewing of others disrobing or engaging in sexual activity, without these persons' knowledge, for one's own sexual gratification. The voyeur usually masturbates during or after his voyeuristic activities. An individual is diagnosed with voyeurism if he meets two main criteria. First, he must have strong desires, fantasies, or behaviors that involve observing unsuspecting individuals disrobing or engaging in sexual activity, and these desires, fantasies, or behaviors must recur for at least six months. Second, his voyeuristic activities must interfere with his work, social life, or other aspects of his life. Voyeurism is usually a chronic disorder, and the age of onset is usually before fifteen. Voyeurs are often so consumed by voyeuristic activities that it is the only sexual activity that they are involved in.

The DSM-IV notes that society accepts a minimal level of voyeurism. For example, it is acceptable to watch pornographic movies or view pornographic magazines, and one may become sexually aroused after accidentally viewing an individual undressing or engaging in sexual activity. The crucial difference is that a voyeur actively seeks out these experiences and becomes invested in these activities to the extent that it impairs everyday functioning.

An article from the *American Handbook of Psychiatry* suggested that popular culture has encouraged the United States to become a more voyeuristic nation; reality television shows such as *Survivor*, *Big Brother*, and *Real World* have cameras that follow their cast members' every activities, and web-cams broadcast individuals' most intimate moments twenty-four hours a day. When *Real World* first aired in 1992, it was the only reality television show of its kind. In the past few years, reality television shows have become much more prevalent in popular culture. The article noted that the range of acceptable voyeuristic activities has broadened, while psychologists are still grappling with how to define and treat the psychopathology of voyeurism. It also suggested that the rise of voyeuristic television shows reflects a societal trend towards voyeurism as a guilty pleasure enabled by the internet and new recording technology.

Etiology and treatment of voyeurism

The DSM-IV speculates that childhood trauma, such as physical and sexual abuse, may cause voyeurism. The article cited previously from the *American Handbook of Psychiatry* used Sigmund Freud's theory of psychosexual development to create a hypothesis about the causes of voyeurism. The article suggested that castration anxieties and failure to successfully complete stages of psychosexual development cause voyeurism. During the anal and oral stage, the child begins to develop sexual associations with parts of the body, including the anus, mouth, eyes, skin, and ears. During the phallic stage, all these meanings are collapsed into the phallus so that the child believes that all bodily sensations reside in the phallus. Fearing that the father will hurt him to win his mother's affection, the child develops castration anxieties. Normal development involves accepting the possibility of castration, and finally no longer seeing the father as an enemy. However, if the individual does not accept the possibility of castration, he will go through his life obsessed with others' body parts, seeking reassurance for his own castration anxieties.

An article from the *Archives of Sexual Behavior* noted that voyeurism and other sexual paraphilias are within the obsessive compulsive spectrum. Another recent study examined the effects of drugs used to inhibit obsessive thoughts and impulses in voyeurs. Serotonin dysfunction is hypothesized to be associated with sexual dysfunction; furthermore, abnormal serotonin levels are associated with an increase in testosterone levels, which in turn increase sexual desires and impulses. The article suggested that treatment for voyeurism should consist of both systematic serotonin reuptake inhibitors and testosterone reduction. There have been no empirical studies examining this hypothesis. Cognitive, behavioral, and psychoanalytic therapies are also used to treat voyeurism. Long-term treatment is necessary in order for treatment to be effective.

History of voyeurism and the law

Criminal statutes protect citizens in their homes from prying eyes and date back more than a hundred years. A voyeur is more commonly known as a Peeping Tom, named after the legendary Tom who defied orders and observed the naked Lady Godiva ride horse-back through town. According to legend, Godiva was married to the Lord of Coventry, who was oppressing his people with heavy taxes. Godiva repeatedly appealed to her husband to lift the taxes, but he refused. She declared that she would ride naked through town to protest the taxes, and so he ordered all citizens of the town to remain indoors and to shut their blinds. A man named Tom disobeyed and observed Godiva through a hole in his window blinds. He was struck blind for his offense. Peeping Tom was first used in 1796 to refer to a voyeur.

Until recent years, voyeurism statutes have prohibited voyeurs from observing individuals disrobing or engaging in sexual activity in the privacy of their homes, bathrooms, tanning rooms, and other private places. However, in recent years, voyeurs have taken advantage of modern technology, such as compact digital cameras and camera phones, that allow them to discretely photograph or film their victims, leading to a new genre of sexual offending, video voyeurism. Video voyeurism made national headlines in 1998, when a woman named Susan Wilson discovered that her neighbor had secretly implanted hidden cameras in her bedroom and bathroom and had been observing her for months.

Different types of video voyeurism

Sorrells' case offered an example of a subgenre of video voyeurism called upskirt voyeurism. Offenders utilize a number of devices including digital cameras, camera phones, and video recorders to capture images up females' skirts. Offenders target women wearing skirts, and they attempt to capture upskirt images in a number of ways, including following a woman as she ascends a stairway and then photographing up her skirt; crouching down next to a woman and pretending to be occupied, then photographing up her skirt; and placing a recording device, with the lens directed upward, in a bag, and then discretely placing the bag next to a woman in order to film up her skirt.

One variation of video voyeurism is downblouse voyeurism, which involves recording images of a woman's breasts down her shirt. Another variation is X-ray voyeurism using night-vision, which records near infrared light, the light that penetrates through clothing and reflects off the body. X-ray voyeurs typically film individuals in wet bathing suits at the beach. The night-vision enables the camera to render images that show victims' nipples and genitalia.

The danger of video voyeurism

What distinguishes voyeurs from other sexual offenders is that they do not cause physical harm to their victims. Victims of video voyeurs, however, do suffer emotional and psychological distress, though only if they discover that they have been unsuspectingly photographed or filmed while disrobing or performing sexual activities.

Video voyeurs normally sell and distribute the images that they have captured online. Sometimes, the victims' faces can be identified in these images. Victims experience a sense of shame and mortification if they are recognized by their acquaintances. Some compare video voyeurism to sexual abuse. Voyeurism is, in effect, the act of disrobing and viewing other individuals' bodies without their consent. An expectation of privacy is that individuals have a right to their bodies and which parts of their bodies are exposed, but when that expectation is stripped away, victims experience a degrading feeling similar to that experienced by sexual abuse victims.

The case

Washington's voyeurism statute in 2001, RCW 9A.44.115, stated that it was illegal to photograph or videotape an individual without his knowledge in a place in which a reasonable person would expect to have privacy. Sorrells' attorney, Ken

Sharaga, acknowledged that his client's actions were inappropriate, but he argued that the current statute did not protect people in public places. Sharaga argued that the current statute protected people in private places such as their homes and bathrooms; the offense occurred at public festival in a public location, and therefore his client's offense did not fall under the jurisdiction of the statute. The Superior Court of King County disagreed and found Sorrells guilty on September 7, 2001. Sorrells was ordered to serve a two-month prison sentence and to undergo a sexual deviancy treatment program. Sorrells appealed his conviction to the Washington State Supreme Court.

A similar case

At around the same time, the Washington State Supreme Court was considering another video voyeurism case involving a man named Sean Glas. In 1999, Glas was caught photographing up the skirts of two employees at a Union Gap mall in Yakima County, Washington. Glas was found guilty by the Superior Court of Yakima County. He appealed his conviction to the Court of Appeals, claiming that the state's voyeurism statute did not protect people in public places. The Court of Appeals refuted Glas's claim and found that the area under a person's clothing constitutes an area in which people would expect privacy from surveillance and other intrusions. Glas also claimed that the statute was unconstitutional because it was vague in designating what constitutes hostile intrusion of an individual's privacy and therefore encroached upon rights protected by the First Amendment. The Court of Appeals rejected his claim that the statute was overbroad, and upheld the statute's constitutionality, claiming that photographing under a woman's skirt clearly constituted hostile intrusion. Glas also noted that he did not intend to use the photographs for sexual gratification. However, he had admitted that he was going to sell the pictures to online websites that specialized in fetishes, and they would then be distributed over the internet. The court noted that the statute prohibited any act of voyeurism that would provide sexual gratification for any persons, not necessarily the person committing the crime himself. The Court of Appeals upheld Glas's conviction. Glas's case went to the Washington State Supreme Court, and the court ruled upon both the Sorrells and Glas cases in *State v. Glas*.

Both Sorrells and Glas contended that since they filmed and photographed their victims in public places, their victims were not protected by the current statute. The Washington State Supreme Court unanimously agreed and overturned both convictions. In his opinion, Judge Bobbe Bridge noted that the area under a woman's skirt was not protected under the current statute, contrary to what the

Court of the Appeals claimed. Legislators who wrote the statute only intended to criminalize breach of privacy in homes, bathrooms, tanning rooms, and similar places in which individuals can expect to disrobe in privacy. Public festivals, malls, and the area under an individual's clothing were not protected under the current statute. Once an individual entered any public location, she could not assume that she was safe from hostile intrusion or surveillance because people are constantly being recorded in public, such as by store surveillance cameras and newsreporters. Therefore, people were not protected from being recorded under that provision in public places. The Washington State Supreme Court noted that Sorells and Glas's actions were wrong, but they could not be convicted under the current written statute. The decision to overturn both convictions was filed in September 2002. Sorells continued to participate voluntarily in the sexual deviancy program after his conviction was overturned. He served a total of thirty-eight days in prison.

State voyeurism statutes

As illustrated in the Sorrells and Glas cases, though most states had voyeurism laws protecting individuals in private places, there were no statutes protecting victims from being filmed or photographed in public places. For instance, in December 2000 the Seattle City Council passed a law that outlawed filming or photographing through or up any individual's clothing without her consent. The penalty for this misdemeanor was up to a year in jail and a five thousand dollar fine. However, this statute did not protect individuals in public places. Furthermore, some statutes required that the prosecutor prove that the defendant intended to use the film or photographs for sexual gratification, thereby protecting owners of websites that distribute these voyeuristic images. Current technology had made it possible for offenders to satisfy their voyeuristic urges without legal consequences since the current legislation was outdated. It became clear to state legislators that voyeurism statutes had to be amended to correspond with the crimes.

Washington state legislators aimed to model their voyeurism statute after California's amended voyeurism statute. California had amended its statute in 2000 to include video voyeurism. The statute explicitly prohibited filming under any individual's clothing. In May 2003, after intense lobbying by Jang and other advocates, Washington state passed a bill that prohibited upskirt voyeurism.

Even though Washington State had closed its anti-voyeurism loophole, most other states had no provisions prohibiting upskirt voyeurism. However, the Sorrells case was one of two major cases that inspired federal legislation prohibiting video voyeurism. The other was the case of Susan and Gary Wilson in Monroe, Louisiana. In 1998, Susan Wilson discovered that her neighbor, Steve Glover, had placed hidden cameras in her bedroom and bathroom and had been watching her for months. To Wilson's shock, there was no statute at the time prohibiting Glover from secretly filming her. Glover was placed on probation for three years for unlawful entry. Susan Wilson lobbied to have an anti-voyeurism bill enacted in Louisiana. With the help of Senator Mary Landrieu, Louisiana passed a bill making video voyeurism a felony in July of 1999.

Federal video voyeurism laws

Through the lobbying efforts of Jang, Wilson, and other advocates, Congress passed the Video Voyeurism Prevention Act, or VVPA, in 2004, which stipulated that it was illegal to film, photograph, or broadcast images of a private part of an individual's body without her consent. The bill defined private parts as the buttocks, undergarment-clad genitalia, pubic area, and breasts. The bill specified that it was illegal to capture these images in places where the individual would reasonably expect that she could undress in privacy, or in instances in which the individual believes that her private area was not visible to others, regardless of whether she was in a public or a private place.

By 2005, forty-four states had some type of video voyeurism statute, but the statute was difficult to enforce because of vague wording and First Amendment rights issues. It was difficult to prohibit those who used video surveillance for voyeuristic activities without banning harmless or beneficial video surveillance. However, Congress passed the VVPA with the hope that state legislators would utilize it as a model to amend their own video voyeurism statutes.

Against video voyeurism statutes

Even though the VVPA was more extensive than previous voyeurism statutes, constant new developments in video recording technology have continued to enable voyeurs to record their victims covertly. For instance, cellular phones have picture-taking and video-recording capabilities, and offenders can disguise their illegal behavior by pretending they are dialing or talking on the phone. Several offenders in Japan, where camera phones are ubiquitous, have been arrested for taking upskirt shots using their cell phones. To prevent offenders from using camera phones for illegal activities, manufacturers have opted to include a function that flashes a light or makes a sound every-time the camera is used.

In creating new legislation to protect individuals from video voyeurism, lawmakers were concerned about outlawing all video surveillance because the legislation could outlaw surveillance used for harmless or even beneficial purposes. Law enforcement officials frequently utilize camera surveillance to record drug dealers, and outlawing all video surveillance would prohibit law enforcement officers from recording drug deals.

Some feared that limiting public video recording would impinge on First Amendment rights or make criminals out of well-meaning people. For instance, a reporter might record footage of an accident victim who had her undergarments exposed. Under a law that prohibits all non-consensual filming of undergarments, this reporter would be violating the law. News reporters would thus be restricted in their work.

Others argued that by manufacturing camera phones with functions that alert others when an image is being recorded, law enforcement officials are inconveniencing the ninety-nine percent of individuals who use camera phones for innocuous purposes. One individual claimed that he used his camera phone to record and then send video clips of a wedding ceremony to family members who could not attend the event. He noted that if his camera phone had emitted disruptive flashes or sounds, he would not have been able to record the images because he would have disrupted the ceremony.

Privacy vs. security

Restriction of video surveillance is a controversial topic that raises right to privacy issues. Following the attack on the World Trade Center on September 11, 2001, the United States federal government opted to install biometric mass surveillance cameras in certain airports. Biometrics is the biological identification of a person. Images of individuals are captured and identified, and features such as the face, ear, eye, fingerprint, hand shape, or gait are recorded. These images are captured either voluntarily or involuntarily, require direct contact with the individual or not, and are recorded either at a distance or up-close. This surveillance system was intended to match recorded images with a database of known terrorists and criminals. Face recognition surveillance systems were tested at Palm Beach International Airport in 2001 and at Boston Logan International Airport in 2002. At Palm Beach, the percentage of true positives was fifty percent. The percentage of true positives at Boston Logan Airport was higher, but an American Civil Liberties Union, or ACLU, representative noted that the number of false positives generated was too high for the system to be practical.

Immediately following the attack on the World Trade Center, eighty-six percent of polled individuals supported having face recognition systems installed in public locations to trace and locate terrorists. Eight months after this initial survey, eighty-percent of polled individuals still supported having face recognition systems installed. Statutes that prohibit or legalize video surveillance need to compromise privacy for security or vice versa. In the case of detecting terrorists, individuals are willing to sacrifice their privacy for security.

However, an incident of mass video surveillance in 2001 sparked debate on the issue of non-consensual video surveillance. At Super Bowl XXV in Tampa, Florida, law enforcement officials captured images of every individual entering the gates of the stadium and used a face recognition system to try to find matches on their terrorist and criminal database. The surveillance was intended to capture terrorists and criminals, but only pickpockets and scalpers were captured using the surveillance and face recognition system. Thomas Colatosti, CEO of Viisage, the company that provided the face recognition system for the 2001 Super Bowl event dubbed as the Snooper Bowl by critics, noted that face recognition systems were effective in combating identity theft and in protecting bank accounts. He also noted that images that were not matches of criminals were discarded, and claimed that face recognition and video surveillance did not violate individuals' rights but instead provided security.

Opponents of this incident, most notably the ACLU, feared that this would be the beginning of an era of video surveillance abuse in which individuals' every move would be recorded and tracked by the government. Colatosti dismissed these concerns, and noted that people are already being recorded by surveillance cameras in convenience stores and banks. He also compared that controversy to the debate over installing X-ray surveillance cameras in airports, and noted that their goal was security and not violation of rights. Colatosti also claimed that a benefit of face recognition technology is that it is impartial. The system did not target one race over another, and objectively compared faces from the database to the recorded image. However, opponents argued that the face recognition system was used disproportionately on African Americans. Ironically, opponents claimed that the camera operators, who are usually male, often captured images of women for voyeuristic purposes.

Conclusion

With the Video Voyeurism Prevention Act of 2004, legislators recognized the potential use of new video recording technology for voyeuristic crimes. However, constant advancement in technology could provide voyeurs with new equipment to bypass the law and render the current statute outdated. Law enforcement officials and legislators need to be aware of developing technology so that they can modify their laws to protect individuals.

Notes about sources

This case was written with the aid of local newspaper articles in Seattle, Washington about Richard Sorrells and Sean Glas's offenses, specifically coverage from the *Seattle Post-Intelligencer* and a *Newsweek* article, and local newspaper articles in New Orleans, Louisiana about Susan Wilson, specifically coverage from the *Times-Picayune*. The author also relied on court cases in which Sorrells and Glas were involved, *Newsweek* and *Technology News* articles about crimes using new video-recording technology, the Video Voyeurism Protection Act, and an article from *Harvard Magazine* about the legend of Lady Godiva and Peeping Tom. The criteria and etiology of voyeurism were obtained from the DSM-IV, and an article from the *American Handbook of Psychology* was used to discuss the possible cause of voyeurism and the idea that the United States is becoming a more voyeuristic nation. An article from the *Archives of Sexual Behavior* was used to discuss the link between voyeurism and obsessive-compulsive behavior. An article from the ACLU website was used to address the debate about restriction of video surveillance.

Sundance Associates, Inc.
Restricting child pornography

Abstract

Title 18 United States Code §2257 was a record-keeping statute intended to combat child pornography. The statute required producers of visual depictions of sexually explicit conduct to create and maintain records of the names and birth dates of the performers in such materials. While the rationale for maintaining such records was straightforward, the language used to define the boundaries of responsibility of those involved in the production of pornography, was hardly simple.

Sundance Associates, Inc., a publisher of pornographic magazines, was involved in one such trial. Sundance argued that it could not be held responsible for maintaining records of the images it published as the definition of producer in the statute was not consistent with 28 Code of Federal Regulations 75, the regulations created to implement it. At the time of this trial, failure to comply would have resulted in fines and imprisonment of up to two years for the first offense, and up to five years but no less than two for subsequent convictions. Thus, if Sundance were convicted, the statute would have been implemented incorrectly.

Sundance had been previously awarded summary judgment by the United States District Court in Colorado, and the case described below is the Attorney General's appeal of this ruling in the United States Court of Appeals, Tenth Circuit.

In 1998, the court ruled in favor of Sundance, upholding the district court's previous ruling, finding that the verbal ambiguity in Congress's legislation should not be interpreted to have alternative meanings. *Sundance Assoc., Inc. v. Reno* became a landmark case for distributors of pornography, as it spared them from being labeled as primary producers, a designation which would have resulted in assuming the obligations of age-verification record-keeping. In 2005, new restrictions not only emphasized the producer's responsibility in record-keeping, but also extended the definition of producer. As a result, the statute and regulations came to be regarded as the first major legislation against child pornography and internet law, as well as what may have become the most effective means of restricting legitimate pornography yet.

Background

Record-keeping requirements for pornography created in the United States are stated under Title 18 United States Code §2257, referred to as 18 U.S.C. §2257. Congress approved 18 U.S.C. §2257 as an amendment to the Child Protection Restoration and Penalties Enhancement Act of 1988 towards the goal of eliminating child pornography. Age-verification legislation was made a priority to combat pedophilic pornography after it was revealed in 1984 that pornographic actress Traci Lords was fifteen, not twenty-two, years of age. The Attorney General created 28 Code of Federal Regulations §75, referred to as 28 C.F.R. §75, to implement the statutory requirements.

18 U.S.C. §2257 had undergone several revisions since 1988, but there were four basic obligations for the producers of visual depictions of sexually explicit acts: the duty to identify and verify ages of the performers involved through valid identification such as a driver's license, the duty to create and maintain retrievable records of the performers' ages and names, the duty to indicate the name and location of the custodian of records in all sexually explicit visual works, and the duty to make the records available to the Attorney General for inspection. While these recommendations were originally relatively straightforward, the increasingly stringent restrictions of the statute would eventually result in legal battles over the changing degrees of responsibility for those involved in the distribution and creation of pornography at every level.

One such trial focused on the responsibility of those involved in the distribution of pornography: Could a party be held liable if its inclusion as a pornographic producer was not consistent with both the definitions put forth in a statute and regulation? Sundance Associates, Inc., a publisher of pornographic magazines, faced criminal liability as a producer under the statute as it stood in 1998. Sundance published five pornographic magazines: *Odyssey, Odyssey Express, Connexion, Looking Glass,* and *UnReal People.* In these magazines, individuals could place personal announcements seeking to contact others with similar sexual interests. These announcements were often submitted with sexually explicit pictures. Sundance's defense was that while they would be legally responsible to maintain records under the statute, they would not be responsible under the regulation.

The legal language issue

The original trial at the district court concerned whether the Attorney General's regulatory definition of producer was inconsistent with the statutory definition as indicated by Congress. Under 18 U.S.C. §2257, Sundance would be forced to maintain records because producers included not only those directly involved in the creation of the actual pornography, but also those responsible for arranging the performers' participation and assembling the resulting sexually explicit visual depictions for distribution. Activities such as mere distribution were exempt.

28 C.F.R. §75 handled the definition of producer a little differently. Producers were further divided into two categories: Primary producers included any individual who actually filmed, photographed, or videotaped a visual depiction of actual sexually explicit conduct, while secondary producers were those who assembled, manufactured, or duplicated visual depictions of the content created by primary producers.

According to Sundance, the inconsistency between the statute and regulation was that activities towards coordinating performers' participation, such as their management or hiring, were included in the statutory but not regulatory definition of producer. Oddly enough, a subsection of the regulation stated that exemptions from being labeled as a producer could include any activity, other than those already identified in the regulation definition, that did not include securing the performers' involvement. If this type of involvement was not even identified in the definition of producer, how could it be a condition for exemption to the definition?

The district court ruled in Sundance's favor, finding the regulation invalid for the purposes of enforcing the statute.

Attorney General's appeal

While the district court had ruled in favor of Sundance, the Attorney General appealed the ruling to the circuit court, questioning whether the district court had been incorrect in finding the regulation to be an erroneous implementation of the statute. The appeal requested a new summary judgment applying the same legal standards used by the district court. Summary judgments were relevant if the arguments and evidence presented demonstrated an insufficient foundation for the ruling.

According to the government, its regulatory definition was justified because the clause of the statute stating which activities were not included under the definition of producer was actually intended to include those very activities.

Next, the government complained that the district court's interpretation of the statute should be rejected because the clause concerning the duplication and reissuing of sexually explicit depictions did not necessarily overlap with the arrangement of performers' participation, and thus the latter condition did not have to be included in the regulatory definition.

Finally, the government argued that its broad conditions in the regulation were necessary because enforcing record-keeping requirements would be difficult if those requirements were placed only on producers who had direct involvement in securing sexual performers' participation.

Court ruling

In 1998, the circuit court affirmed the district court's ruling. The court compared the government's reading of the statute to the confusion in Alice in Wonderland, flatly rejecting the complaint. The court reminded the appellant that it is usually assumed that Congress's language is clear and does not require alternative interpretations, and that the intent of the statute was salient.

The court also rejected the government's argument that the district court had incorrectly interpreted the clause referring to duplication and reissue. The court explained that it was entirely possible for individuals to be duplicating or reissuing material they had originally created, and as a result it was possible for them to be affected by the statute as they would have had sufficient contact with the performers. The court added that although the exemption might render the statute inapplicable to some duplicators, exclusions inherently narrow the field.

The court responded to the government's objection to the overly restrictive definition of producer with the reminder that courts can only uphold laws; Congress is responsible for legislation.

Attorneys involved

Arthur M. Schwartz of Denver, Colorado, defended Sundance. Anne M. Lobell of the United States Department of Justice, Washington, D.C., represented the Attorney General. Circuit Judge Brobry presided. The District Judge from the original trial was Judge Brown.

Related cases

The conflict over what parties should be responsible for record-keeping requirements has been the subject of several other court cases. In 1994, the distinction between primary and secondary producers was indirectly upheld in *American Library Association v. Reno*. The D.C. Circuit Court ruled that it was not unconstitutional on First Amendment grounds for secondary producers, as defined by 28 C.F.R. §75, to maintain records because they could easily comply by using copies provided by primary producers. Critics of the more restrictive regulations enacted in 2005, described below, frequently cited the Sundance case as appropriate precedent, but the Department of Justice favored *American Library Association v. Reno* as the correct interpretation of the law.

In 1998, Connection Distributing Company in *Connection Distributing Company v. Reno* cited First Amendment violations in the record-keeping requirements of 18 U.S.C. §2275. Connection printed magazines similar in concept and content to those from Sundance. Connection argued that the statute infringed on self-expression and free association. The court ruled against Connection, as readers could easily continue to submit photographs anonymously as long as they were not sexually explicit.

In 2002, *Ashcroft v. Free Speech Coalition*, the U.S. Supreme Court ruled that the Child Pornography Protection Act of 1996, known as CPPA, was excessively broad. CPPA attempted to include images that merely appeared to involve children in sexually explicit acts, such as computer-produced artwork, as well as depictions that attempted to convey the impression that the individuals involved were minors. The Supreme Court sided with the plaintiffs as the government had failed to show a significant connection with speech that might incite thoughts resulting in child abuse.

New restrictions

On June 23, 2005, extensive amendments to the Attorney General's regulations implementing 18 U.S.C. §2257 became effective. The most significant change was the inclusion of webmasters and those who digitally manipulated images as secondary producers, as well as the inclusion of computer-generated images under the list of affected depictions of sexually explicit activity. While this was criticized as an unreasonable burden, the Department of Justice defended this amendment citing the aforementioned D.C. Circuit ruling in *American Library Association v. Reno*. As a result, droves of pornographic websites shut down overnight in their efforts to comply with the statute, which now carried a punishment of not more than five years for a first offence, and no more than ten but not fewer than two years for subsequent offenses. This was the most sensitive aspect of the new amendment, as many viewed this as the strongest attack yet on internet pornography, targeting the numerous website owners who would find it virtually impossible to obtain the sufficient records. All websites that sought to continue operation had to display a statement as per the regulation stating that the owners of the site could present records confirming that all performers were over the age of eighteen, and the location of these records.

Other changes related to the statute drew comparisons to the so-called war on drugs. Among the most controversial changes was the provision for records inspections to occur without advance warning or warrant. Inspectors could enter only between regular business hours and in a reasonable fashion, but were permitted to seize any evidence of records-keeping violations. Similar proposed restrictions were found in the Children's Safety Act of 2005, passed in the House in the fall of 2005 and referred to the Senate. The bill, including a proposal to include retail stores under the definition of producers, sought asset forfeiture in child pornography production.

Reactions to new restrictions

Although the new amendments to the regulation were ostensibly drafted to extend the efforts of authorities fighting child pornography, reactions have been polarized towards their practical application. Not surprisingly, the stringent 2005 amendments to 28 C.F.R. §75 were sponsored by conservative politicians. Critics of the new regulations affecting 18 U.S.C. §2257 expressed skepticism towards its child-protection priorities, suspecting that their actual purpose was the restriction of undesirable material that had long been protected by the First Amendment. Unfortunately, politicians were reticent about challenging the statute after it became law, as it was difficult to justify being opposed to legislation aimed at protecting children. Commentary from the adult industry noted that record-keeping legislation would not affect those producing child pornography as their operations had always been illicit for reasons beyond records maintenance.

Psychology and pornography

The debate over the potential dangers of adult pornography generally occurs in moral or psychological paradigms. While there are obvious concerns associated with child pornography and pedophilia, evidence of real psychological harm resulting from long-term exposure to adult pornography has never been clear.

In 1967, The President's Commission on Obscenity and Pornography was formed to investigate the effects of such materials on the American people. The Commission investigated the nature of obscenity, the distribution of pornography, the alleged antisocial effects of pornography on the public, and was charged with recommending any constitutional, advisable, appropriate and effective methods to deal with controlling pornography and obscenity. In 1970, President Richard Nixon was outraged when the commission reported that it could find no harmful effects of such materials on adults. Moreover, it suggested legalizing the sale of pornographic materials, while retaining restrictions on sale to minors. Nixon rejected the report, accusing the commission of having performed a disservice.

In 1987, the Attorney General's Commission on Pornography concluded that there was a causal relationship between exposure to pornography and antisocial effects, including increased levels of violence against women. A study published the same year in *American Psychologist* conducted a scrutiny of the data provided from the studies used in the report. The study found that the commission used data from these studies selectively, and in several cases, made generalizations that were somewhat overbroad given the research provided. For instance, violence in R-rated films with sexual themes but not sexual explicitness resulted in much more aggression towards women than the violence found in pornographic films. The commission inaccurately concluded that pornographic violence was also extremely detrimental. If anything, this finding indicated that violence against women in films pornographic or otherwise is the real threat, not the sexual content. The Attorney General's report also erroneously extrapolated that committing actual acts of aggression was associated with pornography from a study that only concluded that callous attitudes towards rape were correlated with self-reported aggression and sexually degrading pornography. The authors of the article advised not regulating pornography but rather encouraging the public to be better informed about their entertainment, and to examine violent acts against women in all media.

Studies examining possible relationships between the recent increase in rates of rape and violent pornography have not supported a connection between the two, or at least have not been able to find one. A Danish study examining rape data from four countries where pornography is widely available did not find that the availability of pornography had any damaging effects in the form of increased sexual violence. A 1993 study had similar findings using *Hustler* magazine as a pornographic culture bellwether. Over a fourteen-year period, it was determined that depictions of sexual violence tended to be in a relatively small and consistent proportion of pornographic depictions, and it was therefore unlikely that alleged increases in violent pornography was an explanation for increases in rape rates.

Research on pornography in the past fifteen years has tended to be more focused on the effects of violent pornography, rather than general sexual explicitness. As noted above, violence against women independent of sexual content has been demonstrated in laboratory situations to be encouraging of female-directed aggression. Numerous studies have also narrowed the investigation of violent pornography to isolating the effects of the female victim's positive or negative reactions and the connection to arousal. Male subjects were more likely to be aroused by such violent depictions towards pornography where the victim has a positive reaction, and were also more likely to direct aggression towards females in a laboratory environment.

Internet and pornography

The unbridled growth of the internet over the past decade has also presented pornographic issues unique to its structure. Child pornography awareness has visibly increased, as the internet has provided an unprecedented community for pedophiles. This significant audience has resulted in a substantial demand for more images and, as a result, the continued abuse of children.

The internet has also made it possible for children to view pornography freely, no longer restricted to out-of-reach magazine racks or sex stores. This unrestricted access has raised questions about the psychological implications of viewing pornography without being able to process it maturely. A 2003 study examined the effects of unwanted internet pornography on children and their caretakers. This national survey found that the problem of internet pornography was not necessarily restricted to youth seeking out porn, but also by youth who had been exposed to it unwillingly. Most of the youth were not affected by this exposure, but one-quarter felt strongly disturbed and upset afterwards. A similar phenomenon of children stumbling upon sexually explicit material through peer-to-peer file sharing was also observed in a 2004 study, and it was concluded that while an understanding parent-child relationship was the best defense against negative effects, male youths displaying antisocial behaviors had to be particularly well-policed in this circumstance.

Pornography as harmful

Though not a formal psychological study, transcripts from the civil rights hearings conducted by Catharine MacKinnon and Andrea Dworkin provide a look at anecdotal evidence for the damage caused by pornography, especially with regard to female victims. The anecdotes generally involved the individual, including a cast as diverse as former prostitutes and Peter Bogdanovich, and cited pornography as the origin of another's desire to abuse, including enslaving someone into prostitution or being coerced into the adult film industry, the latter being a flamboyant attempt at dispelling the apparent myth of women willingly choosing to work in the adult industry. The hearings were conducted between 1983 and 1992 as part of the two anti-pornography feminists' efforts to circumvent First Amendment defenses of pornography by passing local ordinances declaring pornography to be sexual discrimination. In short, their legal strategy was to argue that pornography should not be protected under the First Amendment because it violated women's civil rights. This strategy was ultimately unsuccessful, but it was nevertheless an innovative effort toward restricting pornography.

Notes about sources

A general background to 18 U.S.C. §2257 and its progress was provided by the pornography interest and news website Fleshbot. Commentary, both legal and otherwise, from the adult industry was found on adult entertainment news websites AVN and Xbiz. The Federal Register provided a detailed summary of the amendments to 18 U.S.C. §2257 when they were proposed in 2004, as well as the objections from various legislators. This record was particularly helpful as it also explained the background and refutations for all criticism in all parts of the new amendments. J.D. Odenberger and Associates compared the original 28 C.F.R. §75, proposed changes, and actual changes on their website; this clarified a number of the legal issues that made the new version so much more controversial than the original. Court cases were provided by the District or Circuit courts. Psychological studies were selected from relevant peer-reviewed journals.

Jesse Timmendequas
Child rape, murder, and Megan's Law

Abstract

In 1994, a young girl named Megan Nicole Kanka was raped and murdered by a neighbor and convicted sex offender, Jesse Timmendequas. Following her death, Megan's Law was passed as an amendment to its preceding statute, the Jacob Wetterling Crimes Against Children and Sexually Violent Offender Registration Act, and required law enforcement to notify communities of the presence of a registered sex offender. As a type of notification law, Megan's Law was one of three statues passed by the U.S. Congress during the mid-1990s in an attempt to fortify procedures of keeping tabs on convicted sex offenders. The other two statutes were Wetterling Act, passed in 1994, and the Pam Lychner Sexual Offender Tracking and Identification Act, also known as the Lychner Act, which was passed shortly after the enactment of Megan's Law in 1996. Under the national enactment of Megan's Law in 1996, each state established its own discretionary criteria for disclosing information about registered sex offenders, but was required to make the information publicly accessible.

Rape and murder of Megan Kanka

Megan Kanka was a seven year old girl living in Hamilton Township of Mercer County, New Jersey. She was last seen around 8 p.m. on Friday, July 29, 1994, speaking with her neighbor, Jesse Timmendequas. Neighbors said they had seen her outside Timmendequas' residence while he was cleaning a boat across the street from the Kanka residence. While young Megan was speaking with Timmendequas, he offered to show her a puppy inside his home. She followed him inside where he pulled her into his room, strangled her with his belt, and raped her. Timmendequas attempted to disguise his crime by wrapping her head in plastic to avoid her blood spilling inside his home, hiding her body in a toy box, and tearing her shorts into shreds. He brought the toy box into his truck and took her body to a park three miles away from Kanka residence. He sexually assaulted her once more and left her body there. Once a neighborhood search started for the missing girl, police began to check the neighborhood using dogs and Timmendequas used ammonia to clean his steps, truck, and toy box to eliminate odors. The next day, he even informed neighbors of Megan's disappearance and volunteered to distribute flyers to help her family find her. On Saturday evening, the Hamilton Township Police found Megan's body hidden in a pile of weeds next to a portable toilet in the park Timmendequas visited the night before. Autopsy records showed that Megan died from acute asphyxia via strangulation. Police arrested and questioned Timmendequas soon after discovering Megan's body and he confessed to committing the crime. Mercer County authorities sought the death penalty as punishment for the crime. Timmendequas currently is on death row at the Capital Sentencing Unit at New Jersey State Prison in Trenton, only several miles away from Megan's neighborhood.

Background of a sex offender

In Jesse Timmendequas' defense during the trial, there was an interview of Jesse's younger brother, Paul Timmendequas, shown on videotape. Paul talked about the childhood misfortunes they shared in their abusive family. According to Paul, Jesse was one of ten children born by his mother, Doris Unangst, by seven different men. Charles Hall, Jesse and Paul's father, was an ex-convict who left New Jersey in 1972 after stabbing a man in Piscataway. Jesse was named after Hall's hero, Jesse James, and his last name, Timmendequas, was an alias his father often went by.

Hall was convicted of burglary when Jesse was a toddler and was paroled when Jesse was about seven years old. His mother was often absent from the home and Charles Hall sexually assaulted the young boys at this time, at least once a week. He would often hold the two together and force himself upon them, but would eventually, according to Paul, impose full abuse on Jesse. Paul recalls hearing the screams of his older brother in the next room while their father beat and raped young Jesse. Hall also forced the young boys to witness the rape of an eight year old girl in his truck. At home, he killed the boys' pet rabbit, drowned the dog, and decapitated the cat. Eventually, he fled to join a white supremacist community in rural California.

At the time of Megan's murder, Jesse Timmendequas was thirty-three years old and had already been convicted twice for sexual assault in Middlesex County of New Jersey. In 1979, he pleaded guilty to attempted aggravated sexual assault of a five year old girl from Piscataway, New Jersey. He received a suspended sentence, but did not attend suggested counseling therapy and consequently served nine months at the Middlesex Adult Correctional Center. In 1981, he was convicted of sexual assault of a seven year old girl. Both of Timmendequas' convicted crimes were pedophilic by targeting young girls under the age of ten with sexually violent acts. After his second crime, he served six years of a ten-year sentence at the Avenel Adult Diagnostic and Treatment Center, a prison for sexual offenders, in New Jersey. At the center, Timmendequas befriended a convicted child molester and another sex offender. At the time of Megan Kanka's murder, Timmendequas lived with these two men and one of their mothers in her home in Hamilton Township of New Jersey.

Existing legislation

Prior to Megan's murder, the Jacob Wetterling Crimes Against Children and Sexually Violent Offender Registration Act was enacted in 1994 as one of Congress's earlier attempts to enforce stricter regulation on protecting children from dangerous criminals. In 1989, an eleven year old Minnesota boy named Jacob Wetterling was abducted at gunpoint by a masked man while he, his brother, and a friend were riding their bicycles near the Wetterling residence. Jacob's body was never found.

The Wetterling Act required convicted child molesters and sexually violent offenders to notify authorities of their whereabouts for ten years after release from prison, parole, or community supervision.

Urging new legislation

Following Megan's murder, the Kanka family and other residents were outraged that the local authorities never informed them of the presence of three convicted sexual offenders living in their neighborhood. Neighbors were unaware of Jesse Timmendequas' criminal history as a sex offender. According to them, he was a diligent, easygoing laborer who lived with two roommates and enjoyed talking to the children in the neighborhood.

Immediately after the arrest of Jesse Timmendequas, Megan's parents, Richard and Maureen Kanka, pushed for a proposal to require sexual offenders to notify local authorities when moving into a community and to release the information via public notification. A rally supporting Take Back the Night, a national organization against the sexual assault and rape of women and children, was originally scheduled the weekend Megan was raped and murdered. With the recent tragedy, the rally took on local significance and Megan's parents collected over a thousand signatures on a petition to urge Governor Christine Todd Whitman on legislative reform that would require local authorities to notify a community within a thousand-foot range of a previous sex offender of his presence. Within the last five years prior to Megan's case, at least twenty-five states required criminals to register with a government agency after their release from prison. Megan's parents and neighbors in the Hamilton Township community sought a reform resembling the law adopted by the state of Washington. In Washington, local authorities were usually required to hand-deliver letters to community centers that notify them of a pending release and arrival of a convicted sex offender.

Dick Zimmer, a state senator for New Jersey and a Congressman, drafted a package of bills suggesting a process of assessing the dangerous risk factor posed to a community by a registered sex offender and notifying a community of the presence of the offender depending on the level of danger. Many New Jersey politicians, including the state's Attorney General Deborah Poritz, Governor Christine Todd Whitman, and other leaders representing both houses of the state legislature advocated the set of bills. Poritz then served as the chief justice of the New Jersey State Supreme Court and Whitman as the head of the federal Environmental Protection Agency.

Less than ninety days following the disappearance of Megan Kanka, the New Jersey State Assembly approved the bills increasing penalties for convicted sex offenders and imposing controls on their whereabouts after release from prison. A bill specifies the requirement of legal authorities to notify a neighborhood, schools, and other community centers of the presence of a nearby convicted sex offender. Other bills passed by the New Jersey Assembly require sex offenders to register with legal authorities once every ninety days; extend prison time for a sexual offense; require life in prison without parole for a second sexual offense; allow the death penalty for the murder of a child; and allow the state to confine sex offenders more often to psychiatric hospitals.

Reactions to Megan's Law

Convicted sex offenders and prisoners' rights groups argued that the proposal unconstitutionally and unjustly added a negative stigma to those criminals who already served their punishment. The defense lawyer for Timmendequas argued that the publicity of Megan's Law made Timmendequas a notorious household name by disclosing private information that is often not even provided to jurors. Three years after Megan's death, Timmendequas was finally scheduled to have a trial for the rape and murder of Megan. His attorney argued that by this time, it was nearly impossible for Timmedequas to find an impartial jury and have a fair trial.

In May 1996, President Bill Clinton signed a federal version of Megan's Law as an amendment to the Wetterling Act. Megan's Law extends the Wetterling Act to make it necessary for the authorities to disclose sexual offender registration information to the public. Criminals continued to argue that the new notification law was unconstitutional by subjecting them to double jeopardy via public humiliation and negative reaction after serving their term in prison. Opponents of the reform argued that the measure would give ex-convicts a tainted reputation and spoiled opportunity to start a new life, thus interfering with the finality of a punishment. In 1998, the Supreme Court rejected the challenge and deemed Megan's Law constitutional.

Communities argued that they had the right to know about the presence of a nearby sex offender to protect children and women from harm. Although the Wetterling Act was also a notification law, the public viewed that stricter legislation as essential for preventive measures. While the Wetterling Act alerted local authorities to the whereabouts of a convicted child molesters and sexually violent criminals for ten years after release from prison, Megan's Law extended the Wetterling Act to disclose private information to the public. Megan's Law advocates argued in support of mandatory public notification for the safety of the members within the community.

Implementation of Megan's Law by state

Since 1996, every state in the United States has adopted its own method of public notification. Some states have implemented a three-tiered system for categorizing sex offenders. Sex offenders are divided among three groups: tier one for lowest risk to the community, tier two for moderate risk, and tier three for highest risk. The state determines which levels of offenders are considered dangerous enough to be essential for public notification. For example, some states require tier two criminals to be reported to schools and day care centers and tier three criminals to be reported to families within a certain radius of the criminal.

Some states have organized an accessible database of sex offender information via local police departments. Others require members of the public to submit a written request to access information, whether free of cost or for a fee. Thirty-seven states adopted sex offender registries online.

Concluding remarks and further legislation

The Kanka family founded the Megan Nicole Kanka Foundation with the mission to ensure the safety of children from sex offenders in their neighborhoods. The Megan Nicole Kanka Foundation is based in New Jersey and continues to advocate education on child safety and improvements on Megan's Law in different states.

In 1996, the Lychner Act amended the Violent Crime Control and Law Enforcement Act of 1994 to require the FBI to draft a national database of offenders and administer sex offender registration and notification for states that were unable to carry out Megan's Law sufficiently on their own. Under the Lychner Act, criminals at the most dangerous risk to society would have to register with public authorities throughout their lifetimes.

In 2002, the United States Supreme Court ruled that internet registries in Alaska and Connecticut did not violate the constitutional rights of an offender.

Currently, members of the foundation are petitioning to update Pennsylvania's Megan's Law to include a three-tiered system and internet registry of criminals available to the public. The internet registry includes the name, address, photo, crimes committed, and license plate number of the sex offender.

On April 30, 2003, President George W. Bush signed the Protect Act of 2003 for child safety to ensure improved protective measures over children, stronger investigation for apprehending offenders, increased sentencing, and stricter child pornography laws.

Notes about sources

For this case, I have used articles from the *New York Times*, *Philadelphia Inquirer*, the *Herald*, the *Washington Post*, *Milwaukee Journal Sentinel*, and the *Pittsburgh Post-Gazette* published around the date of the rape and murder of Megan Kanka. I also used *Psychology and Law* by Bartol and Bartol and *Psychology and the Legal System* by Wrightsman, et al. as references to the legal history of Megan's Law.

Aileen Wuornos
Prostitution and murder

Abstract

Aileen Wuornos was born into instability in 1956, abandoned by her biological mother as a toddler and raised by abusive grandparents. She moved to Florida at the age of twenty where she became a prostitute. She lived a careless life filled with crime and unhealthy relationships. She met Tyria Moore, her lesbian lover for four years, in 1986. From December 1989 through October 1990, the dead bodies of six men were discovered near highways in Florida with .22 caliber gun shot wounds. Investigators tied the murders to a single assailant, and it eventually pointed to Wuornos. In 1992, Wuornos was convicted of the murder of her first victim, Richard Mallory. She was given the death penalty for his murder and later the murders of her next five victims. She claimed to have killed a seventh man, but she was never charged for his murder because a body was never discovered. Wuornos was executed by lethal injection on October 9, 2002, becoming the second woman in Florida and the tenth woman in the United States to be executed since the death penalty had been reinstated in 1976. The story of her life, trial, and death has been portrayed by the media in several forms.

The early life

Aileen Wuornos's childhood was characterized by loss and abuse. Her mother, Diane Wuornos, married Leo Dale Pittman at the age of fifteen and had two children by him, Keith and then Aileen, in Rochester, Michigan. Leo Pittman was a psychopathic child molester, and Diane soon realized that he was a very dangerous man. Fearing for her safety and the safety of her children, she divorced Leo less than two years into the marriage, and Aileen was born a few months later on February 29, 1956 as Aileen Carol Pittman. Leo Pittman was later convicted of raping a seven year old girl and sentenced to life in prison in Kansas. He hanged himself in prison in 1969. Diane raised Aileen and Keith as a single mother until she found the task too difficult, so in 1960 she abandoned her two children.

Aileen and Keith were adopted by their grandparents, Lauri and Britta Wuornos, that same year. Lauri and Britta raised Aileen and Keith with their own children in Troy, Michigan and did not reveal to them that they were not their biological parents. It was not until Aileen was about twelve years old that she and her brother discovered the truth about their parentage. This shocking information caused them to rebel. Lauri and Britta were not particularly good parents, either. Besides hiding the truth from Aileen and Keith, Lauri physically and sexually abused Aileen, and Britta was an abusive alcoholic.

Aileen was sexually promiscuous at an early age. She claimed to have had sex with her brother Keith. She became pregnant at the age of fourteen and gave birth to a baby boy, who was immediately put up for adoption in 1971.

Her first ten years in Florida

In July 1971, Britta Wuornos died of liver failure. Keith died of throat cancer at twenty-one, and Lauri committed suicide. Aileen then left Michigan for Florida at the age of twenty. She received ten thousand dollars from Keith's life insurance policy, only to spend it frivolously in two months. While she was hitchhiking the highways of Florida, she met a sixty-nine year old wealthy man who soon fell in love with her. They married in 1976, but only about a month into the marriage he had the marriage annulled after he found Wuornos to be abusive and a spendthrift.

For the next ten years, she led a destructive lifestyle and was arrested for prostitution, forgery, theft, and armed robbery. She was unsuccessful in her personal life, entering into a number of poor relationships. Aileen was destroying her body with alcohol and other drugs, and all of the self-inflicted abuse took its toll on her emotional health, as well.

The love of her life

With all the loss and abuse she had encountered in her life, Aileen felt alone and upset with the world and had given up dating men by her late 20s. Her luck had a turn for the better when she met twenty-four year old Tyria Moore at a gay bar in 1986. In the beginning of their relationship, everything was nice. Aileen and Tyria loved each other. Aileen assumed the male role, and Tyria assumed the female role. Aileen saw Tyria as her wife, and so she gave herself the responsibility of earning the money for the somewhat nuclear family that they had established. Tyria quit her job as a motel maid for a period of time and lived with Aileen, allowing her income as prostitute to support them. The money Aileen earned as a prostitute was not enough to support the two of them, and Tyria's propensity for alcohol led her to spend freely. They were soon living a meager existence.

Tyria stayed with Aileen as they barely made ends meet, bouncing from one cheap motel to the next and even resorting to sleeping outdoors. Even with their financial woes and instability, this was the most stable time in Aileen's life. She was with someone whom she loved and who loved her, and they depended on each other. Aileen would go to lengths to be with Tyria, and she was willing to do whatever it took, as it soon became apparent, to make a life for Tyria and herself.

Her hustle as a hitchhiking prostitute

Aileen Wuornos made a habit of prostituting herself from the time she was a child. When she came to Florida, it became her primary source of income. In her early years in Florida, prostitution was a relatively stable and reliable means of making money, but as she grew older, her hard lifestyle and lack of care for her physical appearance began to decrease her value as a prostitute. She was over-weight, and she was more masculine in her appearance. She wore cut-off T-shirts, camouflage T-shirts, sneakers, a hat, glasses, and no makeup. She would not have been the first choice for someone who wanted cheap sex.

Despite her casual approach to prostitution, she still had many clients. Her hustle when she got in the car with the men would be to first survey the situation and then show the man pictures of Lori Grody's children and say that those were her children. Lori Grody was the sister of Aileen's aunt. Then she would proceed to tell a story about her family and that she needed money, and then she would negotiate what sexual favors she would do for what price. This was to make up for her diminishing value as a prostitute. It worked for a short while until she realized that her options as a prostitute were becoming slim. Aileen carried a .22 caliber pistol in her bag for protection. She decided that she would use her gun to get her and Tyria more of what they desperately needed: cash.

Devaluation of men

From childhood, Aileen had unhealthy relationships and encounters with men. The first was her father, Leo Pittman, whom she never actually met but who was nonetheless a negative influence on her mother. Aileen began prostituting herself as a child, and so most of her encounters with boys or young men around her age were for their own sexual gratification. She was allowing herself to be used and abused. Many of the young men who had sexual encounters with her would humiliate her in public; she notably became an outcast in her own community. Her grandfather, who was the closest thing she had to a father, repeated physically abused her. This was witnessed by people who grew up with her and was attested to by even her. It was even rumored by those who lived near Aileen when she was younger that she had sexual intercourse with her brother Keith. A man, who reportedly lost his virginity to Aileen, said from the age of nine she had sex with boys in exchange for cigarettes. He also said that he witnessed Aileen and Keith having sex.

Aileen had endless cheap and meaningless sexual encounters with men as a hitchhiking prostitute in Florida, which was her main occupation throughout her life. Her brief marriage to an older gentleman in Florida proved how reckless she was in relationships with men; it ending with him seeking an annulment after several incidents of her physically and verbally abusing him.

The only positive relationship Aileen ever seemed to have had was with Tyria, and she was prepared to do anything to keep her. By the time she was in a well established relationship with Tyria, men had become largely the object of her hatred and disdain. Men were the source of many of the negative turns in her life, and they became very dispensable.

Six bodies found

Aileen soon found a new way to sustain Tyria and herself: murder and theft. Dead bodies of men began popping up along highways in Florida in late 1989, and at first nothing linked Aileen to the murders.

On December 13, 1989, the badly decomposed body of Richard Mallory was found close to Interstate 95 in Volusia County, Florida. He had been shot in the head three times from a .22-caliber gun. On June 1, 1990, the naked body of David Spears was found in the woods in Citrus County, Florida; he had been shot several times with a .22 caliber gun. On June 6, 1990, the naked, decomposed body of Charles Carskaddon was discovered a few miles off Interstate 95 in Pasco County. There were nine bullets found in his remains, belonging to a .22 caliber gun. The body of Troy Burress was discovered on August 4, 1990 off Highway 19 in the Ocala National Forest. It had two .22 caliber bullets in it. The body of Dick Humphreys was found on September 12, 1990 in Marion County; he had been shot seven times with a .22 caliber gun. Walter Gino Antonio's naked remains were found in October 1990. Six men had been killed by a .22 caliber gun in the span of less than a year.

Two women suspected

On July 4, 1990, Florida resident Rhonda Bailey, while sitting on her porch, watched a car swerve off the road into the brush in front of her home near Orange Springs, Florida, and two women emerged from the vehicle haphazardly. The two women were Aileen Wuornos and Tyria Moore. They were driving the stolen 1988 grey Pontiac Sunbird of Peter Siems, who went missing the month before on June 7 after leaving his home in Jupiter, Florida. The incident aroused suspicion. After they abandoned the vehicle and began on foot, Wuornos and Moore were approached by Hubert Hewett of the Orange Springs Volunteer Fire Department in response to a call on the car accident. John Wisnieski of the Jupiter Police, who was on the Peter Siems case, posted a nationwide teletype containing descriptions of the two women. He also registered the case, including sketches of the women, in the Florida Criminal Activity Bulletin.

The commander of the Marion County Sheriff's Criminal Investigation Division began to piece together the murder cases of the men in neighboring counties in Florida. Knowing that the days of readily picking up hitchhikers was gone, he theorized that the murderer or murderers would be female and was or were not initially threatening to the men. His primary suspects at that time were the two unnamed women who had wrecked Peter Siems's car and walked away. Beginning in late November, the press ran stories about the killings, along with police sketches of these two women.

Following the leads

Leads began pouring in for the same two women, revealing the different identities that Wuornos used. A computer check produced the driver's license and criminal record for Tyria Moore and Wuornos's numerous aliases. The identification information for one of the aliases, Cammie Marsh Green, gave police investigators sufficient information to track Wuornos's location. Volusia County,

Florida police officers found that in Daytona, Florida, Cammie Marsh Greene had pawned a camera and a radar detector. Her thumbprint was left on the receipt. It was discovered that the camera and radar detector belonged to Richard Mallory, her first victim. In Ormand Beach, Florida, a woman under the name Cammie Marsh Greene pawned a set of tools that apparently belonged to David Spears, Wuornos's second victim.

The thumbprint on the receipt proved to be the best piece of evidence in tracking Wuornos. In Volusia County, Florida, a manual hand search of fingerprint records yielded a match. The fingerprint was linked to a Lori Grody through a weapons charge and outstanding warrant. Lori Grody's prints were found in the blood-stained interior of 1988 Pontiac Sunbird belonging to Peter Siems, whose body was never recovered. The compiled information was made available on the National Crime Information Center. After receiving tips from Michigan, Colorado, and Florida, the aliases Lori Grody, Susan Blahovec, and Cammie Marsh Greene were all linked to Aileen "Lee" Carol Wuornos. The investigation allowed the police to pinpoint her location and develop a relatively seamless plan for bringing her into custody.

The arrest

On January 5, 1991, the search for Aileen Wuornos was fully underway. Two undercover police officers, Mike Joyner and Dick Martin, posed as drug dealers from Georgia named "Bucket" and "Drums". On January 8, they hung out with Wuornos at the Port Orange Pub and then later met her at the Last Resort, a biker bar, nearby. She spent what would be her last night as a free woman sleeping on an old car seat in the Last Resort.

On the afternoon of January 9, the decision was made to arrest Wuornos. Wearing transmitters to keep the police aware of the entire discourse, Joyner and Martin as "Bucket" and "Drums" again met up with Wuornos at the Last Resort biker bar. Because bikers would be arriving shortly for a barbeque at the bar, police sped up matters. Wuornos accepted an offer from "Bucket" and "Drums" to go back to their motel and wash up, and they left the bar together. It was at this point that Volusia County police arrested her on the outstanding warrant of Lori Grody. The police intentionally left out all information pertaining to the murders and did not allow the media to be privy to the arrest of a suspect. They were cautious because they did not have a murder weapon or Wuornos's lesbian partner, Tyria Moore. The police were developing their case.

Confession

The police tracked Tyria Moore down the next day on January 10 at her sister's residence in Pittston, Pennsylvania. Jerry Thompson of Citrus County, Florida and Bruce Munster of Marion County, Florida flew in to Pennsylvania to interview Moore. She was read her rights and sworn in. At this point Moore was not charged with anything, but Munster made sure she knew what perjury was to compel her to tell the whole truth. Moore stated that from the beginning she knew about the murders, starting when Wuornos came home with Richard Mallory's Cadillac. Wuornos openly confessed to murdering him, but Moore did not want Wuornos to talk about it. As the murders continued, Moore asked Wuornos not to tell her the details of her crimes. She reasoned that if she knew the full extent of what Wuornos did, she would feel obligated to turn Wuornos in to authorities. Moore did not want to jeopardize her own safety since Wuornos was more physically capable than her, despite Wuornos telling her that she would never hurt her.

Moore joined Munster and Thompson on their flight back to Florida to continue the investigation. The police wanted a confession from Wuornos to make their case airtight, and they needed Moore to accomplish that. Munster and Thompson explained to her that she would contact Wuornos in jail from a Daytona motel, saying that she came down to Florida with money from her mother to gather the remainder of her belongings. Investigators would tape Moore's phone conversations with Wuornos in which she was instructed to say that the authorities had been asking her family many questions and that she thought that Florida authorities would charge her, Moore, with the murders. This was supposed to provoke Wuornos to confess to Moore out of genuine concern and devotion to her.

Moore talked to Wuornos in jail on January 14–16, telling of her worries about the police falsely linking the murders to her. At this time Wuornos still believed that she was only in jail for the weapons violation on Lori Grody, one of her aliases. She at first did not divulge any information that would reveal that she murdered the men found along Florida highways because she knew that the phones in the jail were monitored. Patience and persistence would pay off for investigators. On January 16, 1991, Wuornos confessed to the murders so that Moore would not be implicated.

Her stance

Though she gave a full confession, she portrayed herself in a positive light, saying that she killed all the men in self-defense. Wuornos emphasized that each of her victims had threatened, assaulted, or raped her. She was careful not to incriminate herself, going to lengths to construe every detail in her favor. She told the police that she had been raped on numerous occasions in the past, and that she did not want it to happen again. Wuornos also said that fear motivated her to kill the men when they showed belligerence. Her confession, however, seem ridiculous to Michael O'Neill, the public defender, and the police officers who were present.

When the media heard about her story, book and movie offers began pouring in. Wuornos felt like a star and was confident in telling her version of what happened to anyone who would listen.

An unlikely defender

Amid all the frenzy, Wuornos would get a third chance at having a mother. Arlene Pralle and her husband read about Aileen's story in the newspaper and felt a special connection to her. After two and a half weeks of prayer, Arlene Pralle, a forty-four year old Christian, wrote Wuornos in jail and explained that Jesus Christ had told her to do so. Pralle allegedly said that Aileen asked God when she was arrested to send a Christian woman into her life to show her love. If that was true, then Aileen got her wish. Pralle gave Wuornos her contact information, and they communicated via telephone and letters. Their relationship became close very quickly; Pralle gave her advice and spoke well of her to the media. On November 22, 1991, Arlene Pralle and her husband legally adopted Aileen Wuornos at, what Pralle asserted, was the command of God. Arlene Pralle's ulterior motives and true intentions would surface later on after Aileen was convicted of murder and sentenced to death many times over.

The trial for the murder of Richard Mallory

The trial for the murder of Richard Mallory, the first of the seven men that Aileen Wuornos is known to have killed, began on January 14, 1992. From the beginning, the evidence and witnesses against Aileen Wuornos seemed to seal her fate, leading unequivocally to her guilt. The medical examiner who had done the autopsy on Richard Mallory testified that Mallory had taken ten to twenty minutes to die, showing that it was a particularly slow and torturous death. Tyria Moore, Wuornos's ex-lover, stated that Wuornos appeared obviously anxious, upset, and intoxicated when she told her that she killed Mallory. Twelve men came forward and testified that they had encountered her along Florida's highways in the past.

The Williams Rule made the case against Aileen Wuornos exponentially more damaging. The Williams Rule was a Florida law that allowed evidence from other crimes to be admitted if it aids in showing a pattern of behavior. Along with the murder of Mallory, the jury was made aware of the murders of six more men. Including her videotaped confession of the murders, the additional information made Wuornos's claim of self-defense totally implausible.

Against the advice of her public defenders, Wuornos took the stand to tell her side of the story. At this point in the trial, her version of events had changed considerably from her initial taped confession. She now claimed that Mallory had raped, sodomized, and tortured her. During her cross-examination, any credibility that she may have had was destroyed. Twenty-five times, she invoked her Fifth Amendment privilege against self-incrimination. She was the only witness for the defense, and her testimony ended up being quite detrimental to her case.

Guilty of murder

In less than two hours, the jury found Aileen Wuornos guilty of first-degree murder on January 27, 1992. Wuornos was furious and verbally expressed her rage to the jury. During the penalty phase of her trial, psychologists who testified on behalf of the defense said that Wuornos was mentally ill, suffering from borderline personality disorder. They also pointed to her unfortunate, torturous childhood as the precursor for her later trouble-ridden, destructive life. Tricia Jenkins, one of Wuornos's public defenders, pleaded with the jury not to give her the death penalty. Despite the efforts of the defense, the jury unanimously recommended to the judge that he sentence Wuornos to die via the electric chair. On January 31, 1992, he sentenced Wuornos to die via electrocution for the murder of Richard Mallory.

A poor defense

Aileen's public defenders were criticized for not making the court aware of the fact that Richard Mallory had served ten years for attempted rape. This would have bolstered Aileen's testimony of her violent sexual encounter with Richard Mallory, which was particularly graphic. Her testimony was so detailed and convincing that many people believed it. Aileen testified that Richard Mallory had violent anal sex and vaginal sex using rubbing alcohol and Visine eye drops in her rectum, vagina, and mouth. She also said he got a thrill out of her crying and screaming. Aileen stated on the stand that in an attempt to protect herself, she shot him two times with her pistol.

If her public defenders had entered into evidence Richard Mallory's sexually violent past, combined with her believable testimony, then perhaps it would have resulted in her receiving something short of the death sentence.

A new lawyer

With the advice of her new adoptive mother Arlene Pralle, Aileen fired her public defenders and hired Steven P. Glazer, or Dr. Legal as his television commercial called him. He did not prove to be any more experienced or helpful than her previous lawyers, and he was criticized for it. Arlene and Steve convinced Aileen to plead no contest to her other murder charges. Arlene said it was the Christian thing to do so that she could get right with God. Steve told her that if she did not plead no contest, which is essentially the same thing as pleading guilty, that he would be forced to resign as her lawyer because he did not have the knowledge or resources to put together a full defense if it went to trial.

More death sentences

Aileen heeded their advice. On March 31, 1992 she expressed a desire to clear her conscience and therefore pleaded no contest to the murders of David Spears, Troy Burress, and Dick Humphreys. She declared that Richard Mallory, her first victim, did in fact rape her but that the other men never had the chance to do so. She was then given her second, third, and fourth death sentences.

In June 1992, she pleaded guilty to the murder of Charles Carskaddon, and in November 1992, she was given her fifth death sentence. In February 1993, she pleaded guilty to the murder of Walter Gino Antonio and was given her sixth death sentence. As for her seventh victim, Peter Siems, his body was never recovered, so no charges were ever brought against Wuornos for his murder.

After she was given her six death sentences, new evidence surfaced, revealing that Richard Mallory, her first victim, had served ten years in prison for sexual violence. With this new evidence, Wuornos's attorneys felt that she should receive a new trial for the murder of Richard Mallory because the jurors would view the case in a different light. As stated earlier, Wuornos was never granted a second trial. The State Supreme Court of Florida affirmed her six death sentences.

Declining psychological state of mind

Anyone who knew or observed Aileen could see that she was psychologically unstable to some degree, whether she was born that way or whether her overall negative life contributed to it. In interviews conducted with Nick Broomfield, the director of the two documentaries about her, her psychological condition was apparent and it noticeably declined throughout her time on death row in prison. She had paranoid delusions that her mind was being controlled by radio waves beamed into her cell on death row. Her lawyers challenged her execution on the grounds that she was not mentally competent, but it was to no avail. A final example of her declining psychological state arose in her last interview, when she said that someone had been using sonic pressure on her head in her cell since 1997, and the pressure would be turned up every time she wanted to write something. She also thought the television or the mirror in her cell was rigged. She said that the continual increase of sonic pressure, harassment, and inedible food was all concocted against her so that people would believe she was crazy and therefore would not believe anything she had to say.

Her execution

In 2001, Wuornos began to seek an expedited execution. She petitioned the Florida Supreme Court for the right to fire her lawyers and for all appeals to cease. She also petitioned to get the form of execution changed from the electric chair to lethal injection. The Florida Supreme Court granted both of her petitions. Wuornos was clearly mentally unstable on some level, so Governor Jeb Bush ordered a stay of execution so she could be given a mental exam. Three psychiatrists interviewed Wuornos and concluded that she fully comprehended that she was going to die and understood completely the reasons for her impending execution. As a result, Governor Jeb Bush lifted the stay of execution during the first week of October 2002.

At 9:47 a.m. on Wednesday, October 9, 2002, Aileen Wuornos, 46, was executed by lethal injection at Florida State Prison near Starke, Florida. She became the tenth woman in the United States and the second woman in Florida to be executed since the death penalty was reinstated in 1976. The execution of Aileen Wuornos was carried out in the midst of a fiery controversy over capital punishment.

One true friend

In the end it can only be said that Aileen had one true friend. Dawn, her best friend from childhood, was there for Aileen until her execution. Tyria Moore, Arlene Pralle, Steve Glazer, and all the others deserted Aileen eventually. Dawn and Aileen were pen pals throughout Aileen's ten-year stay on death row. Dawn said that she would get up at 5 a.m. every morning to write to her. The night before her execution, Dawn was her only personal visitor. When Aileen was executed, her ashes were spread on Dawn's property.

Media interest

The life, trial, and death of Aileen Wuornos garnered much publicity. It led to several works, including books, a made-for-television movie, two documentaries, and an acclaimed film titled *Monster*. Charlize Theron, who played Aileen Wuornos in *Monster*, was awarded the Academy Award for Best Actress in 2003.

Notes about sources

The information for the Aileen Wuornos case was drawn primarily from crimelibrary.com and the documentaries *Aileen Wuornos: The Selling of a Serial Killer* and *Aileen: Life and Death of a Serial Killer*.

Bibliography

Abbey, A., Clinton-Sherrod, A., McAuslan, P., Zawacki, T., and Buck, P. (2003). The relationship between the quantity of alcohol consumed and the severity of sexual assaults committed by college men. *Journal of Interpersonal Violence*, 18, 813–833.

Abouesh, A. and Clayton, A. (1999). Compulsive voyeurism and exhibitionism: A chemical response to paroxetine. *Archives of Sexual Behavior*, 28.

Abraham, Y. (1998), September 24–October 1. Life After Death. *Boston Phoenix*. Retrieved February 20, 2006. <http://www.bostonphoenix.com/archive/features/98/09/24/JEFFREY_CURLEY.html>

Addington v. Texas (1979). 441 U.S. 418.

Alberts v. California (1957). 354 U.S. 476.

Alexander, D. The Bernie Baran story. *Choir Boy Regime*. Retrieved October 19, 2005. <http://www.choirboyregime.com/baran.html>

Alexander, R., Jr. (1997). Reconstructing sex offenders as mentally ill: A labeling explanation. *Journal of Sociology and Social Welfare*, 25, 65–76.

All about ECT. Med Help International. Retrieved January 9, 2006. <http://www.medhelp.org/lib/ect.htm>

American Civil Liberties Union (1996), August 19. Brief of *amicus curiae* for Hendricks. *Kansas v. Hendricks*.

American Civil Liberties Union (2002), March 1. Freedom of expression. Retrieved February 20, 2006. <http://www.aclu.org/natsec/gen/12472res20020301.html>

American Library Association v. Reno (1994). 33 F.3d 78.

207

American Psychiatric Association (1994). *Diagnostic and statistical manual of mental disorders* (4th Ed.). DSM-IV. Washington, D.C.: American Psychiatric Association.

American Psychiatric Association (1996), August 16. Brief of *amicus curiae* for Hendricks. *Kansas v. Hendricks.*

Analysis for the Homeland Security Act of 2002. (2002). White House. Retrieved February 18, 2006.
<http://www.whitehouse.gov/deptofhomeland/analysis/>

Andrews, S. (2005), August 11. Curley family: NAMBLA paying killer. *Cambridge Chronicle.*

Andriette, B. (1999), January. America's sex gulags. *Guide.* Retrieved February 18, 2006.
<http://www.guidemag.
com/magcontent/invokemagcontent.cfm?ID=E6B2CF88-031D-11D4-
AD990050DA7E046B&Method=GuideFullDisplay>.

An erosion of due process (1997), June 26. *Boston Globe*, A22.

Ashcroft v. Free Speech Coalition (2002). 535 U.S. 234.

Assault on Common Sense (2000), July 27–August 2. *Boston Phoenix.* Retrieved February 20, 2006. <http://www.bostonphoenix.com/archive/features/00/07/27/
EDITORIAL.html>

Associated Press (1994), August 1. Man charged in 7-year-old neighbor's killing. *New York Times*, B5.

Associated Press (2005), July 30. States track sex offenders by GPS. *Wired News.* Retrieved February 18, 2006.
<http://www.wired.com/news/technology/0,1282,68372,00.html?tw=rss.POL>

Association for the Treatment of Sexual Abusers (2001). Civil commitment of sexually violent offenders. Retrieved February 18, 2006.
<http://www.atsa.com/ppcivilcommit.html>

Attorney General's Commission on Pornography: Final report. (1986). Washington, D.C.: U.S. Department of Justice.

Baro, M. (1997), May 8. Medical, legal experts debate merits of castration bill. Associated Press. In *Abilene Reporter-News*. Retrieved February 20, 2006. <http://www.texnews.com/texas97/ouch050897.html>

Bartley, N., Harris, C., and Clarridge, C. (1998), January 7. Letourneau's freedom restricted: Former Highline teacher begins 3-year treatment as sex offender. *Seattle Times*, B1.

Bartol, C. and Bartol, A. (2004). *Psychology and law: Theory, research, and application* (3rd Ed.). Belmont, CA: Wadsworth.

Bass, E. and Davis, L. (1988). *The Courage to heal*. New York: Harper and Row.

Bell, R. Michael Bruce Ross: Staring death in the face. Retrieved February 18, 2006. <http://www.crimelibrary.com/serial_killers/predators/michael_ross/index.html>

Berman, D., Lock, C., Rainey, R., and Taub, L. (2004), June 18–24. The trials of Bernard Baran. *The Boston Phoenix*. Retrieved February 20, 2006. <http://www.bostonphoenix. com/boston/news_features/top/features/documents/03917095.asp>

Berman, D. Rainey, R., and Taub, L. (2004), June 25–July 1. Undoing injustice. *The Boston Phoenix*. Retrieved February 20, 2006. <http://www.bostonphoenix. com/boston/news_features/other_stories/documents/03936949.asp>

Birkland, D. and Brown, C. (1998), February 3. Letourneau arrested again: Ex-teacher found in car with youth she had raped. *Seattle Times*, A1.

Biskupic, J. (1997), November 27. Justices to rule on "decency" standards for arts funding: 1990 law on NEA grants in dispute; Case on Disabilities Act and HIV also accepted. *Washington Post*, A4.

Bivins, T. (1997). Voluntary castration for sex offenders—S.B. 123 (1997). Highlights of the 75th Texas State Legislature. Retrieved October 31, 2005. <http://www.senate.state.tx.us/SRC/75HiLite/Sec3.htm>

Blenkinsopp, A. (2005). Honesty v. expedience: The deficient jurisprudence of punishment and the legal labeling game. Unpublished thesis. Social Studies. Harvard University.

Boston Globe (2003). *Betrayal: The crisis in the Catholic Church.* Boston: Back Bay Books.

Boston Globe Staff (2003). Geoghan's troubled history. Retrieved October 12, 2005.
<http://www.bishop-accountability.org/service-records/service-archive/Geoghan-John-J-History.htm>

Bottoms, B., Shaver, P., and Goodman, G. (1991). Profile of ritualistic and religion-related abuse allegation reported to clinical psychologists in the United States. Paper presented in the 99th Annual Convention of the American Psychological Association, San Francisco.

Bowman, L. (2001), March 9. Firm defends "Snooper Bowl" technology. *CNET News.* Retrieved February 20, 2006.
<http://news.com.com/Firm+defends+snooper+bowl+technology/2100-1023_3-253884.html>

Brailey, D. (2003), April 8. The prosecution of a false memory: An update on the Ingram case. Retrieved November 11, 2005.
<http://members.aol.com/IngramOrg>

Brewer, K. (2005), May 24. New 2257 regulations: "Yes, they are going to change the way this business is conducted." *AVN Online.* Retrieved November 10, 2005.
<http://www.avnonline.com/
index.php?Primary_Navigation=Web_Exclusive_Features&Action=View_Article&Content_ID=227704>

Brooke, S. (2004). Is cyber peeping causing future shock? *Expository Magazine*, 4.

Broom, J. (1998), February 7. Letourneau's failure not a surprise; she resisted therapy officials say. *Seattle Times*, A1.

Broom, J. and Bartley, N. (1998), February 6. Letourneau appeared ready to flee; she gets 7 ½ years; vehicle contained passport, $6000, baby clothes; and her rape victim. *Seattle Times*, A1.

Broomfield, N. (Director). (1992). *Aileen Wuornos: The selling of a serial killer.* Lafayette Films.

Broomfield, N. and Churchill, J. (Directors). (2002). *Aileen Wuornos: Life and death of a serial killer*. Lafayette Films.

Brown, L. (1999), November 10. Sicari's friend killed boy, lawyer argues. *Daily Free Press* (Boston University). Retrieved February 20, 2006. <http://www.dailyfreepress.com/media/paper87/DFPArchive/cityscope/1110982.cfm>

Brown U. settles 2-year-old date-rape dispute. (1998), January 9. *The Chronicle of Higher Education*.

Brownmiller, S. (1975). *Against Our Will: Men, Women, and Rape*. New York: Simon and Schuster.

Burge, K. (2003), September 27. Geoghan ruling sparks anger: Alleged victims protest erasure of conviction. *Boston Globe*, B1.

Burgess, A. and Holmstrom, L. (1974). Rape trauma syndrome, 133, 981–986.

Bush, G. (2000). Question of the day. *Web White & Blue*. Retrieved October 31, 2005. <http://www.markle.org/markle_programs/program_highlights/policy_for_a_networked_society/public_engagement/web_white_blue/debate/2000-10-13/bush/question/>

Can pedophiles be treated? (2005). *Why Files*. Retrieved January 9, 2006. <http://www.whyfiles.org/154pedophile/3.html>

Care, treatment and rehabilitation of sexually dangerous persons: Definitions. Massachusetts General Laws, Chapter 123A: Section 1.

Ceci, S. and Bruck, M. (1995) *Jeopardy in the courtroom: A scientific analysis of children's testimony*. Washington, D.C.: American Psychological Association.

Center for Sex Offender Management. An overview of sex-offender treatment for a non-clinical audience: A training curriculum. Retrieved January 9, 2006. <http://www.csom.org/train/treatment/index.html>

Center for Sex Offender Management (2000). Myths and facts about sex offenders. Retrieved February 18, 2006. <http://www.csom.org/pubs/mythsfacts.html>

Center for Sex Offender Management (2001). Recidivism of sex offenders. Retrieved February 18, 2006. <http://www.csom.org/pubs/recidsexof.html>

Chatelle, B. Help us free Bernard Baran! Retrieved October 19, 2005. <www.freebaran.org>

Chatelle, B. Bernard Baran: The first day care conviction. Retrieved October 19, 2005. <http://www.justicedenied.org/bernie.htm>

Clarke, K. (2003), November. Double jeopardy: Thousands of crimes go unreported because they happen behind prison bars. Why? *U.S. Catholic*, 40.

Clements, D. (1997), July. From the president. *Voice of Justice*. Retrieved February 20, 2006. <http://www.jfa.net/VOJ/July97.html>

CNN (1996a), April 2. Pedophile warns he will strike again. Retrieved October 31, 2005. <http://www.cnn.com/US/9604/02/child_molester/index.html>

CNN (1996b), April 8. Molester faces lock-and-key parole. CNN.com. Retrieved October 31, 2005. <http://www.cnn.com/US/9604/08/molester/>

Coastal United Fetish Society—Maine (2001), October. Paddleboro is over! Ben Davis is found not guilty! *CUFSmaine Newsletter*. Retrieved January 1, 2006. <http://www.cufsmaine.org/newslett9.htm>

Cocca, C. (2004). *Jailbait: The politics of statutory rape laws in the United States*. New York: State University of New York.

Coe, C. (2003). Lady Godiva: The naked truth. *Harvard Magazine*, 105. Retrieved February 20, 2006. <http://www.harvard-magazine.com/on-line/070377.html>

Cohen, G. Mandatory supervision. Cohen Law Firm. Retrieved October 31, 2005. <http://www.parolelaw.com/MandatorySupervision.htm>

Commitment and retention of dangerous persons. *Massachusetts General Laws*, Chapter 123: Section 7.

Commitment of alcoholics or substance abusers. *Massachusetts General Laws*, Chapter 123: Section 35.

Commitment of sexually violent predators. *Kansas Statutes Annotated*, Chapter 59: Article 29.

Connection Distributing Co. v. Reno (1998). 154 F.3d 281.

Corbett, R., and Fersch, E. (1985). Home as prison: The use of house arrest. *Federal Probation*, 49, 13–17.

Crimes against chastity, morality, decency and good order. *Massachusetts General Laws*, Chapter 272: Section 24.

Criminal History Systems Board of Massachusetts (2004). Sex offender registry board: Registration, classification and dissemination. Retrieved February 18, 2006. <http://www.mass.gov/Eeops/docs/sorb/sor_regulations.pdf>

Crowe, R. (2005), May 10. Expert: Castration no cure for pedophilia; Drugs, surgery may temper drive, but sexual interest won't "normalize." *Houston Chronicle*, B1.

Curtis, K. (2003), January 8. California "loses" 33,000 sex offenders. *CBS News*. Retrieved February 18, 2006.
<http://www.cbsnews.com/stories/2003/01/08/national/main535654.shtml>

Davis, K. (2000), October 18. Cornell alumnus arraigned for 1982 murder of girl. *Cornell Daily Sun*. Retrieved February 18, 2006.
<http://www.cornellsun.
com/media/paper866/news/2000/10/18/News/Cornell.
Alumnus.Arraigned.For.1982.Murder.Of.Girl-1324145.shtml>

Davison, G., Neale, J., and Kring, A. (2004). *Abnormal psychology* (9th Ed.). Hoboken, NJ: Wiley.

Dean, S. (1997), April. Taking the stand: Who should decide the consequences of students' bad behavior? Increasingly, committees such as Brown's disciplinary council are going on trial themselves. *Brown Alumni Magazine*.

Defense: Self-defense: Tennessee criminal pattern jury instructions, Section 40.06. Retrieved February 18, 2006.
<http://www.tncrimlaw.com/TPI_Crim/40_06.htm>

Dembner, A. (1997), May 18. Disciplinary boards attacked from both sides. *Boston Globe*, A27.

Dershowitz, A. (1969), February. The psychiatrist's power in civil commitment: A knife that cuts both ways. *Psychology Today*, 2, 43–47.

Disorder Information Sheet: Voyeurism. *Psychnet-UK*. Retrieved November 3, 2005. <http://www.psychnet-uk.com/dsm_iv/voyerism_disorder.htm>

Donner, M. (alias) (2005), October 16. Interview by C. Watts-Fitzgerald with a dominant on Bondage Discipline Sado Masochism culture and practices.

Donnerstein, E. and Berkowitz, L. (1981). Victim reactions in aggressive erotic films as a factor in violence against women. *Journal of Personality and Social Psychology*, 41, 710–724.

Dowd, M. (1999). The "battered women's defense": Its history and its future. *FindLaw.com*. Retrieved February 18, 2006.
<http://library.findlaw.com/1999/Dec/1/130513.html>

Drug Policy Alliance. (2002). Personal liberties and the war on drugs. Retrieved November 15, 2005.
<http://www.drugpolicy.org/library/factsheets/personallibe/fact_liberties.cfm>

Elliott, M. (1996), April 29. Michael Ross: Why a killer offers to die. *Connecticut Law Tribune*. Retrieved February 18, 2006.
<http://www.courttv.com/archive/map/library/capital/special.html>

Emery, T. (2003), August 27. Geoghan killing could void conviction. *Associated Press*.

Ennis, B. and Litwack, T. (1974). Psychiatry and the presumption of expertise: Flipping coins in the courtroom. *California Law Review*, 62, 693–752.

Facts about sexual harassment. (2002). U.S. Equal Employment Opportunity Commission. Retrieved February 18, 2006.
<http://www.eeoc.gov/facts/fs-sex.html>

Farragher, T. (2002), September 20. Settlement doesn't heal victims' hearts: After Geoghan case, victims feel defeat. *Boston Globe*, A1.

Feinsten, S. Castration works. *212.net.* Retrieved January 9, 2006. <http://www.212.net/crime/castrate.htm>

Feister, J. (2002), May 31. Editorial: Clergy sexual abuse: Put children first. *St. Anthony Messenger*, 23.

Fersch, E. (1970). The relation between students' experience with restricted-access erotic materials and their behaviors and attitudes. In *Report of the President's Commission on Obscenity and Pornography*, 153–156, 167. Washington, D.C.: U.S. Government Printing Office.

Fersch, E. (1971). Don't ask. *Yale Magazine*, 34, 28–29.

Fersch, E. (1974). Court clinic treatment in Massachusetts: Mental health care v. civil rights. *International Journal of Offender Therapy and Comparative Criminology*, 18, 275–282.

Fersch, E. (1975). When to punish, when to rehabilitate. *American Bar Association Journal*, 61, 1235–1237.

Fersch, E. (1976). The approach of a Massachusetts court clinic in the probate court. *International Journal of Offender Therapy and Comparative Criminology*, 20, 178–182.

Fersch, E. (1979). *Law, psychology, and the courts.* Springfield, IL: Charles C Thomas.

Fersch, E. (1980). Ethical issues for psychologists in court settings. In Monahan, J. (Ed.), *Who is the Client?*, 43–62. Washington, D.C.: American Psychological Association.

Fersch, E. (1980). *Psychology and psychiatry in courts and corrections.* New York: John Wiley & Sons.

Fersch, E. (1982), November 22. Guilty but mentally ill? *The Harvard Crimson.*

Fersch, E. (1982). Law and psychiatry. *International Journal of Offender Therapy and Comparative Criminology*, 26, 157–175.

Fersch, E. (2005). *Thinking about the insanity defense.* Lincoln, NE: iUniverse.

Fersch, E., Goldfine, P., and Vrabel, J. (1978). The need for sanctuary from the community. *International Journal of Offender Therapy and Comparative Criminology*, 22, 68–79.

Fikac, P. (1997), April 15. Senate passes surgical castration bill. Associated Press. In *Abilene Reporter-News*. Retrieved February 20, 2006. <http://www.texnews.com/texas97/cast041597.html>

Fisher, B., Cullen, F., and Turner, M. (2000). The sexual victimization of college women. *U.S. Department of Justice, Office of Justice Programs*. Retrieved February 18, 2006. <http://www.ncjrs.org/pdffiles1/nij/182369.pdf>

Fisher, W. (1994). Violent pornography, antiwoman thoughts, and antiwoman acts: In search of reliable effects. *Journal of Sex Research*, 31, 23–38.

Fitten, R. (1997a), March 4. Teacher bad sex with boy, charges say. *Seattle Times*, B1.

Fitten, R. (1997b), July 18. Teacher says she'll plead guilty to child rape: 35 year old had sex with 13-year-old boy. *Seattle Times*, B1.

Fitten, R. (1997c), July 25. Burien teacher's sex with student leaves lives and trust shattered: Prison possible but she hopes to raise the 14-year-old's baby. *Seattle Times*, A1.

Fitten, R. (1997d), August 11. Teacher's dad had affair, too: Conservative politician lost career. *Seattle Times*, B1.

Fitten, R. (1997e), November 14. Teacher won't go to prison for rape: She gets 80 days in jail followed by treatment. *Seattle Times*, A1.

Fitten, R. (2002), May 21. Jury rejects negligence claim by Vili Fualauu. *Seattle Times*, A1.

Flanagan, A. Attitudes to sex and sexuality. *About.com*. Retrieved January 6, 2006. <http://buddhism.about.com/cs/ethics/a/Sexuality.htm>

Fleshbot. (2005). Retrieved October 10, 2005. <http://www.fleshbot.com>

Forstein, M. (2004). The pseudoscience of sexual orientation change therapy: An "old" problem with relevance today. *British Medical Journal*. Retrieved January 9, 2006. <http://bmj.bmjjournals.com/cgi/content/full/328/7445/E287>

Foster, J. (2000), June 9. Kids, sex, the Internet: ISP for child-molesters' website targeted in wrongful-death suit. *WorldNetDaily*. Retrieved October 1, 2005. <http://www.worldnetdaily.com/news/article.asp?ARTICLE ID=17905>

Foucault, M. (1978). *The history of sexuality*. New York: Vintage.

Fredrickson, R. (1992). *Repressed memories: A journey to recovery from sexual abuse*. New York: Simon & Schuster.

Free Speech Coalition, Inc. (2005). Retrieved November 15, 2005. <http://www.freespeechcoalition.com>

Fryer, A. (2000), April 14. Boy seeks damages in Letourneau rape case: $1 million or more may be sought. *Seattle Times*, A1.

Gawande, A. (1997), July 13. The unkindest cut. *Slate*. Retrieved February 18, 2006. <http://www.slate.com/id/2660>

Geoghan sentenced to maximum for molestation (2002), February 21. *NBC30.com*. Retrieved October 12, 2005. <http://www.nbc30.com/print/1245646/detail.html>

Giordano, K. (2000), March 1. The chemical knife: Will Tennessee be the next state to approve castration for sexoffenders? *Salon.com*. Retrieved October 31, 2005. <http://www.salon.com/health/feature/2000/03/01/castration/>

Glaberson, W. (1997), May 29. Prosecutors in Megan case credit defense after editorial. *New York Times*, B4.

Glaser, B. (1998). Psychiatry and paedophilia: a major public health issue. *Australian and New Zealand Journal of Psychiatry*, 32, 162–167.

Gleitman, H., Fridlund, A., and Reisburg, D. (2003). *Psychology* (6th Ed.). New York: Norton.

Goldstein, D. (2004), May 31. He said, she can't remember: the Adam Lack case. *Brown Daily Herald*. Retrieved February 18, 2006.

<http://www.browndailyherald.com/media/paper472/news/2004/05/31/
Commencement2004/He.Said.She.Cant.Remember.The.Adam.Lack.
Case-726506.shtml>

Goldstein, M. (2000), November 2. Prosecutor defends police handling of sado-masochist party. *Providence Journal*, B3.

Goldstein, M. (2001), March 27. Attleboro S&M party detective: Suspicion of prostitution led to arrests. *Providence Journal*, B1.

Greenfield, P. (2004). Inadvertent exposure to pornography on the Internet: Implications of peer-to-peer file-sharing networks for child development and families. *Journal of Applied Developmental Psychology*, 25, 741–750.

Greer, C. (2003). *Sex Crime and the media: Sex offending and the press in a divided society.* Portland, OR: Willan.

Grob, G. (1994). *The mad among us: A history of the care of America's mentally ill.* New York: Free.

Hanna, C. (2001). Sex is not a sport: consent and violence in criminal law. *Boston College Law Review*, 42, 239–290.

Harris, A. (2005). *Civil commitment of sexual predators: A study in policy imple-mentation.* New York: LFB Scholarly Publishing.

Hennessey, R. (1994). July 31. Murdered girl found. *Princeton Metro: The Times.*

Herek, G. Attempts to change sexual orientation. Retrieved January 9, 2006. <http://psychology.ucdavis.edu/rainbow/html/facts_changing.html>

Herman, S. (2005). Rape (law). *Microsoft Encarta Online Encyclopedia 2005.* Microsoft Corporation.

Hethcock, B. and Correll, D. (2005), September 26. A lifetime of supervision. *Gazette.* Retrieved December 13, 2005. <http://www.gazette.com/display.php?secid=27>

Hibbert, M. (1999). DNA databanks: Law enforcement's greatest surveillance tool? *Wake Forest Law Review*, 34, 767–825.

Hider, J. (2005), July 28. Muslim veil descends on Iraqi women. *Australian*.

Higgins, M. (1999). Acid test: DNA databases help nail slippery criminals, but their potential uses make privacy advocates nervous when it comes to arrestees and ordinary citizens. *American Bar Association Journal*, 85, 64.

Hilgers, J. (1910). Index of prohibited books. *The Catholic Encyclopedia* (Vol. VII), online edition. Retrieved February 20, 2006.
<http://www.newadvent.org/cathen/07721a.htm>

Hoffman, J. (1994), August 4. New law is urged on freed sex offenders. *New York Times*, B1.

Holmes, R. and Holmes, S. (2002). *Current perspectives on sex crimes*. Thousand Oaks, CA: Sage.

Howe, A. (1998). *Sexed crime in the news*. Sydney: Federation.

Hucker, S. (2005). Psychiatric aspects of risk assessment. *PsychDirect*. Retrieved February 18, 2006.
<http://www.psychdirect.com/forensic/Criminology/risk/riskassess.htm>

Hyman, I. and Billings, F. (1998). Individual differences and the creation of false childhood memories. *Memory*, 6, 1–20.

In re Hendricks (1996). 259 Kan. 246.

In re P.S. (1997). 167 Vt. 63.

Inspection of Records Relating to Depiction of Sexually Explicit Performances. *Code of Federal Regulations*, Title 28: Part 75.5.

Irons, P. (2005). *Cases and controversies: Civil rights and liberties in context*. Upper Saddle River, NJ: Pearson Prentice Hall.

Jackson v. Indiana (1972). 406 U.S. 715.

Janus, E. (2000). Sexual predator commitment laws: Lessons for law and the behavioral sciences. *Behavioral Sciences and the Law*, 18, 5–21.

Johns, C. Civil commitment for sexual predators. Retrieved February 18, 2006.
<http://www.cjjohns.com/c_law/civil_sexual.html>

Johnson, G. (1997), October 7. Death penalty unlikely for boy's killers. Associated Press. In *SouthCoastToday.com*. Retrieved February 20, 2006. <http://www.southcoasttoday.com/daily/10-97/10-07-97/a01sr002.htm>

Johnson, T. (2002), September 20. Filming up women's skirts is ruled legal: Law doesn't ban voyeurism in court, Supreme Court says. *Seattle Post-Intelligencer*, A1.

Jones v. United States (1983). 463 U.S. 354.

Josephson, D. (1998), March 20. Unfinished business at Brown: The settlement of the Lack case. *Providence Journal-Bulletin*, 6B.

Justice for Women. Battered women's syndrome: Help or hindrance? Retrieved October 27, 2005. <http://www.jfw.org.uk/BWS.HTM>

Just the facts about sexual orientation & youth: A primer for principals, educators and school personnel. (2006). *American Psychological Association*. Retrieved February 18, 2006. <http://www.apa.org/pi/lgbc/publications/justthefacts.html>

Kansas v. Crane (2002). 534 U.S. 407.

Kansas v. Hendricks (1997). 521 U.S. 346.

Kennedy, D. (2001), June 28–July 5. The fourth annual Muzzle Awards: Ten who undermined freedom of speech and personal liberties: Attleboro Police. *Boston Phoenix*. Retrieved February 20, 2006. <http://www.bostonphoenix. com/boston/news_features/top/features/documents/01692185.htm>

Ko, M. (1997), March 4. Judge lifts no-contact order. *Seattle Times*, B1.

Ko, M. (2004), August 4. Letourneau release from prison due today: Child rape term ends; Victim, now 21, unsure of his feelings. *Seattle Times*, B1.

Krauthammer, C. (1996), December 13. Throw away the key. *Washington Post*, A23.

Kutchinsky, B. (1991). Pornography and rape: Theory and practice? Evidence from crime data in four countries where pornography is easily available. *International Journal of Law and Psychiatry*, 14, 47–64.

Lalumiere, M., Harris, G., Quinsey, V., and Rice, M. (2005). *The causes of rape: Understanding individual differences in male propensity for sexual aggression.* Washington, D.C.: American Psychiatric Association.

Landry, P. and Lutton, C. (1994), August 1. After a child is killed, shock and calls for action. *Philadelphia Inquirer.*

Langevin, R. and Lang, R. (1985). Psychological treatment of pedophiles. *Behavioral Science & the Law*, 3, 403–419.

Larson, A. (2003). Megan's law. *ExpertLaw*. Retrieved February 18, 2006. <http://www.expertlaw.com/library/criminal/megans_law.html>

Lavoie, D. (2004), February 3. Report: Defrocked priest, slain in prison, was wrongly placed in high security prison unit. *Associated Press.*

Lawrence v. Texas (2003). 539 U.S. 558.

Lee, R. and Crowe, R. (2005), May 4. Castrated pedophile begins work release: Prison officials say he'll be under watch at all times. *Houston Chronicle*, B1.

Lessard v. Schmidt (1972). 349 F.Supp. 1078.

Lewin, T. (1992), March 7. Texas court agrees to castration for rapist of 13-year-old girl. *New York Times*, 1.

Lieb, R. (1996). *Washington's sexually violent predator law: Legislative history and comparisons with other states.* Olympia, WA: Washington State Institute for Public Policy.

Lilienfeld, S. (2002). When worlds collide: Social science, politics, and the Rind et al (1998) child sexual abuse meta-analysis. *American Psychologist*, 57, 176–188.

Linz, D., Donnerstein, E., and Penrod, S. (1987). The findings and recommendations of the Attorney General's Commission on Pornography: Do the psychological "facts" fit the political fury? *American Psychologist*, 42, 946–953.

Loftus, E. and Ketcham, K. (1994). *The Myth of Repressed Memory*. New York: St. Martin's.

Loftus. E. (1993). The reality of repressed memories. *American Psychologist*, 48, 518–537.

Lotto, D. (1994). On witches and witch hunts: ritual and satanic cult abuse. *Journal of Psychohistory*, 21.

Lutton, C. (1994), August 2. Promise of puppy lured her to death. *Philadelphia Inquirer*.

MacKinnon, C. and Dworkin, A. (1997). *In harm's way: The pornography civil rights hearings.* Cambridge, MA: Harvard University Press.

MacLeod, M. Aileen Wuornos: Killer who preyed on truck drivers. *Court TV Crime Library.* Retrieved December 12, 2005.
<http://www.crimelibrary.com/notorious_murders/women/wuornos/>

Mahoney, P. (1998). The wife rape information page. Retrieved February 18, 2006. <http://www.wellesley.edu/WCW/projects/mrape.html>

Maibom, H. (2005). Moral unreason: The case of psychopathy. *Mind & Language*, 20, 237–257.

Manhood for chop (Editorial). (1997), May 17. *Economist*, 30.

Markam, J. (alias) (2006), October 16. Interview by C. Watts-Fitzgerald with submissive on masochism and submissiveness in a Bondage Discipline SadoMasochism relationship.

Mary Kay Letourneau preps for her wedding (2005), May 12. *ET Online.* Retrieved November 20, 2005. <http://et.tv.yahoo.com/celebrities/11259/>

McCloskey, R. (2005). *The American Supreme Court.* Chicago: University of Chicago.

McDermott, T. (1997), November 16. Letourneau, Billie: Similar cases but different outcomes. *Seattle Times*, B1.

McElroy, W. (2002), October 28. Battered women's syndrome: Science or sham? *Independent Institute.* Retrieved November 10, 2005.
<http://www.independent.org/newsroom/article.asp?id=11>

McGrath, C. (2005), September 24. Now at 50, "Lolita" still has power to unnerve. *New York Times*, B9.

McGuire, T. (2000). Correctional institution based sex offender treatment: A lapse behavior study. *Behavioral Sciences and the Law*, 18, 57–71.

McNulty, F. (1980). *The Burning Bed*. New York: Harcourt Brace Jovanovich.

McNulty, K. (2005), October 23–26. Personal communication with D. Musante.

McQuay, L. (1994), May. The case for castration, part 1: Punishment for sex offenses against children. *Washington Monthly*.

McShane, P. (2005), October 28. Personal communication with M. Gubbins.

McVicar, D. (1996), December 15. Brown's handling of sexual assault complaint splits campus: A disciplinary council punished a student for having sex with another student who may have been drunk, provoking a bitter debate. *Providence Journal Bulletin*, 1A.

McVicar, D. (1997a), January 30. 20/20 Vision? Tempest over sexual assault outdoor rally at Brown denigrates into rhetorical melee with TV reporter. *Providence Journal-Bulletin*, 1B.

McVicar, D. (1997b), February 8. Student sues Brown, accuser: He says sexual-misconduct case damaged his reputation. *Providence Journal-Bulletin*, 1A.

McVicar, D. (1998), January 1. Student settles suit with Brown, accuser; Adam Lack says he's been cleared of sexual misconduct in an incident in which he had sex with a student who was drunk. *Providence Journal-Bulletin*, 1A.

McVicker, S. (1995), August 24. The trouble with Larry. *Houston Press*. Retrieved February 20, 2006.
<http://www.houston-press.com/issues/1995-08-24/feature.html>

Megan's killer (1997), July 31. *Pittsburgh Post-Gazette*, A9.

Meloy, J. (2002). *The psychopathic mind: Origins, dynamics and treatment*. Northvale, NJ: Aronson.

Menzies, R., Webster, C., and Sepejak, D. (1985). The dimensions of dangerousness: Evaluating the accuracy of psychometric predictions of violence among forensic patients. *Law and Human Behavior*, 9, 49–70.

Metzl, J. (2004). Voyeur nation? Changing definitions of voyeurism, 1950–2004. *Harvard Review of Psychiatry*, 12.

Michigan Battered Women's Clemency Project. Clemency for battered women in Michigan: A manual for attorneys, law students and social workers. Retrieved February 18, 2006.
<http://www.umich.edu/~clemency/clemency_manual/manual_intro.html>

Miller, R. (1987). *Involuntary civil commitment of the mentally ill in the post-reform era*. Springfield, IL: Thomas.

Miller v. California (1973). 413 U.S. 15.

Mitchell, K., Finkelhor, D., and Wolak, J. (2003). The exposure of youth to unwanted sexual material on the internet: A national survey of risk, impact, and prevention. *Youth and Society*, 34, 330–358.

Mitchell, S. (2002). The psychoanalytic treatment of homosexuality. *Studies in Gender and Sexuality*, 3, 23–25.

Montoya v. Sibbett (2003). 2003 UT App 398.

Murder and rape of child made US legal history. (2000), August 7. *Herald* (Glasgow), 4.

Murdock, D. (2005). End it, don't mend it. *National Review Online*. Retrieved October 31, 2005.
<http://www.nationalreview.com/murdock/murdock200507070851.asp>

Nabokov, V. (1991). *Lolita*. New York: Vintage.

Nathan, D. and Snedeker, M. (1995). *Satan's silence*. New York: Basic.

National Association of State Mental Health Program Directors (1997). Position statement on laws providing for civil commitment of sexually violent criminal offenders. Retrieved February 18, 2006.
<http://www.nasmhpd.org/general_files/position_statement/sexpred.htm>

New England Leather Alliance (2000), July 21. Arrests in Attleboro information page. Retrieved October 12, 2005. <http://www.nelaonline.org/attleboro.html>

New Jersey closer to new Megan's law. (2000), December 19. *Realty Times*. Retrieved February 18, 2006. <http://realtytimes.com/rtcpages/20001219_njrule.htm>

Newton, M. (2000). *The encyclopedia of serial killers*. New York: Checkmark.

New York v. Ferber (1982). 458 U.S. 747.

N.J. Assembly passes sex-offender legislation. (1994), October 21. *Washington Post*, A2.

Norris, J. (1991). Social influence effects on responses to sexually explicit material containing violence. *Journal of Sex Research*, 28, 67–76.

Ockerbloom, J. (2005). Banned books online. *Online Books Page*. Retrieved November 15, 2005. <http://onlinebooks.library.upenn.edu/banned-books.html>

O'Conner, M. (2005), September 14. New 2257-related bill could spell big trouble for industry. *Xbiz*. Retrieved October 10, 2005. <http://www.xbiz.com/news_piece.php?id=10324>

O'Connor, T. (2001), October 23. Serial killer sentenced in death of Valley Central student. *The Times Herald-Record*. Retrieved February 18, 2006. <http://www.th-record.com/archive/2001/10/23/toross.htm>

O'Connor v. Donaldson (1975). 422 U.S. 563.

Odenberger, J. (2005). The Attorney General's changes to the Section 2257 regulations. *Xxxlaw*. Retrieved November 15, 2005. <http://my.execpc.com/~xxxlaw/2257Tables5.24.05.htm>

Ostrum, C. (1998), February 15. Bipolar disorder: valid excuse for Letourneau? *Seattle Times*, A1.

Palermo, G. and Farkas, M. (2001). *The dilemma of the sexual offender*. Springfield, IL: Thomas.

Parker, P. (2001a), June 28. Most charges dropped in S&M party hearing. *Providence Journal*, B1.

Parker, P. (2001b), September 25. Judge refuses to dismiss charge in Attleboro sex case. *Providence Journal*, C1.

Parkin, A. (1996). *Explorations in cognitive neuropsychology*. Oxford: Blackwell.

Pearman, B. (1998). Note: *Kansas v. Hendricks*: The Supreme Court's endorsement of sexually violent predator statutes unnecessarily expands state civil commitment power. *North Carolina Law Review*, 76, 1973–2015.

Petrunik, M. (1994). Models of dangerousness: A cross-jurisdictional review of dangerousness legislation and practice. Report for the Policy Branch, *Ministry of the Solicitor General of Canada*. Retrieved November 25, 2005.
<http://www.psepc-sppcc.gc.ca/publications/corrections/pdf/199402_e.pdf>

Pfeiffer, S. and Kurkjian, S. (2002), September 1. Rights of priests an issue at probes. *Boston Globe*. Retrieved February 18, 2006.
<http://www.boston.com/globe/spotlight/abuse/stories3/090102_priests.htm>

Pogrebin, M. (2004). *About criminals: A view of the offender's world*. Thousand Oaks, CA: Sage.

Poletiek, F. (2002). How psychiatrists and judges assess the dangerousness of persons with mental illness: An expertise bias. *Behavioral Sciences and the Law*, 20, 19–29.

Pollitt, K. (2000), February 21. Justice for Bernard Baran. *Nation*, 10.

Pollitt, K. (2003), July 14. Lost innocents. *Nation*, 9.

Pollock, B. (1998). Note: *Kansas v. Hendricks*: A workable standard for "mental illness" or a push down the slippery slope toward state abuse of civil commitment? *Arizona Law Review*, 40, 319–349.

Proceedings to commit dangerous persons. *Massachusetts General Laws*, Chapter 123: Section 8.

Prosecutor urges death for Megan's killer. (1997), June 10. *Milwaukee Journal Sentinel*, 8.

Rabinowitz, D. (2003). *No Crueler Tyrannies*. New York: Free Press.

Rapping, E. (2002). The politics of representation: Genre, gender violence and justice. *Genders*, 32. Retrieved November 2, 2005.
<http://www.genders.org/g32/g32_rapping.html>

Record keeping requirements. *U.S. Code*, Title 18: Section 2257.

Reilly, T. (2003). The sexual abuse of children in the Roman Catholic archdiocese of Boston: a report by the attorney general. Office of the Massachusetts Attorney General. Retrieved February 18, 2006.
<http://news.findlaw.com/hdocs/docs/abuse/maag72303abuserpt.pdf>

Reisner, R., Slobogin, C., and Rai, A. (1999). *Law and the mental health system: Civil and criminal aspects*. St. Paul, MN: West.

Reparative therapy (2004). *glbtq*. Retrieved January 9, 2006.
<http://www.glbtq.com/social-sciences/reparative_therapy.html>

Reparative therapy: idealized homosexuality. *Political Research Associates*. Retrieved January 9, 2006.
<http://www.publiceye.org/equality/x-gay/X-Gay-04.html>

Report of the President's Commission on Obscenity and Pornography. (1970). Washington, D.C.: U.S. Government Printing Office.

Right to counsel. (2005). *FindLaw*. Retrieved November 9, 2005.
<http://criminal.findlaw.com/crimes/criminal_rights/
criminal_rights_courtroom/right_to_counsel.html>

Rind, B., Bauserman, R., and Tromovich, P. (2000). Debunking the false allegation of "statistical abuse": A reply to Spiegel. *Sexuality and culture*, 4, 101.

Rind, B., Tromovich, P., and Bauserman, R. (1998). A meta-analytic examination of assumed properties of child sexual abuse using college samples. *Psychological Bulletin*, 124, 22–53.

Robbins, M. (1997), April 15. Bill approved for voluntary castration. Morris News Service. In *Lubbock Avalanche-Journal*. Retrieved February 20, 2006.
<http://www.lubbockonline.com/news/041597/bill.htm>

Rodriguez, E. (1996), December 2. Sex predators: Throwing away the key. *American Lawyer News Service.*

Rolde, E., Fersch, E., Kelly, F., Frank, S., and Guberman, M. (1973). A law enforcement training program in a mental health catchment area. *American Journal of Psychiatry* 130, 1002–1005.

Rolde, E., Fersch, E., Kelly, F., Frank, S., and Guberman, M. (1975). A law enforcement training program in a mental health catchment area. In Monahan, J. (Ed.), *Community mental health and the criminal justice system*, 82–86. New York: Pergamon.

Rollman, E. (1998). "Mental illness": A sexually violent predator is punished twice for one crime. *Journal of Criminal Law & Criminology*, 88, 985–1014.

Ross, M. (1999). It's time for me to die. *Whole Earth.*

Roth v. United States (1957). 354 U.S. 476.

Rothman, D. (2002). *The discovery of the asylum: Social order and disorder in the new republic.* New York: de Gruyter.

Rubenstein, K. (2001). Massachusetts v. Salvatore Sicari: "Molestation murder trial." *CourtTV.com.* Retrieved October 4, 2005.
<http://www.courttv.com/archive/verdicts/sicari.html>

Rules and Regulations. (2005). *Federal Register*, 70.

Salter, A. (2003). *Predators: Pedophiles, rapists, and other sex offenders: Who they are, how they operate, and how we can protect ourselves and our children.* New York: Basic.

Sandler, L. (2003), December 29. Women under siege. *Nation.* Retrieved February 18, 2006. <http://www.thenation.com/doc/20031229/sandler>

Santana, A. (1998), March 15. Imprisoned Letourneau is pregnant—former teacher who bore child by ex-student is expecting again. *Seattle Times*, A1.

Sapinsley, B. (1991). *The private war of Mrs. Packard.* New York: Paragon.

Schacter, D. (1996). The memory wars: Seeking truth in the line of fire. In *Searching for Memory* (pp. 248–279). New York: Basic Books.

Schacter, D. (2001). The sin of persistence. In *The Seven Sins of Memory* (pp. 161–183). Boston: Houghton Mifflin.

Schwartz, M. and DeKeseredy, W. (1997). *Sexual assault on the college campus: The role of male peer support*. London: Sage.

Sears, A. and Osten, C. (2005). *The ACLU v. America: Exposing the agenda to redefine moral values*. Nashville, TN: Broadman & Holman.

Sensible decision: Keep man locked up (1996), December 12. *Omaha World Herald*, 28.

Setup for a sham (1997), June 26. *St. Petersburg Times*, 18A.

Sex Weekly Plus. (1997), April 28. Provision of castration bill in Texas. Retrieved October 31, 2005. <http://www.newsrx.com/issue_article/SW/1997-04-28/199704283333SW.html>

Shapiro, F. (1997a). Two Strikes Law for Sex Offenders: S.B. 46. *Highlights of the 75th Texas State Legislature*. Retrieved October 31, 2005. <http://www.senate.state.tx.us/SRC/75HiLite/Sec3.htm>

Shapiro, F. (1997b). Sex Offender Registration Program: S.B. 875. *Highlights of the 75th Texas State Legislature*. Retrieved October 31, 2005. <http://www.senate.state.tx.us/SRC/75HiLite/Sec3.htm>

Skinner v. Oklahoma (1942). 316 U.S. 535.

Slobogin, K. (2001), January 7. Rights and wrongs. *CNN & Time*. Retrieved October 29, 2005. <http://transcripts.cnn.com/TRANSCRIPTS/0101/07/impc.00.html>

Slovenko, R. (1999). The mental disability requirement in the insanity defense. *Behavioral Sciences & the Law*, 17, 165–180.

Smith, M., & Prader, L. (1980). *Michelle remembers*. New York: St. Martin's.

Snyder, J. The Adam Lack sexual misconduct case. *Brown University ACLU.* Retrieved February 18, 2006.
<http://www.brown.edu/Students/ACLU/ILack.html>

Socarides, C. (1978). The sexual deviations and the Diagnostic Manual. *American Journal of Psychotherapy*, 32, 414–427.

Spiegel, D. (2000). The price of abusing children and numbers. *Sexuality and culture*, 4, 63.

Spousal rape laws: 20 years later (2004). *Victim Policy Pipeline.* Retrieved February 18, 2006.
<http://www.ncvc.org/ncvc/main.aspx?dbName=
DocumentViewer&DocumentID=32701>

Stanley v. Georgia (1969). 394 U.S. 557.

State of Washington v. Glas (2002). 145 Wn.2d 1033.

State supreme court decision: A victory for treatment (2002). *Treatment Advocacy Center.* Retrieved February 18, 2006.
<http://www.psychlaws.org/StateActivity/Wisconsin/StatevsDennisH.htm>

Staying the course (1996), April 29. *Legal Times*, 3.

Steiker, C. (1997). Punishment and procedure: Punishment theory and the criminal-civil procedural divide. *Georgetown Law Journal*, 85, 775–819.

Stevenson, R. (2005), January 17. White House again backs amendment on marriage. *The New York Times.*

Stossel, J. (1998), January 2. When yes means no. *20/20.* ABC News.

Stratford, L. (1988). *Satan's underground.* New York: Pelican.

Stuart, D. (2005), July 19. Testimony before the Senate Judiciary Committee. Retrieved February 18, 2006.
<http://www.usdoj.gov/ovw/docs/testimony07192005.pdf>

Sundance Associates, Inc. v. Reno (1998). 139 F.3d 804.

Talanian, N. (2003). The Homeland Security Act: The decline of privacy; the rise of government secrecy. *Bill of Rights Defense Committee.* Retrieved February 18, 2006. <http://www.bordc.org/resources/hsasummary.pdf>

Terry, K. and Furlong, J. (2003). *Sex offender registration and community notification: a "Megan's Law" sourcebook.* Kingston, NJ: Civic Research Institute.

Texas Department of Public Safety Crime Records Service. Sex offender record details. Retrieved October 31, 2005. <https://records.txdps.state.tx.us/soSearch/soDetail.cfm?ShowNav=False&dps_number=04244419>

The Olympia Press. (1971). *The Obscenity Report.* Great Britain: Oxley Press.

The pervert freaks are coming out of the woodwork (1996). KFI AM 640. Retrieved October 31, 2005. <http://www.kfi640.com/sexoffenderrelease.html>

Truell, M. (1996), December 9. Court to weigh allowing confinement of sexual predators. *Associated Press.*

Tsang, D. (1996), September 18. A sex-crime law for the dark ages. *Los Angeles Times,* B9.

Turvey, B. (1996), March. Dangerousness: Predicting recidivism in violent sex offenders. *Knowledge Solutions Library.* Retrieved November 25, 2005. <http://www.corpus-delicti.com/danger.html>

Ullman, S., Karabatsos, G., and Koss, M. (1999). Alcohol and sexual assault in a national sample of college women. *Journal of Interpersonal Violence,* 14, 603–625.

Valetk, H. (2003), August 5. Keeping Tom from peeping: New law will not protect all victims of high-tech voyeurs. *New York Law Journal,* 5.

Vander, A., Sherman, J. and Luciano, D. (2001). *Human physiology: The mechanisms of body function.* Boston: McGraw Hill.

Verhovek, S. (1996a), April 5. Texas agrees to surgery for a molester. *New York Times,* A16.

Verhovek, S. (1996b), April 9. Texas frees child molester who warns of new crimes. *New York Times,* B7.

Video Voyeurism Prevention Act (2004). S.1301. Retrieved November 3, 2005. <http://thomas.loc.gov/cgi-bin/query/z?c108:S.1301.ENR:>

Virginia State Crime Commission. (2002). SJR 381: not guilty by reason of insanity: a bill referral study. Retrieved February 18, 2006. <http://leg2.state.va.us/dls/h&sdocs.nsf/By+Year/RD312004/$file/RD31.PDF>

Wakefield, H. and Underwager, R. (1991). Sex offender treatment. *Institute for Psychological Therapies*, 3. Retrieved January 9, 2006. <http://www.ipt-forensics.com/journal/volume3/j3_1_2.htm>

Walker, L. (1979). *The battered woman.* New York: Harper and Row.

Wallace, D. (1998), March 17. Convicted molester repeats request for castration. Associated Press. In *Abilene Reporter-News.* Retrieved October 31, 2005. <http://www.texnews.com/1998/texas/molest0317.html>

Washington v. Letourneau: Original sentencing from November 14, 1997 (1998), April 18. *CourtTV.com.* Retrieved October 31, 2005. <http://www.courttv.com/trials/letourneau>

Weiss, J. (1999a), January 10. Voyeur prompts DA to propose peeping Tom law. *Times-Picayune* (Louisiana), A1.

Weiss, J. (1999b), April 7. Bills attack "video voyeurism;" but ban on high-tech peeping may snag private eyes, media. *Times-Picayune* (Louisiana), A3.

Weiss, J. (1999c), April 13. Creating a crime. *Times-Picayune* (Louisiana), B4.

Weiss, M. (2004). Beware! Uncle Sam has your DNA: Legal fallout from its use and misuse in the U.S. *Ethics and Information Technology*, 6, 55–63.

Welner, M. (1998). Defining evil: A depravity scale for today's courts. *Depravity Scale.* Retrieved February 18, 2006. <http://www.depravityscale.org/depravity5.htm>

Weslander, E. (2005a), June 3. Notorious molester now in rural Lawrence. *Lawrence Journal-World.* Retrieved February 18, 2006. <http://www2.ljworld.com/news/2005/jun/03/molester/?sexual_predator_law>.

Weslander, E. (2005b), September 25. Sex predators: What goes on at Larned facility may shock some taxpayers. *Lawrence Journal-World*. Retrieved February 18, 2006.
<http://www2.ljworld.com/news/2005/sep/25/
sex_predators_what_goes_larned_facility_may_shock_/?sexual_predator_law>.

Wex (2005). Civil procedure. *Legal Information Institute*. Retrieved November 9, 2005. <http://www.law.cornell.edu/wex/index.php/Civil_procedure>

White, D. (2002), September 17. Harvard's new sex harassment policy: brilliance at last. *Yale Daily News*. Retrieved September 18, 2006.
<http://www.yaledailynews.com/article.asp?AID=19686>

Williams, D. (2004). Sexual offenders' perceptions of correctional therapy: What can we learn? *Sexual Addiction & Compulsivity*, 11, 145–162.

Williams, K. (2005), February 14. Policing video voyeurs: The feds join the battle against perverts with cameras. *Newsweek*, 35.

Winick, B. and La Fond, J. (2003). *Protecting society from sexually dangerous offenders: Law, justice, and therapy*. Washington, D.C.: American Psychological Association.

Wright, L. (1994). *Remembering Satan*. New York: Vintage.

Wrightsman, L., Greene, E., Nietzel, M., and Fortune, W. (2002). *Psychology and the legal system* (5th Ed.). Belmont, CA: Wadsworth.

Yee, Y. (1995). Criminal DNA data banks: Revolution for law enforcement or threat to individual privacy? *American Journal of Criminal Law*, 22, 461–490.

Zgoba, K., Sager, W., and Witt, P. (2003). Evaluation of New Jersey's sex offender treatment program at the Adult Diagnostic and Treatment Center: preliminary results. *The Journal of Psychiatry & Law*, 31, 133–164.

978-0-595-39092-2
0-595-39092-7

Printed in the United States
202680BV00003B/280-363/A